TELEVISION STUDIES IN QUEER TIMES

This timely collection of accessible essays interrogate queer television at the start of the twenty-first century. The complex political, cultural, and economic milieu requires new terms and conceptual frameworks to study television and media through a queer lens. Gathering a range of well-known scholars, the book takes on the relationship between sexual identity, desire, and television, breaking new ground in a context where existing critical vocabularies and research paradigms used to study television no longer hold sway in the ways they used to. The anthology sets out to confound conventional categories used to organize queer television scholarship, like "programming," "industry," "audience," "genre," and "activism." Instead, the anthology offers four interpretive frames – historicity, temporal play, ideological limitation and industrial contextualization – in the interest of creating new queer tools for studying digital television in the contemporary age.

This collection is suitable for scholars and students studying queer media studies, television studies, gender studies, and sexuality studies.

F. Hollis Griffin is Associate Professor in the Department of Communication and Media and the Department of Film, Television, and Media at the University of Michigan, where he is also affiliated with the Digital Studies Institute and the Institute for Research on Women and Gender. He is the author of *Feeling Normal: Sexuality and Media Criticism in the Digital Age* (2017), which was named an "Outstanding Academic Title" by *CHOICE,* the publication of the American Library Association. He has published research in *Television and New Media, Journal of Cinema and Media Studies, New Media & Society, International Journal of Cultural Studies, Popular Communication, Journal of Popular Film and Television, Feminist Media Histories,* and the anthologies *Ryan Murphy's Queer America, The Companion to*

Reality Television and *The Routledge Companion to Urban Media and Communication*. He serves on the editorial boards of *Journal of Cinema and Media Studies, Television and New Media, Communication, Culture, & Critique, Film Criticism,* and *Queer Studies in Media & Popular Culture*. He has also served on the Board of Directors for the Society of Cinema and Media Studies, where he was Secretary.

TELEVISION STUDIES IN QUEER TIMES

Edited by F. Hollis Griffin

Routledge
Taylor & Francis Group
LONDON AND NEW YORK

Designed cover image: Getty/ferrantraite #823025764 'Millennial Pink'

First published 2023
by Routledge
4 Park Square, Milton Park, Abingdon, Oxon OX14 4RN

and by Routledge
605 Third Avenue, New York, NY 10158

Routledge is an imprint of the Taylor & Francis Group, an informa business

British Library Cataloguing-in-Publication Data
A catalogue record for this book is available from the British Library

Library of Congress Cataloging-in-Publication Data
Names: Griffin, F. Hollis, editor.
Title: Television studies in queer times / edited by Hollis Griffin.
Description: Abingdon, Oxon ; New York, NY : Routledge, 2023. |
Includes bibliographical references and index.
Identifiers: LCCN 2022051054 (print) | LCCN 2022051055 (ebook) |
ISBN 9780367623517 (hardback) | ISBN 9780367623418 (paperback) |
ISBN 9781003109044 (ebook)
Subjects: LCSH: Homosexuality on television. | Gender identity on television. |
Television–Social aspects–United States–History–21st century. |
LCGFT: Television criticism.
Classification: LCC PN1992.8.H64 T45 2023 (print) |
LCC PN1992.8.H64 (ebook) |
DDC 791.45/653–dc23/eng/20221212
LC record available at https://lccn.loc.gov/2022051054
LC ebook record available at https://lccn.loc.gov/2022051055

ISBN: 978-0-367-62351-7 (hbk)
ISBN: 978-0-367-62341-8 (pbk)
ISBN: 978-1-003-10904-4 (ebk)

DOI: 10.4324/9781003109044

Typeset in Bembo
by Newgen Publishing UK

CONTENTS

FIGURES

CONTRIBUTORS

Ron Becker is Professor of Media and Communication at Miami University. He is the author of *Gay TV and Straight America* (Rutgers University Press, 2006) and coauthor of *Media and Culture: Mass Communication in a Digital Age* (Bedford/St Martin's, 2021). His work has also appeared in publications like *The Craft of Criticism*; *The Television Studies Reader*; *How to Watch TV*; *Reading the Bromance*; *The Velvet Light Trap*; *Queer Studies in Media and Popular Culture*; and *Historical Journal of Film, Radio and Television*.

Faithe Day is Assistant Professor in the Department of Black Studies at the University of California at Santa Barbara, having earned a B.A. in English and Digital Humanities, as well as a Ph.D. in Communication Studies. Her research and writing analyzes the roles that race, gender, class, and sexuality play in the production and consumption of media, data, and technology. Her work has been published in *Transformative Works and Cultures*, *Social Media + Society*, and the *Journal of Lesbian Studies*.

Michael DeAngelis is Professor of Cinema and Media Studies at DePaul University. He is the author of *Gay Fandom and Crossover Stardom: James Dean, Mel Gibson, and Keanu Reeves* (Duke University Press, 2001) and *Rx Hollywood: Cinema and Therapy in the 1960s* (Wayne State University Press, 2017). He also edited the volume *Reading the Bromance: Homosocial Relationships in Film and Television* (SUNY Press, 2014). Michael's work has been published in *Camera Obscura*, *Cultural Critique*, *Celebrity Studies*, *Film Criticism*, *Literature/Film Quarterly*, *The Velvet Light Trap*, *Spectator*, and numerous anthologies.

Slava Greenberg is an assistant professor of Film Studies in Department of Media Studies at the University of Amsterdam, and author of *Animated Film and Disability:*

Cripping Spectatorship (Indiana University Press, 2023). His articles have appeared in *Film Quarterly, TSQ: Transgender Studies Quarterly, Animation, The Moving Image, Journal of Feminist Studies in Religion, Review of Disability Studies, and Jewish Film and New Media*. He has also contributed to anthologies on disability and documentary, accent studies, queer television studies, and new media. He is currently working on a second book project, entitled *Gender Dysphoria: An Unauthorized Biography*, focusing on the history and visual culture of dysphoria through the lens of trans and crip theories.

Melissa Hardie is Associate Professor in the School of Arts, Communication, and English at the University of Sydney. With Meaghan Morris and Kane Race, she edited *The Year's Work in Showgirls Studies*, forthcoming from Indiana University Press. With Kate Lilley, she edited a pandemic-adjacent special issue of *Southerly*, *The Way We Live Now*. Other recent publications include articles on Ivana Trump's novel *For Love Alone* and its televisual adaptation, *Charlie's Angels* and bitcoin, and Marielle Heller's *Can You Ever Forgive Me?* in *Textual Practice*, *Australian Humanities Review*, and *Film Quarterly*. She is working on a book about the closet.

Hunter Hargraves is Associate Professor in the Department of Cinema and Television Arts at California State University, Fullerton. He is the author of *Uncomfortable Television* (Duke University Press, 2023). His research traverses the intersection of spectatorial affect and popular television cultures and can be found in journals such as *Camera Obscura*, *Television & New Media*, *Communication, Culture & Critique*, and *JCMS*.

Lauren Herold is Visiting Assistant Professor of Women's and Gender Studies at Kenyon College. Her current book project argues that public access cable TV programming made by and for LGBTQ+ people mediated and amplified the structures of feeling circulating in queer communities from the 1970s to 2000s. Her work has appeared in *Jump Cut*, *New Review of Film and Television Studies*, and *Television & New Media*. She holds a PhD in Screen Cultures from Northwestern University.

Julia Himberg is Director and Associate Professor of Film and Media Studies at Arizona State University. She is the author of *The New Gay for Pay: The Sexual Politics of American Television Production* (University of Texas Press, 2018). Her work has appeared in journals such as *Communication, Culture, & Critique*, *Television & New Media*, and *Journal of Cinema and Media Studies* and in books such as *Ryan Murphy's Queer America* and *From Networks to Netflix: A Guide to Changing Channels* (2nd ed). She served as the Special Features Editor for the *Journal of Cinema and Media Studies* from 2017 to 2022.

Lynne Joyrich is Professor of Modern Culture and Media at Brown University. She is co-editor of the journal *Camera Obscura* and the author of *Re-viewing*

Reception: Television, Gender, and Postmodern Culture (Indiana University Press, 1996). Her pieces on film, television, feminist theory, and queer theory have appeared in such journals as *Critical Inquiry*, *Cinema Journal; differences; Discourse; Journal of Visual Culture*, and *Transformative Works and Cultures*, and such books as *Inventing Film Studies*; *Logics of Television*; *Mad Men, Mad World*; *New Media/Old Media*; *Private Screenings*; *Ryan Murphy's Queer America*; *Queer TV*; and *Unwatchable*.

Bridget Kies is Assistant Professor of Film Studies and Production at Oakland University. Her research examines queerness in television and fan communities. She is the co-editor of *Fandom, the Next Generation* (University of Iowa Press, 2022), and her work has been published in numerous journals, including *Feminist Media Histories*, *Television & New Media*, and *VIEW Journal of European Television History and Culture*.

Candace Moore is Assistant Professor of Gender, Women's, and Sexuality Studies and Cinema and Media Studies at Carleton College. Moore's research has been published in *Feminist Media Histories, Cinema Journal, GLQ,* and numerous anthologies, including *Sisters in the Life: A History of Out African American Lesbian Media-Making; Loving* The L Word: *The Complete Series in Focus; Production Studies: Cultural Studies of Media Industries; Televising Queer Women: A Reader;* and *Gender, Race, and Class in Media: A Critical Reader.*

Robert Payne is Associate Professor in the Department of Communication, Media and Culture at the American University of Paris. He is the author of *L'Homme blessé* in the series Queer Film Classics (McGill-Queen's University Press, 2022), *The Promiscuity of Network Culture: Queer Theory and Digital Media* (Routledge, 2015), and articles on various aspects of queerness and masculinity in media and popular culture published in journals such as *Cultural Studies*, *Continuum*, and *International Journal of Cultural Studies*. He has also co-edited special issues of *Sexualities* and *Cultural Studies Review*.

Jake Pitre is a PhD candidate in Film and Moving Image Studies at Concordia University in Montreal. His work has appeared in *Television & New Media*, *The Velvet Light Trap*, *Global Storytelling: Journal of Digital & Moving Images*, *Transformative Works and Cultures*, and *New Media & Society*. He also appears in the edited collections *Representation in Steven Universe* and *Serial Killers in Contemporary Television: Familiar Monsters in Post-9/11 Culture*. He is also an active journalist and has been published at *The Globe and Mail*, *Pitchfork*, *Jacobin*, *Lapham's Quarterly*, *Senses of Cinema*, and elsewhere.

Nick Salvato is Professor of Performing and Media Arts at Cornell University and the author of four books: *Uncloseting Drama: American Modernism and Queer Performance* (Yale University Press, 2010), *Knots Landing* (Wayne State University Press, 2015), *Obstruction* (Duke University Press, 2016), and *Television Scales* (punctum books, 2019). His essays have appeared in such venues as *Camera Obscura*, *Critical Inquiry*, *Criticism*, and *Discourse*.

Maria San Filippo is Associate Professor in the Department of Visual and Media Arts at Emerson College and editor of the *New Review of Film and Television Studies*. She authored the Lambda Literary Award-winning *The B Word: Bisexuality in Contemporary Film and Television* (Indiana University Press, 2013), *Provocauteurs and Provocations: Screening Sex in 21st Century Media* (Indiana University Press, 2020), and the Queer Film Classics volume *Appropriate Behavior* (McGill-Queen's University Press, 2022), and edited the collection *After "Happily Ever After": Romantic Comedy in the Post-Romantic Age* (Wayne State University Press, 2021).

Sarah E. S. Sinwell is Associate Professor in the Department of Film and Media Arts at the University of Utah. She has published essays in *Journal of Cinema and Media Studies, Women's Studies Quarterly, Jump Cut, The Projector, Mai*, and *Flow*. Examining shifting modes of independent film distribution and exhibition on YouTube, Hulu, Netflix, and SundanceTV, her book *Indie Cinema Online* (Rutgers University Press, 2020) redefines independent cinema in an era of media convergence. Sarah teaches both undergraduate and graduate courses, including Diversity in Film and Media, Women Directors, Queer Media, Independent Cinema, and Convergence Cultures.

Amy Villarejo is Professor and Chair of the Department of Film, Television, and Digital Media at the University of California at Los Angeles. She was previously the Frederic J. Whiton Professor of Humanities in the Department of Performing and Media Arts and the Department of Comparative Literature at Cornell University. She is the author of the books *Lesbian Rule: Cultural Criticism and the Value of Desire* (Duke University Press, 2003), which won the Katherine Kovacs Award for best book from the Society of Cinema and Media Studies, *Ethereal Queer: Television, Historicity, Desire* (Duke University Press, 2013) and *Film Studies: The Basics* (Routledge, 2013). She is also the co-editor of *The Oxford Handbook to Queer Cinema* (Oxford University Press, 2021). Her essays have appeared in a range of peer-reviewed journals including *New German Critique*, *Social Text*, *GLQ*, *Film Quarterly*, and *Cinema Journal*, now *Journal of Cinema and Media Studies*. She serves on the editorial boards of *Film Quarterly* and *JCMS*. She regularly teaches television studies and history, queer media, feminist media studies, the history of global cinema, third cinema, and critical theory.

INTRODUCTION

Queer Tools for Studying Digital Television

F. Hollis Griffin

I had just finished my first year as a graduate student in media studies when I attended a high school friend's wedding in June 2006. During the reception, I was seated with a bunch of the bride and groom's friends, none of whom were students or worked in higher education, though all were fascinated by the fact that I was starting a dissertation on the relationship between lesbian, gay, bisexual, transgender, queer (LGBTQ+) politics and television. "Is there even enough to study?" they wondered, asking me what it meant to write about such a topic. Between the soup and salad courses, the conversation turned to the other wedding guests listing as many LGBTQ+ characters and LGBTQ+-themed "very special episodes" as they could recall. In that conversation, people remembered classic, one-off episodes, like the episode of *All in the Family* (CBS, 1971–1979) wherein the homophobic main character's best friend turns out to be gay, and the episode of *Roseanne* (ABC, 1988–1997, 2018) in which the main character goes to a lesbian bar. They also recalled recurring queer characters from programs in eras past, like Jodie Dallas on the 1970s-era sitcom *Soap* (ABC, 1977–1981) and Stephen Carrington on the 1980s primetime soap opera *Dynasty* (ABC, 1981–1987)—though all were quick to point out that neither character actually *stayed* queer over the course of the series. Still others remembered problematic episodes that dealt with LGBTQ+ issues, like the AIDS-themed episodes of programs like *Touched by an Angel* (CBS, 1994–2003) and *Designing Women* (CBS, 1986–1993) in which HIV+ gay men appear only to die by the end of the narrative, or the murder*ous* bisexuals of *24* (Fox, 2001–2010) and *Nip/Tuck* (FX, 2003–2010), or *Buffy the Vampire Slayer* (WB, 1997–2001; UPN, 2001–2003). My fellow guests agreed that they loved the network sitcom *Will & Grace* (NBC, 1998–2006; 2017–2020), liked the music in the cable drama *Queer as Folk* (Showtime, 2000–2005; Peacock, 2022), and thought Ellen DeGeneres's comeback after the cancellation of her sitcoms in the 1990s and 2000s as a talk show host was long overdue. As the wedding segued from salad to the main course,

DOI: 10.4324/9781003109044-1

the table had decided that if I were to study LGBTQ+ issues as they are made manifest on television, my archive would be small and a little sad—and the project itself was noble if also perhaps somewhat pointless. *Aren't things "better now," with entire programs and television networks devoted to LGBTQ+-themed content? Isn't the internet going to replace television anyway?* I attempted to launch a spirited defense: *But there are many ways of studying LGBTQ+ politics and television beyond merely looking at characters and episodes! What about industries and audiences? What about the changes to television production and consumption precipitated by the development of digital technologies? What about the centrality of television to discussions of LGBTQ+ activism? What did it mean that they could all rattle off all of these programs and episodes and characters and they were not even studying them?* None of them were receptive to what I had to say. No one even asked me what I thought of any of the programs and episodes and characters they mentioned because whatever knowledge there was to be gleaned from them was treated as being self-evident. And while my investments were treated as being *honorable*, they did not think I was doing anything *important.*

What a difference a few years makes…

Nearly 15 years later, I received a message on a social media network from one of the very people I sat with at that wedding. I had not spoken to her in the intervening years but she told me she was thinking about me because she remembered talking to me about my research so many years earlier. More specifically, she was reaching out because she had come across *Bad Girls* (ITV, UK, 1999–2006), a lesbian-themed British series set in a women's prison, on a streaming platform more than a decade after it initially aired. She wanted to know if I had seen it and what I thought of it. The woman admitted to being a big fan of the program but was nearly apologetic in telling me so, explaining that she felt as though her own heterosexuality should have mitigated her affection for the lesbian plots and characters. I wish I could say that I then coached this woman toward a deeper appreciation of the capacity for television to cultivate improbable affinities between its audiences and its representations. But I thanked her for the email, told her I would look for the program because I had not, in fact, seen it, and that I would get back to her when I had something intelligent to say about it. In the years since I attended that wedding, that exact exchange has happened more times than I can count. Someone who knows what I do for a living—teach and research LGBTQ+ media culture, especially as it occurs on television and new media—will reach out to ask what I think about this or that television program and I, wholly flattered to be asked what I think about anything, promise to look into it and get back to them. To be clear, I think this phenomenon has less to do with me than it does with the moment in which this book is published.

Nearly 15 years removed from the wedding reception where I struggled to tell a table full of people why studying LGBTQ+ content on television is important, it is no longer so out-of-the-ordinary to suggest that studying LGBTQ+ programming yields important information about television as a whole, the industry that creates it, the audiences that consume it, and the world in which it circulates. That there are scholars who devote their lives to studying these issues, with entire college courses built around such analysis, is no longer novel. Many people understand it to be crucial work that yields important insights. The expansion of the television universe and the multiplication of delivery platforms in the context of digital production, distribution, and reception has helped precipitate a glut of LGBTQ+-themed content in the contemporary media ecosphere that reaches and speaks to many different types of viewers. Moreover, issues related to same-sex desires and non-normative sexual identities enjoy new centrality in cultural conversations of all kinds. I now keep a running list of LGBTQ+-themed television in an app on my cellphone so that any time anyone recommends something, I can add it to the long list of things I have yet to see but desperately want to watch—or at least suspect I "should" watch.

In short, it is a "queer time" to be studying television. Issues related to sexual identity and desire are front and center in conversations of politics, economy, and culture across the globe. Sexual minorities have won rights and recognitions all over the world, not just same-sex marriage rights in the United States, Ireland, and Ecuador but also the decriminalization of homosexuality in India and Angola, new protections for transgender people in Sweden, parity in the age of consent in Canada, and the formal denunciation of homophobia by the Brazilian Supreme Court. But the rise of conservative populism makes these gains tenuous, at best. "Bathroom laws" demonize transgender people and religious freedom initiatives seek to disenfranchise sexual minorities and dial back whatever strides they have made. Politicians are often elected to office by virtue of their homophobic and transphobic rhetoric. Moreover, the politics of race, ethnicity, gender, and class complicate easy determinations about who, exactly, has benefited from these "gains" in the first place. At the same time, the medium we've known as "television" is an increasingly dispersed object. New modes of television production, distribution, and reception co-exist alongside more traditional programming and practices. The overlaps, parallels, tensions, and contradictions that characterize broadcasting, cable, streaming, and other online modalities make it difficult to generalize what, precisely, television is. That fact also makes it hard to parse out how the medium participates in the politics of sexuality. The power dynamics at work in the medium's representations of bodies, desires, lives, and cultures shape discourses on television in ways that often trumpet the diversity enabled by online platforms. But too-familiar, limiting images and narratives persist. The insularity and gatekeeping functions of industry circles can limit the career trajectories for queer media professionals of color. Finally, the logic of capital shapes television's programming and practices in ways that contour any ideas about sexual identity and desire that circulate there.

These complicated political, economic, and cultural milieux require new terms and conceptual frameworks. Existing critical vocabularies and research paradigms used to analyze television no longer hold sway in the ways they used to. For instance, "least objectionable programming" describes the business philosophy that prevailed in the era of television broadcasting in the United States, from the mid to late twentieth century. Here, U.S. television networks' imperative to court large, varied audiences resulted in programming that endeavored to remain palatable to diverse viewerships. The result was images of and narratives about sexual minorities that some viewers found pleasurable, though many others found bland, predictable, and neutered. But in the second decade of the twenty-first century, a context wherein networks court narrow market demographics with content imagined for evermore finely conceived audiences, representations of sexual minorities do not have to be designed that way. The result is programming that speaks to the specificities of LGBTQ+ lives and cultures, like a web series that uses elements of fantasy to reimagine the history of AIDS by foregrounding bondage and sadomasochism (BDSM) activities among gay men, or a sketch comedy program that pokes fun at the cultural mores of transmen dating lesbians. But the relatively small audiences of these more contemporary programs raise the question of whether or not "television," as a medium, performs the kind of cultural work it used to–especially when compared with the large audiences and broad cultural dialogues that characterized television in prior eras. In an effort to think about these issues in new ways, this anthology confounds conventional categories used to organize scholarship on LGBTQ+ television, like "programming," "industry," "audience," "genre," and "activism." Rather than reproduce staid terminologies for a decidedly different historical moment, I have organized the book using four modes of criticism that scholars use to study LGBTQ+ television in the context of digital production, distribution, and reception: historicity, temporal play, ideological limitation, and industrial contextualization. I have collected four examples for each of the modalities in an effort to articulate the kinds of questions, arguments, and objects of analysis LGBTQ+ television scholarship might take up in the contemporary moment.

Historicity: Placing Television Programming and Practices in Historical Context

When scholars of LGBTQ+ television take up issues of historicity, they tackle issues related to historical actuality. In these instances, scholars are essentially asking: how does programming speak to the cultural moment in which it is initially created and consumed? One example: scholarship on 1970s network sitcoms that details how references to queer sexual practices were often the butt of jokes that made them titillating but inoffensive to broad, heterogeneous audiences during the Sexual Revolution.[1] Another example: scholarship on YouTube-distributed web series that highlights how the lack of regulatory and financial constraints on business practices enables the representation of queer communities of color in content that circulates there.[2] In the anthology's first chapter, "Queer Power: Multicultural Empowerment Narratives on Digital-Era TV," author Ron Becker argues that changes to the economic and technological base of television in the streaming era have precipitated changes in the medium's superstructure that, in turn, require queer television critics to shift their modes of critique. He argues that the splintering of television's audience into ever-finer audience demographics makes queer audiences an actual target demographic for the first time. Looking at the cable television reality contest *RuPaul's Drag Race* (Logo, 2009–2017; VH1, 2017–) alongside the oeuvre of openly gay television showrunner Ryan Murphy and the Marvel Universe's television programming on Netflix, Becker sees contemporary representations of sexuality difference as a move away from the industry practices of prior historical moments, in which LGBTQ+-themed content was used by the television industry to target demographics of all kinds. In this milieu, Becker sees television taking up queer vernaculars and LGBTQ+-specific cultural practices in new ways. In the anthology's second chapter, "Briggs, *Family*, Queer," authors Melissa Hardie and Amy Villarejo, examine a specific moment in time—the late 1970s—to consider the structures of affect at work in a lesbian-themed episode from the U.S. television drama *Family* (ABC, 1976–1980). They consider the episode against the backdrop of its cultural moment, especially in light of California Proposition 6 of 1978. Informally known as the Briggs Initiative after its sponsor legislator, California Proposition 6 sought to ban gays and lesbians from working in California's public schools. Villarejo and Hardie mobilize a critique that considers questions of identity and desire promulgated by the medium by linking television's affective capacities to the discourses in which they were bound at a specific cultural moment. In both essays, the authors historicize television in the discourses of sexual desire and identity that circulated in the United States at particular moments in time.

In contrast, the anthology's third chapter looks backward in time to articulate a mode of criticism that examines questions of historicity in search of new approaches to queer television scholarship. In "In the Queer-View Mirror: Looking at 1991," author Nick Salvato considers how different media texts produced and distributed in 1991 simultaneously—and co-constitutively—stake queer ground and make reflexive claims about television as a medium in transition as the network model gave way to new practices and industry formations. The essay emphasizes notions of resonance: the attachments, identifications, and desires enabled by television under specific conditions of regulation and capital. Similarly, the anthology's fourth essay looks back at a scheduling practice that prevailed on an Australian television channel in the 1980s and 1990s and the kinds of queer pleasures it engendered for audiences. In "Like Living in a Different Time Zone: SBS's Queer Orientations," author Robert Payne considers the queer pleasures of off-peak television schedules. In connecting viewer memories and a television network's business practices, Payne parses out the serendipity of finding unlikely representations of sexual minorities on television at certain moments of the day.

Temporal Play: Queer Histories and Possibilities

Television programs often foreground non-normative experiences of time and history, providing scholars of the medium with opportunities to think about how this play with temporality fosters new understandings of non-normative sexualities. Representations of the past and stories that jump around in time confound conventional markers of chronology and duration, like death, marriage, and reproduction. One example: scholarship on science fiction television often highlights how the genre is organized by breaks in the space-time continuum that facilitate the representation of non-normative bodies and desires.[3] Another example: scholarship that examines how LGBTQ+-themed programming comments on the politics of television's representations from prior eras, or animates ideas about queer histories.[4] In the anthology's fifth chapter, "Making Things Perfectly Sketch: Reflexive Queer and Trans Themes in Sketch Comedy," author Candace Moore limns the representational possibilities of sketch comedy by revisiting touchstone LGBTQ+-themed skits on *Saturday Night Live* (NBC, 1975–) and analyzing transgender-themed skits from the more contemporary *The Black Lady Sketch Show* (HBO, 2019–). In doing so, she analyzes the role humor plays in destabilizing LGBTQ+ stereotypes and circulating ideas about queer histories to more mainstream, heterogeneous audiences. Given live, improv-style comedy's reliance on intertextuality and tendency to construct parodies and satirical bits around popular culture, sketch shows critique and even historicize queer and trans media representations. As such, the chapter considers current debates in LGBTQ+ and trans communities about jokes related to LGBTQ+ and trans lives and identities, thinking through how appeals to heterogeneous audiences' "land" with varied viewerships.

In "Realizing Unrealizable Joy: Forming Queer Utopia in *The Fathers Project*," Hargraves considers representations of AIDS history in the web series *The Father Project*. Financed by donations from audiences and distributed via non-traditional means, *The Fathers Project* imagines a future where the AIDS crisis of the 1980s and 1990s did not happen–because its challenges were met by a fictive separatist colony comprised of queer communities steeped in the practices of gay male sexual subcultures. Hargraves considers how a narrative world focused on sexual practice and predicated on historical fantasy is enabled by *The Father's Project*'s alternative modes of financing and distribution. Like Hargraves, author Bridget Kies also considers how television's representation of the queer past can do transformative cultural work. Looking specifically at crime programs, "Murdering Our Queer Past," outlines how historically set murder mysteries deal with questions of queer villainy and queer cultural history. While many of these programs foreground the mistreatment and ostracism of queer people in prior eras, Kies argues that they often do so by erasing important historical realities in favor of flattened depictions of diversity, tolerance, and acceptance. In contrast, Michael DeAngelis identifies transgressive possibilities in television's play with narrative temporality in the anthology's eighth chapter. In "Obscure Temporalities: *Dark* and the Queering of the Time Travel," he examines how *Dark* (Netflix, 2017–), a time-travel series set in a small town, disrupts the logical segmentation of time into neatly discernible fields of past, present, and future. In this series, characters inhabit temporal fields 33 or 66 years apart but then interact and converse with younger and older versions of themselves. These temporal manipulations queer identity norms by disavowing conventional markers of time (e.g. marriage, death) and then further disrupt heteronormativity by foregrounding queer desires that disorient familial relations.

Ideological Limitations: The Boundaries of What's Possible

When scholars of LGBTQ+ television identify the conditions and constraints on the medium's representations of sexual minorities, they locate the boundaries of television as a cultural practice through which people might encounter ideas about non-normative sexual identities, cultures, and desires. Some things are just not possible in a given context: like, perhaps, sexually explicit dialogue in content created for broad audiences, or appeals to heterogeneous audiences through culturally specific representations of sexual practices. One example: scholarship that examines the restrictions on professionals' ability to engage in activist media practice in industry settings.[5] Another example: television scholarship that identifies how genre norms impinge on storytelling possibilities for LGBTQ+ characters.[6] In the anthology's ninth chapter, "The Television-Industrial Closet," Julia Himberg uses documentaries about LGBTQ+ television to consider the experiences of LGBTQ+ people who work in the media industries. She pays particular attention to how the documentaries emphasize even the most "out" television personalities have careers that are as shaped by agency and autonomy as they are by fears of invisibility and confinement. Lynne Joyrich considers the limitations of "outness" in a representational sense in the anthology's tenth chapter, "TV's Ins and Outs, or (Bat) Signals and (Caped) Crusades." Looking at the protagonist of the superhero-themed program *Batwoman* (CW, 2019–2022), Joyrich challenges the notion that "out" characters are free of the power dynamics of the closet. Focusing on the narrative tropes characteristic of superhero-themed programs, like secret identities and dramatic reveals, Joyrich charges that television's treatment of all LGBTQ+ identities is always characterized by the power dynamics associated with "closetedness," especially in a historical moment like the 2010s and 2020s, wherein an empowered conservative movements seek to roll back the political gains of women, racial and ethnic minorities, and LGBTQ+ people.

Similarly, Slava Greenberg considers the representational limits of the docuseries. In the anthology's 11th chapter, "How Do Trans Men Make Babies? *Transkids* and Reproductive Fantasies," Greenberg examines how the docuseries *Transkids* (yesDocu, Israel, 2019) narrates issues related to reproduction, specifically how the series depicts transmen anticipating future infertility by freezing their eggs. For Greenberg, the docuseries disguises heteronormative fantasies with documentary aesthetics, reinforcing conservative ideologies of reproduction in its depiction of transmen who undergo questionable medical procedures. Greenberg sees the docuseries ultimately closing down the radical potential of transgender by naturalizing the privatized heterosexual couple and romanticizing the quest for a conventional family. Where Himberg focuses on the ideological limitations of professionals and Joyrich and Greenberg focus on the ideological limitations of textual paradigms, Jake Pitre focuses on the ideological limitations of technological formations. In the anthology's 12th chapter, "Queer Aesthetics in the Streaming Age," Pitre argues that logic of streaming television is averse to queerness from the start. Looking at a representative sample of queer-themed programming developed for Netflix and

Amazon Prime, Pitre charges that streaming platforms are generally averse to creating content that employs queer aesthetics of transgression and transformation. By gathering data in service of creating firm definitions and strict categorizations, algorithms provide little space for the unconventional or the unpredictable. Pitre argues that because algorithms are designed to provide users with what they want, their parameters are inevitably shaped by what television users have selected and watched previously. For Pitre, the very logic of such a system is averse to the kinds of liminality and possibility that often structure queerness.

Industrial Contextualization: Studying Production Processes

Scholars often study the practices through which media professionals conceptualize, create, and circulate television programs. Sometimes scholars attempt to understand how the identities of LGBTQ+ media professionals shape the work they do in industry settings.[7] Other times, scholars attempt to understand the decision-making processes of people who make LGBTQ+-themed content.[8] These analyses often reveal a great deal about how the politics of sexuality come into play when LGBTQ+ cultures and identities are used for the purposes of commerce. In the anthology's 13th chapter, "Televising Lesbian Feminist Love-Politics on *Dyke TV*," Lauren Herold examines the labor of lesbian producers who created a magazine-format program for public access television. Analyzing the program's production and distribution practices alongside its textual aesthetics, Herold demonstrates how *Dyke TV* (1993–2006) celebrated queer women's community-oriented cultures. Drawing on interviews with the producers of the show as well as close readings of episodes, Herold discusses how the program's national distribution provided producers with the opportunity to incorporate a wider variety of stories into its episodes, as well as how declining resources limited the show's ability to produce programming on a regular basis and eventually caused the show to stop production entirely. In contrast, Sarah Sinwell examines a more conventional television production context in the anthology's 14th chapter, "Producing Inclusion and Intersectionality: Queer Showrunners of Color in Contemporary Television." Sinwell looks at how LGBTQ+-identified people of color and showrunners such as Janet Mock, Lena Waithe, and Tanya Saracho create LGBTQ+-focused series that are inclusive not only of the queer community, but also of women and people of color. Looking at industry discourses related to casting, Sinwell analyzes the showrunners' rhetorical maneuvers when discussing how they cast queer people of color. She argues that the showrunners' press statements offer valuable insights about the relationship between industry norms, the agency of media professionals, and the discursive limits of television's representations.

Where Sinwell looks at a group of queer television showrunners, Maria San Filippo focuses on one queer showrunner in the anthology's 15th chapter, "Living in the Gray Area: Bisexual Resignifications in Desiree Akhavan's *The Bisexual*." Looking at a variety of materials related to the promotion of *The Bisexual* (Hulu, 2018–), San Filippo examines how the showrunners' interviews and social media activity nuance the program's representation of bisexuality. She argues that they add layers of racial and class diversity that are not as readily apparent in the program itself. San Filippo argues that the showrunner's own performance of bisexuality places the program's representation of bisexuality amid a constellation of other racial and class-based identifications for users who follow her on social media. Like San Filippo, Faithe Day also examines the relationship between television narration and social media activity. In the anthology's final essay, "Visual Pleasure and Video-Sharing Platforms: *If I Was Your Girl* and the Representation of Black Sexuality," Day analyzes the mutuality and reciprocity of black queer web series creators and the black queer audiences who watch this programming. Day sees the representation of black female masculinity on the web series *If I Was Your Girl* (2012) instantiating a debate on the series' comment thread that complicates easy determinations about who watches the program and what viewing pleasures they find there. Day sees the series bringing multiple black audiences into the fold by way of culturally specific viewing pleasures that emerge from a back-and-forth between creators and viewers in the comment section on YouTube.

These four modes of criticism—historicity, temporal play, ideological limitation, and industrial contextualization—constitute a set of interpretive frames that can be taken up by others in their own efforts to study television's LGBTQ+ politics in the context of digital production, distribution, and reception. Each of the 16 essays provide an avenue for better understanding television's creators and consumers, its texts and practices, as well as its politics and pleasures in a moment when the medium's shifting political economy and changing technological makeup are no longer novel. Multiple forms of program financing and diverse modes of content delivery are the new norm. As the chapters detail, such changes alter the medium's politics of representation in crucial ways. What queer television studies needs is novel approaches to timeless questions. I am hopeful that the essays collected here provide readers with both models to conduct their own work as well as useful insights as they consume LGBTQ+ television in the contemporary moment.

Notes

1 Elana Levine, *Wallowing in Sex: The New Sexual Culture of 1970s American Television.* Durham, NC: Duke University Press, 2007.
2 Aymar Jean Christian, "Beyond branding: The value of intersectionality on streaming TV channels." *Television & New Media* 21, no. 5 (2020): 457–474.
3 Alexis Lothian, *Old Futures: Speculative Fiction and Queer Possibility.* New York: NYU Press, 2018.
4 Anna McCarthy, "Ellen: Making queer television history." *GLQ: A Journal of Lesbian and Gay Studies* 7, no. 4 (2001): 593–620.
5 Julia Himberg, *The New Gay for Pay: The Sexual Politics of American Television Production.* Austin, TX: University of Texas Press, 2018
6 Joy V. Fuqua, "'There's a queer in my soap!.' The *homophobia/AIDS story line of One Life to live*." In Allen, R. C. (Ed) *To be Continued….. Soap Operas around the World.* London: Routledge (1995): 199–212.

7 Himberg, *The New Gay for Pay*; Katherine Sender, *Business, Not Politics: The Making of the Gay Market*. New York: Columbia University Press, 2005; Lisa Henderson, "Queer Relay." *GLQ: A Journal of Lesbian and Gay Studies* 14, no. 4 (2008): 569–597.

8 F. Hollis Griffin, *Feeling Normal: Sexuality and Media Criticism in the Digital Age*. Bloomington, IN: Indiana University Press, 2017; Alfred L. Martin Jr., *The Generic Closet: Black Gayness and the Black-Cast Sitcom*. Bloomington, IN: Indiana University Press, 2021.

PART I

Historicity

Placing Television Programming and Practices in Historical Context

1

QUEER POWER

Multicultural Empowerment Narratives on Digital-Era TV

Ron Becker

In this essay, I think through certain aspects of television and the practice of TV studies in today's queer times by revisiting the concept of *straight panic*—a term I originally coined to help understand the context that shaped and was in turn shaped by gay content on U.S. prime-time network TV in the 1990s.[1]

While much has changed since the 1990s (both in terms of television and the socio-political landscape), many contours of our recent political, cultural, and media environments took shape during that period. Thus, returning to the 1990s and to the concept of straight panic provides a reference point against which we can gauge continuities and discontinuities that have played out as Americans and American television responded to the nation's deepening diversity and the continued normalization of LGBTQ+ visibility. One symptom of those shifting dynamics, I argue, is the growing presence of multicultural empowerment narratives on U.S. television—a programming trope that reflects a culture in which calls to celebrate diversity (including LGBTQ+ diversity) are no longer new but, rather, are the new normal. After briefly exploring how that trope plays out in media texts like *Hollywood*, *RuPaul's Drag Race*, and others, I conclude by identifying three interrelated issues we should ponder when studying the relationship between straight panic and multiculturalism in today's queerer times.

Straight Panic Revisited

In the 1990s, conservatives claimed that America was in the midst of a culture war. To some extent, they were right. Of course, as a nation founded on colonization, immigration, and slavery, America has always grappled with deep divisions. Despite (or perhaps because of) those divisions, the idea of America as a melting pot where a diverse population was united through a shared culture operated as a powerful myth. That myth long had an especially strong hold over those in dominant and

DOI: 10.4324/9781003109044-3

majority groups whose way of life others were expected to assimilate into. Its hold was particularly strong after World War II when industrial mass culture helped construct a notion of "the mainstream." By the 1990s, however, the idea that America should be or ever had been a melting pot became hotly contested as views on social difference shifted.

That shift was fueled by various factors that coalesced in the 1990s. Decades of identity-based civil rights activism had revealed the discrimination operating under the guise of mainstream American values, and an increasingly fragmented media environment provided fewer shared cultural touchstones and more content tailored to narrower interests and markets. Rather than a melting pot, America was increasingly framed as a multicultural society where differences weren't assimilated away but celebrated. It was also framed as a society whose diversity was destined to deepen. Widely reported 1990 U.S. census figures, for example, painted a demographic picture of a white majority losing ground to racial minorities. Experts predicted that by 2050, non-Hispanic whites would no longer form a majority, leading *American Demographics* magazine to argue, "In the future, the white Western majority will have to do some assimilation of its own."[2] The gay rights movement and the increasing visibility of gay people in mainstream culture (especially on TV) added to the sense of America's expanding diversity and undermined heteronormativity's taken-for-granted status.

Such developments shaped the era's structure of feeling, fueling what I call straight panic—the anxieties felt by those whose identities and values had existed largely unchallenged at the center of mainstream American culture as they confronted a rapidly changing landscape where monoculturalism seemed increasingly maligned and social difference celebrated. Members of a once naïve majority (those who long had the luxury of ignoring what it meant to be white, male, straight, etc.) found it harder to assert the universality of their experience and were often required to navigate a culture where racial, gender, and other identities were valued in new ways.

People's experiences of and responses to straight panic varied across the political spectrum. They were also exploited and channeled by politicians and media producers. On the right, a conservative coalition that included the Religious Right, Contract-with-America Republicans, talk radio hosts like Rush Limbaugh, and Fox News (launched in 1996) marshalled the culture-war discourse to decry what it saw as multiculturalism's moral relativism. They fed straight, white, and male anxieties by framing cultural inclusion as a zero-sum game and making gay rights, affirmative action, and calls for sensitivity to the politics of language (what they denounced as political correctness) symbols of multiculturalists' agenda to take over America. They often targeted their message to blue collar and rural workers who felt left out of the emerging global digital economy.

On the far left, progressive activists and academics in the 1990s argued for a radical multiculturalism—one that dismantled economic, political, and ideological barriers to equity and inclusion. Meanwhile, a much more cautiously liberal version of multiculturalism—one that emphasized the celebration of cultural differences and envisioned a mostly frictionless pluralism—became hegemonic. It shaped university curricular requirements, transformed corporate policies, and became central to the Democratic party platform. During his 1992 presidential run, for example, Bill Clinton repeatedly promised: "If you vote for me, I will give you an Administration that looks like America." Dovetailing well with the logics of market segmentation and narrowcasting, it also spread throughout the media landscape, from TV shows like *The Real World* (MTV 1992–2017) to films like *Pocahontas* (1995).

It also spurred the increase of gay material on prime-time network TV in the mid-1990s. In an increasingly crowded media environment, broadcast networks used gay content on shows like *Seinfeld* (NBC, 1989–1998), *ER* (NBC 1994–2009), and *Ellen* (ABC, 1994–1998) to attract what I have called the Slumpy (socially liberal, urban-minded, professional) audience—a quality audience imagined to be mostly upscale, white, heterosexual 18- to 49-year-olds who prided themselves on being hip and having a cosmopolitan sensibility. Used as a narrowcasting tool, gay content was often narrativized through tropes that reflected the historically specific anxieties of liberal straight Americans trying to reconcile a desire to celebrate diversity with residual investments in their majority status and heteronormative privilege. Gay characters in supporting roles, for example, didn't de-center heterosexuality, but watching such shows could help establish one's hip credentials. A common trope—sitcom plotlines in which a straight character is mistakenly assumed to be gay and eventually has to come out as straight—played on the ambivalent anxieties viewers may have had about the stability of straight identity and privilege at a time when the moral distinctions between homo- and heterosexuality were being challenged.

Straight Panic and Today's Queer Times

Since the 1990s, an evolving landscape has altered the ways straight panic has played out. For those more sympathetic to multiculturalism, straight panic anxieties seemed to have eased, shifting the sensibilities of today's cosmopolitan viewers and the media targeted to them. What was new for many people in the 1990s—celebrating diversity and recognizing one's own privilege—has now become the new normal.

Television helps us gauge that shift, in part because it played a role in producing it. Watching a lesbian wedding on *Friends* in 1995, for example, felt like one was part of an edgy subversion of the mainstream; today that episode and its straight-panic-fueled version of gay inclusion feels like a heterocentric relic of a bygone era. That difference isn't simply because gay marriage is legal. It is also because a steady exposure for over two decades to discourses about monoculturalism's inequities and multiculturalism's benefits has shifted how some people think and feel about "the mainstream" and about social difference more broadly. Those discourses were often encountered through television—through reruns of gay-inclusive series from the 1990s and new TV content accessed through ever more fragmented technologies and tailored even more narrowly to their evolving sensibilities. Slumpy anxieties in the 1990s reflected an experience of and even identification with "the mainstream," even as it was being undermined and problematized (hence the ambivalence central to so much slumpy TV). In today's queerer times, by contrast, "the mainstream" has lost much of its resonance as a site of identification. That may be especially so for those who came of age since 2000. Rather than discovering the problems with monoculturalism, more people today feel that they already know it's a problem.

Today's television industry is thoroughly entangled in these shifts. Activist movements like #OscarsSoWhite and #TimesUp have pressured Hollywood to address issues of diversity, equity, and inclusion in front of and behind the camera. In response, many in the media industries have embraced (or at least deployed) multiculturalist discourses, especially those that dovetail with their business goals. In 2021, for example, Nielsen launched a partnership with a data analytics firm to track levels of diversity in terms of race, gender, ethnicity, and sexual identity on broadcast, cable, and streaming programs. "Audiences today actively seek out programs that highlight people who resemble them and experiences that reflect their own," Tina Wilson, head of analytics at Nielsen, explained. "Under these circumstances, it's critical that the entertainment industry create authentic content which resonates with underrepresented groups."[3] While the TV industry had made nods to serving the needs of diverse audiences for decades, more intense competition for viewer attention paired with decreasing expectations that they should or could appeal to a mass audience has allowed and/or compelled executives to deploy such discourses more forcefully.

Amid these shifting dynamics, TV content has also evolved. The anxious ambivalence about the relationship between the majority and minorities that characterized so much slumpy programming in the 1990s has faded. Gone, for example, are the mistaken sexual identity plotlines and their nervous preoccupation with the line between gay and straight; straight characters (and perhaps a lot of straight viewers) don't seem that worried about that boundary. Meanwhile, some recent programs construct pluralistic utopias where cultural differences are acknowledged but not stressed over. HGTV's *House Hunters*, for example, includes a diverse mix of home buyers in terms of race, ethnicity, sexuality, and household structure. In each episode, interviews with the house hunters usually provide enough details for viewers to get a sense of their social identities: A straight white divorcee looks to downsize in Little Rock; an interracial, bisexual throuple wants a bathroom with three sinks in Colorado Springs; a Black college grad tries to find a sunny apartment near her family in Atlanta. In the rigid formula that operates across episodes, however, the house hunters are interchangeable. Thus, social differences matter (since they often inform the house hunt and maybe viewer pleasure), but those differences aren't problematic (since they never cause narrative complications). As such, a show like *House Hunters* may speak to and fuel some viewers' desire for frictionless multicultural communities.

If straight panic anxieties have eased for many on the left, they seem to have only intensified on the right. For some, the election of a Black president, the legalization of gay marriage, and the #MeToo, Black Lives Matter, and Trans movements seemed to confirm their worst fears about marginal groups pushing aside "normal" Americans. In an ever more fragmented digital media environment, far-right outlets like One America News and Breitbart have transformed fear and resentment into an alt-right movement and Trumpist populism. Right-wing straight panic fuels anti-immigration sentiments. It pops up in the All Lives Matter discourse and was on frightening display as neo-Nazis chanted "Jews will not replace us" in Charlottesville. Within right-wing discourses, the mainstream media's embrace of multiculturalism is part of the problem and confirmation of the left's cultural power.

Multicultural Narratives of Empowerment

I want to spend time exploring a trope I see as increasingly common in content that targets viewers sympathetic to a multicultural future and may fuel conservatives' sense of marginalization: multicultural narratives of empowerment. Stories about underdogs who overcome long odds to find success have always been fruitful ground for Hollywood. In today's media environment, however, we see a specific subgenre of such stories—one in which the obstacles that are faced and overcome are the systems of discrimination that have kept women, people of color, queer people, and others disempowered.

This trope is woven throughout the fabric of the TV landscape—in an ABC evening news story recognizing the first Black woman serving as an official in the National Football League (NFL); in the acceptance speeches delivered at awards shows; in CBS's coverage of Lee Elder, the first Black golfer to compete at the Masters, becoming an honorary starter in 2021; and in countless other moments large and small. Since disempowered groups have often been marginalized in media representation and defined by limiting media stereotypes, television's empowerment narratives are often self-redemptive and self-congratulatory. They are often about the media and media creators and their ability to promote positive change in the world. The trope can also circulate around TV; for example, while *House Hunters* may not overtly frame the throuple's appearance on the show as an empowering milestone for queer households, it can be experienced, promoted, or discussed as one. Given the limited space I have, I focus on a few examples that can help us get a sense of some of the contours of this increasingly common trope.

Ryan Murphy, one of the most prolific TV producers of the last two decades, is something of a multicultural-empowerment-narrative auteur. Many of his programs are organized around it, including *Glee* (2009–2015), the hit Fox musical melodramedy about misfit high school kids who find empowerment through glee club. The series was celebrated for its diversity, which includes students and teachers who are white, Black, Latina, and Asian American; openly identify as straight, gay and bisexual; are cis-gender, non-binary and trans; and are able-bodied and have disabilities. The show didn't present a frictionless pluralism, however. The show's founding premise emphasized the main protagonists' marginalization within the school where they are repeatedly bullied.

Although their membership in the glee club is a source of the teens' marginalization, musical performances often serve as affectively rich moments of empowerment. In the pilot's emotional climax, for example, the cast sings Journey's "Don't

Stop Believin'." With lyrics that resonate with a hopeful longing to escape, the number came to represent *Glee*'s core theme—that this group of misfits could win nationals and, in the process, create a future for themselves. Later in season one, Kurt, the series' first openly LGBTQ character, captures the multicultural nature of *Glee*'s empowerment narrative perfectly when he tells his concerned father, "Being different made me stronger. At the end of the day, it's what's going to get me out of this cow town."

Although the glee club is diverse, the series often foregrounds white, cis-het characters like Rachel and Finn. That is especially true early on. In the iconic "Don't Stop Believin'" number, for example, Rachel and Finn sing lead, turning gay, non-white, and disabled members into backup singers. Centering their budding hetero relationship in the pilot may have been seen as necessary for a series produced for broadcast network TV and thus expected to draw a relatively large audience. At the same time, the series works hard to queer them. Rachel is ostracized for her nerdy ambition to be the next Barbra Streisand; Finn, the star quarterback, risks his social capital by joining glee. In this way, the show provides entry points for white, cis-het viewers to enjoy the show's affects of marginalization and empowerment.

Hollywood (2020), Murphy's alternative history of movie making in the Golden Age of the 1940s, is an unmistakable example of a multicultural empowerment narrative. The limited series produced for Netflix (ten years after *Glee* and within notably different development conditions) tells the story of a diverse group of aspiring young hopefuls that includes Raymond (a director who is part Filipino); his girlfriend Camille (a Black actress); Archie (a gay, Black screenwriter); his actor boyfriend Rock Hudson; and Jack (a straight, white actor). The group battles against an industry repeatedly shown to be racist, sexist, anti-Semitic, and homophobic. With the help of sympathetic studio insiders, however, they overcome the system by getting *Meg*, a movie about a young Black starlet's struggles in Hollywood, produced at a major studio. In Murphy's alternative-universe, the movie becomes a blockbuster; Archie, Raymond, and Camille win Oscars; and Rock and Archie come out on the red carpet.

In *Hollywood*'s utopic re-imagination of what could have been had Hollywood not discriminated against talented minorities, media representations matter—a claim Murphy, rarely known for subtlety, lays on thick. At one point, Meg's fate rests in the hands of Avis Amberg, the wife of Ace Studio's boss. When her husband falls into a coma, Avis finds herself in charge. When the studio's money men tell her that casting a Black actress as the lead will be a financial disaster, she hesitates. But then former first lady Eleanor Roosevelt intervenes. "Think about it, what it might mean to a dirt-poor little Black girl living in a shanty in some cotton town—what it would mean to see herself up there on that screen, vaunted, dignified, valued." Roosevelt tells Avis. "My time in Washington taught me a lot of things. I used to believe that good government could change the world. Well, I don't know that I believe that anymore. However, what you do…can change the world."

While Ryan Murphy tends toward the hyperbolic, the assumption that media representations can be empowering in and of themselves is woven throughout the logic of today's multicultural empowerment narratives. It is, for example, a central theme in an episode of Disney+'s *616*, a behind-the-scenes docuseries that is part cultural analysis and part Marvel self-promotion. The episode ("Amazing Artisans," 2020) examines the impact a new generation of diverse content creators are having at Marvel. Through interviews with academics and content creators, the episode explains why Marvel is diversifying on both sides of the page. According to Saladin Ahmed, a writer for Marvel's *Miles Morales: Spider-Man*, "When you get creators coming from different places and have different life experiences informing what they think a superhero is, the stories only get better."

Marvel also weaves the multicultural empowerment trope into and around its blockbuster movies. A brief moment in the final battle scene from *Avengers: Endgame* is especially instructive. Captain Marvel's arrival turns the tide of the fight; she singlehandedly destroys the villain's ship and is asked to do what various male superheroes hadn't been able to do: get the gauntlet off the battlefield. As Peter Parker hands it to her and looks at the enemy troops gathering, he expresses concern: "I don't know how you're gonna get it through all of that." At just that moment, all of the female superheroes amass around her in dramatic fashion. "Don't worry," Wanda Maximoff says. "She's got help," adds Okoye. The moment is an exclamation point of female power, and its presence in the film only makes sense within the logic of the multicultural empowerment trope. Asserting the solidarity of these superheroes *as women*, the moment is a deliberate recognition and repudiation of sexism—in society, in the history of the superhero genre, and perhaps also in some of its traditional fanbase. The moment's affective punch comes from simultaneously seeing sexism defeated and imagining a future where sexism (like Thanos) is defeated.

There isn't (nor can there be) a parallel scene for men—a fact that reveals an obvious yet significant aspect of multicultural empowerment narratives and of our current structure of feeling. Of course, there are many scenes where male superheroes amass; the battle sequence actually starts with Captain American, Thor, and Iron Man doing just that. But that moment isn't (at least within the narrative's preferred meaning) meant to be an overt statement about their gender but about their history as core Avengers. Although the central role they play in the franchise is linked, in no small part, to them being men, their gender is effectively exnominated—a feature that reflects the very systemic privilege that the female empowerment moment pushes against. In essence, then, men (as well as straight and white people) are excluded from the heart of multicultural narratives of empowerment, because as men (or as straight people or as white people) they are already *in* power. Of course, characters in those dominant social subject positions often have preferential access to other kinds of narratives. In *Endgame*, for example, it is Iron Man who gets to be the ultimate hero and defeat Thanos in a narrative that is about redemption and sacrifice rather than empowerment.

So what roles do men, straight people, white people, or members of any dominant group tend to play within multicultural narratives of empowerment? They can certainly play the villains—agents of the system of discrimination that needs to be overcome. But they can also play other roles. They can, for example, play the role of witness who simply observes and by doing so acknowledges the empowerment. As the audience for the assembly of the female superheroes, Peter Parker plays that role in *Endgame*. So too, of course, does the film's male audience.

They can also be supportive secondary characters who assist a character on their path to empowerment. That is certainly the case on *RuPaul's Drag Race*, the long-running reality competition show in which drag queens vie to be America's next drag superstar. The series is replete with multicultural empowerment moments. Competitors frequently recount the homophobia, racism, and gender discrimination they experienced coming out as gay and as drag performers and appearing on the show is repeatedly framed as empowering in and of itself.

In a reversal of heteronormative culture, the show is dominated by queer men who appear not only as contestants, but also as judges and choreographers. For the straight men and women who appear, the show's queer-centrism positions them as supportive allies and perhaps affords them a degree of queerness (akin to *Glee*'s Rachel and Finn). That is certainly true for judge Michelle Visage, but also for the many straight and cis-gendered men and women who have participated in challenges in which contestants make over members of the show's production team, members of their own family, or super fans. In contrast to so much of the gay-themed programming of the 1990s that put straight characters and their straight panic anxieties at the center, *Drag Race* keeps its focus on the queens.

When they provide entry points for members of the groups who benefit from those systems, multicultural empowerment narratives work as a multicasting tool. In the age of narrowcasting, networks, cable channels, and streaming services face conflicting imperatives: provide content tailored narrowly enough to the interests of a specific audience so you can attract their attention in a very crowded media environment, but also look to grow your viewership by appealing to other audiences.[4] The multicultural empowerment trope can help achieve these conflicting goals by speaking to viewers who feel marginalized by a certain system of discrimination and to modern-day male (or straight, white, cis-gender, etc) slumpies who see themselves as allies in that political struggle. Thus, television's programming strategies intersect with, leverage, and perhaps deepen the psychographics of our highly polarized political culture.

Implications for TV Studies

I want to spend the rest of this essay raising a number of interconnected issues TV scholars might ponder, given the evolving dynamics of straight panic and the emergence of multicultural empowerment narratives. From its inception, critical TV studies has been deeply invested in critiquing television's normative and monocultural power. Of course, it has also been adapting many of its assumptions in response to the changing nature of its object of study. This discussion is meant to contribute to that effort.

First, what I think might be the easiest issue to address: the limitations of multicultural empowerment narratives. Such narratives appear to challenge the systems of oppression TV has long been criticized for reproducing. And at times, writers' rooms and sound stages seem to be increasingly staffed by a new generation of content creators who often seem invested in the kind of critique of TV that TV scholars have been advancing for decades. While some of the rhetoric may be industry self-promotion, much of it also reflects meaningful changes in Hollywood production cultures. And many multicultural empowerment narratives ask viewers to think about systems of power in new ways.

Those changes, however, don't close down the need to explore the complex nature of representation, authorial intent, and industrial television production. We still need to ask: How and why do multicultural empowerment narratives vary? How can they work toward different political ends? And how are they interpreted by diverse audiences? The history of multiculturalism, for example, underscores just how easily multiculturalism can be integrated into neoliberalism in ways that can greatly limit modes of thinking about social inequality.

House Hunters' vision of a frictionless pluralism, for example, rests on the exclusion of people who don't have money to buy a house. While the show does reflect some degree of economic diversity, the web of forces shaping the show's production limit just how inclusive the show is in terms of class status. Similar analysis must be done to expose the ways white supremacy, heteronormativity, cis-genderism, ableism, and other structures of thinking are perpetuated by multicultural narratives of empowerment. Even as the trope makes TV more inclusive, exclusions remain and new ones created. That, after all, is the frustrating nature of representation. Exploring such limitations is the easiest issue to address, I suggest, because such skepticism is baked into TV studies' fundamental orientation.

A second issue I want to address is more fraught and one many scholars are less apt to ponder: how might multicultural empowerment narratives complicate the calculus we use to understand privilege? Exploring this issue can help us think through the relationship between TV, culture, and politics in today's queerer times. Multicultural empowerment narratives' most powerful points of identification and affects are organized around the experience of overcoming socio-political marginality. As such, they are more easily accessible to people marginalized by some aspect(s) of their social identity. Conversely, they are less accessible or even inaccessible to people who aren't marginalized and/or who don't want to imagine themselves or others as marginalized because they don't buy into the idea of systemic oppression or group-based advancement. Thus, as such empowerment narratives become more prominent, they help normalize specific multicultural values, sideline or even censure monoculturalist views, and channel a certain form of cultural capital toward marginalized groups and their allies and away from those who oppose or simply prefer to disregard them.

In raising this issue, I don't want to validate simplistic discourses about male or white victimhood. To be clear, men, white people, straight people, and members of other dominant groups continue to be structurally advantaged economically, politically, legally, and socially, even amid dramatic changes that challenge the monoculturalism upon which those advantages rest. There are also plenty of cultural tropes that work to normalize specific forms of monocultural privilege. The rise of multicultural empowerment narratives, however, push us to consider the complexity of power and of the experience of being (dis)advantaged in today's queerer times by considering (to adapt Althusser) the growing autonomy of the cultural sphere. TV's practices and products certainly remain deeply entangled structurally and ideologically with the economic, political, and social spheres. Compared to the 1970s, however, when early TV scholarship was understandably focused on revealing the tight alignments that existed between network-era TV and other spheres, today's media landscape pushes us to also pay attention to the misalignments and possible disconnections that can exist.

Such a suggestion immediately draws us into the long debate about the relationship of industrial popular culture to the economic, political, legal, and social spheres—a debate that, in the case at hand, comes down to the question: what do TV's multicultural empowerment narratives actually do? No one would (or at least should) claim that they offer a transparent window onto political life or viewers' attitudes about social difference. But some scholars would argue that they actually mask and thus enable continued injustice by offering feelgood fantasies of progress. They would be right, to some extent. Undoubtedly such narratives can obscure as much or more than they reveal. They can underestimate the depth and breadth of systems oppression and may fuel complacency and self-satisfaction rather than self-reflection and indignation. As such, analyzing them and acknowledging their limitations is essential.

Yet multicultural empowerment narratives can simultaneously do other things. As a media and cultural studies scholar, I believe that representations and the affects they can generate are real and that, despite their inevitable limitations, seeing one's self, one's values, and one's way of life validated in the stories a society tells about itself is meaningful.[5] It can spark hope, pride, a sense of belonging and of being understood. That is why many minority groups have fought to increase and improve TV's representations of themselves. That begs the question: if multicultural empowerment narratives are becoming a common and even dominant way in which America thinks about itself, does feeling that you are excluded from them or marginalized within their logics matter? I say yes.

The stakes involved are raised further by a key aspect of multicultural empowerment narratives. Focused as they usually are on overcoming the past and the present, they are often about the future in a way that narratives linked to being *in* power often aren't. If you are someone who was happy with the way things used to be or who sees politics as a zero-sum game where others' gains come at your expense, then multicultural empowerment narratives could feel like a threat to your status and your role in the nation's future. Such fears, I argue, lie at the heart of conservatives' straight panic. For those with privilege, as progressive activists have put it, equality can feel like oppression.

That adage might help people who value diversity and equality work through the blind spots of their dominant social positions, but it doesn't really address the heart of the matter: People have fundamentally diverging visions of America's future that reflect different definitions of equality and incompatible investments in multi- and monoculturalism. Those differences form a deep fault line in American society. If we describe what is going on in today's queerer times as a "culture war" or a "battle for the soul of America," then it seems clear that a moderately left-of-center multiculturalism controls large swaths of the cultural sphere, especially mainstream popular media culture like TV. Of course, holdouts remain (Fox News being the most obvious), and victory in the cultural sphere doesn't mean equal ground has been won in the economic, political, legal, or social spheres.

But acknowledging that a version of multiculturalism, however compromised it may be, has become hegemonic on U.S. television helps us navigate today's socio-political landscape. That includes understanding Trumpism's populist appeal. How so? For one thing, it might lead us to complicate basic assumptions we may have about the nature and experience of privilege. If we hope to move beyond today's dysfunctional polarization, developing a richer sense of why some of those who don't see themselves in the multicultural future validated in so much television feel marginalized or disadvantaged will be a useful first step. It can also help us remember that America's multicultural future isn't inevitable and that the moral superiority of a value system that challenges monoculturalism isn't an objective fact but rather an argument that must be continually advanced. As multicultural narratives become increasingly common and even hegemonic, it can be easy to lose sight of that fact and fall into an overly confident moral fundamentalism that forgets key lessons from queer experience/theory. If that happens, we may find it even harder to extend whatever progress is made in the cultural sphere (and elsewhere) into greater political, legal, social, and economic justice.

I want to conclude by raising a third issue related to straight panic: the need to think through the changing relationship between the mainstream and the majority. While the version of "the mainstream" that coalesced in middle of the twentieth century (alongside the rise of TV) had its detractors, it was generally seen as reflecting experiences and values shared by most Americans and was easily conflated with the majority and consensus American values. In our highly fragmented, politicized, and polarized moment, the concept of "the mainstream" has come to function quite differently. It is increasingly something against which one positions oneself (e.g., hipsters' rejection of bland corporate products; conservative discourses about the lamestream media). And in our increasingly fragmented media culture, it can seem like a relic of the past—something you can either nostalgically long for or celebrate having moved beyond.

While "the mainstream's" cultural relevance seems uncertain, the 2016 and 2020 presidential elections made many people hyperaware of the importance of building a political majority. Trump's norm-busting campaign and volatile presidency suggested what politics might look like when political culture is no longer tempered by any pretense of serving the kind of common cause historically understood in terms of mainstream American values. Trump, one could argue, masterfully deployed post-mainstream political strategies, using rallies, tweets, and policies to narrowcast to voters who felt ignored by the lamestream news media, the multiculturalism of Hollywood elites, and both the Democratic and Republican parties.

We live at a time when people desperately want to be in the political majority but fewer and fewer, it seems, identify with the mainstream. That combination will almost certainly shape U.S. political culture in the near future. A Trumpian right, committed as it seems to be to white, Christian monoculturalism, will likely need to rely on gerrymandering, voter suppression, and other anti-democratic measures in order to build a political majority in a diversifying society. On the left, a positive orientation toward diversity offers the potential for a coalitional politics. Building coalitions that are meaningfully inclusive is difficult, of course. To succeed, I'd argue, such an approach requires moving beyond straight panic and nurturing a new social imagination where people are capable of seeing themselves in—and rooting for overcoming—a range of struggles.

In this context, what should we make of and what can we do with multicultural empowerment narratives like *Hollywood* and *RuPaul's Drag Race*, and their cast of empowered characters and straight-ish sidekicks? I will end by arguing that we see them as opportunities— as tools to help develop the kind of imagination we all need in order to build alliances across social differences. A radically elastic deployment of queerness that would see *Glee*'s Rachel and Finn and RuPaul's straight allies as queer can help too. When defined as the universal gap that exists between lived experience's messy complexity and the social order's idealized norms— queerness can help bridge social differences by helping anyone recognize and lean into their own queerness rather than invest in an unattainable ideal. I recognize that I am ending with a utopian flourish, one that critical theory might dismiss as naïve or complacent about the ways men, straight people, or white people can co-opt the rhetoric of marginality to reproduce rather than dismantle hierarchies. But there is value (what Eve Sedgwick might call reparative value) in remembering that television texts can harm and heal. Approaching them in that way may help us create a queerer future.

Notes

1 Ron Becker, *Gay TV and Straight America* (New Brunswick: Rutgers UP, 2006).
2 Martha Farnsworth Richie, "We're All Minorities Now," *American Demographics*, October 1991, 28.
3 Nardine Saad, "Ratings Firm Nielsen Begins Tracking Diversity and Inclusion in TV," *Los Angeles Times*, February 17, 2021, https://www.latimes.com/entertainment-arts/tv/story/2021-02-17/ratings-firm-nielsen-begins-tracking-diversity-and-inclusion-in-tv
4 Katherine Sender, "Dualcasting: Bravo's Gay Programming and the Quest for Women Audiences," in *Cable Visions: Television beyond Broadcasting*, eds. Sarah Banet-Weiser, Cynthia Chris, and Anthony Freitas (New York: New Your University Press, 2007): 302–318; Julia Himberg, "Multicasting: Lesbian Programming and the Changing Landscape of Cable TV," *Television & New Media* 15, no. 4 (2014), 289–304.
5 F. Hollis Griffin, *Feeling Normal: Sexuality and Media and the Digital Age* (Bloomington: Indiana UP, 2017).

2

BRIGGS, *FAMILY*, QUEER

Melissa Hardie and Amy Villarejo

Eve Kosofsky Sedgwick's essay "How to Bring Your Kids Up Gay" asked something of us at the time it was published that we want to foreground now to revisit its stakes anew. It is an essay about *teachers* and it asked how *teachers could help* queer students. What's more, its simple rhetorical inversion, coding "how to" bring your kids up gay as both a desideratum and a workshop, gives the idea of actively raising kids to become gay rather than thwarting them a real possibility, one that has to be nourished as much in the family as in the classroom. These sites, furthermore, are wedded through the discursive category of adolescence rather than posed as places of *bildung* differentiation.

Her pedagogy of gay cultivation has a history, and one of the places to understand its stakes comes in the debates in the 1970s over the place of gay and lesbian teachers in America's classrooms, put to test in the 1978 California referendum known colloquially as the Briggs Initiative, which attempted to require the firing or termination of teachers in California schools found to have engaged in homosexual activity or conduct. More on this failed attempt to shore up a fantasmatic family, we promise. Popular culture responded to the contemporary news, leading up to the ballot measure with topical treatments, yet the programming mandates of network television required that these plots balance accommodationist and transformative logics. The ABC drama *Family*, which ran from 1976 to 1980, gave unusual attention for a network drama to topical storylines ranging from alcoholism to suicide to homosexuality to breast cancer to adoption to dementia. An episode from 1977, "We Love You, Miss Jessup," focuses on the teenage Buddy (Kristy McNichol) growing attached to a teacher revealed to be a lesbian. It provides an extraordinary place to glimpse "How to Bring Your Kids Up Gay" as a televisual exercise in queer pedagogy.

DOI: 10.4324/9781003109044-4

Sedgwick Revisited

We had remembered Eve Sedgwick's essay "How to Bring Your Kids Up Gay," first published in *Social Text* in 1991, for what we took to be its signal gesture of affirmation in light of a widespread wish for gay people simply *not to be*: we should try, Sedgwick averred, to bring kids up gay, that is, *to rear them and school them* as happy, thriving, humans, widening the space for gay becoming or, a more loaded term, development. Upon rereading and in retrospect, it turns out that Sedgwick's essay provides a much more complicated account of that journey, from childhood to adulthood and from expressions of gender and sexuality along the way and in revisiting it, two decades now after its initial publication, its strengths in illuminating what it might mean actively to affirm queer and trans kids are more attenuated, even blunted. Let us explain how.

As with much of her supple and still-influential scholarship, Sedgwick's interest in the psychodynamics of queer life becomes a writing practice that helps (largely academic humanist) readers become conversant with actually existing methods of treating patients within various ideological apparatuses of violence and erasure, including the mental health professions, schools, the military, mass culture, the law, penal institutions, and so on. In this essay, her focus lands not on what she calls the "mother texts" (Freud *et al.*) but on movements in revisionist psychoanalysis, including ego psychology, especially movements following upon the publication of the Diagnostic and Statistical Manual-III (DSM-III) in 1980, which marked the elimination of "homosexuality" as a pathological diagnosis and the introduction of Gender Identity Disorder (GID) as a new clinical category for diagnosis and treatment.[1] At the time she published this essay, less the case today, lots of academic humanists were indeed riveted intensively to the mother texts and not particularly conversant in developments in many and varied actual psychiatric or therapeutic practices, and so Sedgwick acted as a kind of wise guide for scholars and activists whose heads were literally elsewhere. What is more, she became, for us, a fierce critic of this literature and its associated institutions and practices, willing to indict them for their lies and complicity:

> What the books I have been discussing, and the institutions to which they are attached, demonstrate is that the wish for the dignified treatment of already-gay people is necessarily destined to turn into either trivializing apologetics or, much worse, a silkily camouflaged complicity in oppression—in the absence of a strong, explicit, *erotically invested* affirmation of many people's felt desire or need that there be gay people in the immediate world.
>
> *26, emphasis in the original*

The need for such affirmations has not abated. And yet, the two key framing devices of this essay (the motivating citation of the 1989 publication of a report on youth suicide and the relationship between the suspension of "homosexuality" as a diagnosis and introduction of GID as a diagnosis in the DSMIII) have rightly come under scrutiny.

With regard to suicide, Sedgwick takes for granted the report's contention that "young gays and lesbians are two to three times more likely than other young people to attempt and to commit suicide" (18), a claim experts have disputed not simply as a matter of quantification and sampling but as a matter of continued pathologization via misinformation and the melodramatizing rhetoric of life versus death.[2] Thinking that she was standing with pain, she may have reinforced the barriers between humanities and social scientific knowledge that would have enabled more scrutiny over the study she cites. More important, to reinforce the idea that gay kids kill themselves scarily risks amplifying the sense that that's what gay kids ought to do or contemplate or feel. In an essay that purports to grapple with gay kids, they appear to have little agency or capacity to enunciate their destinies. We will want to stress how media and scholarship might make better room to hear these voices.

With regard to the "homosexuality" versus GID issue, Sedgwick introduces more vexing and consequential misapprehension of the relationship between sexuality and gender that Grace Lavery, in an insightful essay published in *TSQ*, calls "egg theory," namely the "type of reasoning that trans people use, prior to transition, to prove transition's impossibility or fruitlessness."[3] Egg theory, for Lavery, names a generalized hostility to the logic of transition, one that in queer thought entails, for example, "the friction between the life of the 'tr★nny' and that of the queer others whose transness has been sublimated into a more nuanced, sophisticated orientation toward gender" (386). In "How to Bring Your Kids Up Gay," Sedgwick's egg theory wants to line up gender and sexuality in ways that foreclose trans becoming in favor of neatly aligned ascension from "proto-gay" child to gay adult, and just as assuredly from "effeminate boy" to gay man. To note that queer theory was an emergent discourse in 1991, with Sedgwick at its most articulate heart, is not to dismiss the way that trans★ lives and imaginaries are *conceptually* and *consequentially* disabled by its arguments; an affirmation of trans★ lives indeed animates the present attempt to think about TV.

Scholarship on childhood in the past decade or more confirms that such alignments as those presupposed in Sedgwick's essay are rarely neat; we could take Katherine Bond Stockton's *The Queer Child, or Growing Sideways in the Twentieth Century* as luscious evidence, furthermore, that "ascension" and "development" as names for becoming likewise foreclose a whole range of growth she calls "horizontal" and which solicits attention to the *fantasmatic* status of childhood (as "something we are *not*" and in fact never were).[4] Jules Gill-Peterson's book *Histories of the Transgender Child*, concludes with a fitting corrective to "egg theory," a chapter called "How to Bring Your Kids Up Trans."[5] In this conclusion, Gill-Peterson adjusts our frame of reference to show how the terms/frames of trans policing may be new to a situation in which a long history of gender legibility, racial fertility and reproduction, and conservative rhetoric have collectively shaped American responses to trans children. Both of these texts center the voices and imaginaries of children, whether through literature or through the archives, in ways that *allow them to teach us* about the coordinates and processes of gendered and sexual becoming.

And so what is ultimately at stake for Sedgwick, that is to say teaching and learning (she speaks, after all, as a concerned professor), is a question shared by all the thinkers whose work we have just surveyed, namely the question of pedagogy. Transmission. Modeling. Rearing. Educating. In short, TV.

Briggs

The Briggs initiative was a (failed) California state ballot initiative in the election of November 1978. Sponsored by the Orange County far-right representative John Briggs (and based upon the successes of another "orange," the Florida citrus spokeswoman Anita Bryant), the measure would have *required*, not just allowed, California public schools to fire any "certificated" employee (predominantly teachers and their aides and counselors) who had engaged in any public homosexual activity or conduct. [The former entailed public or indiscreet acts of perversion or sodomy under the penal code; the latter was the much wider category of activity that was seen to promote or advocate for homosexual behavior.]

The preamble to the proposed law is a primer in ideological theories of the family:

> One of the most fundamental interests of the State is the establishment and the preservation of the family unit. Consistent with this interest is the State's duty to protect its impressionable youth from influences which are antithetical to this vital interest. This duty is particularly compelling when the state undertakes to educate its youth, and, by law, requires them to be exposed to the state's chosen educational environment throughout their formative years.... As a result of continued close and prolonged contact with schoolchildren, a teacher, teacher's aide, school administrator or counselor becomes a role model whose words, behavior and actions are likely to be emulated by students coming under his or her care, instruction, supervision, administration, guidance and protection.

And in case we missed the point, the text of the measure reiterates the state's interest in "preserving and perpetuating the conjugal family unit." This emphasis on "family values" coincided with the rise of the Christian right-wing of which the Briggs ballot measure was a signal initiative. And while the Church of Jesus Christ of Latter Day Saints (colloquially the Mormon Church or abbreviated as LDS) did not fund Briggs, it funded subsequent "sexual propositions," including the Proposition 8 campaign in 2008, which returned to the threat that gay and lesbian teachers were said to pose to "innocent" students.[6]

Opponents in the "No on 6" movement, notably Harvey Milk and Sally Miller Gearhart, debated Briggs and handily refuted these fear-mongering arguments he and his supporters made on behalf of the ballot measure, including the idea that because homosexuals somehow are unable to reproduce, they must recruit, vampire-style. Although much is known about Milk due to his assassination and subsequent media around his activism, Gearhart deserves more than a footnote. A professor for more than three decades and one of the first openly lesbian professors to hold a tenure track appointment (at San Francisco State University), Gearhart's contributions to the anti-Briggs struggle included grassroots organizing and impassioned debate (although her appearance against Briggs, glimpsed in *The Times of Harvey Milk*, was edited out of *Milk*, the feature film). As Sara Smith-Silverman explains in her history of teachers' activism against Briggs, "Gearhart's ability to use her influence as a lesbian professor points to the centrality of queer educators in efforts to defeat the initiative."[7]

In any case, the willingness of teachers across the state to organize at a grassroots level and to come out of the closet to their families, students and their parents, and colleagues led to the defeat of Proposition 6. The work of remembering the fight against Briggs has led to research by academic historians and exhibitions at historical archives such as the GLBT Historical Society in San Francisco.[8] In almost all of this material, the "gays and lesbians" under discussion are the teachers threatened with discriminatory action and with the climate of fear stoked by the measure's proponents; the students—certainly to the "yes" crowd but implicitly in the "no" crowd, too—are presumptively straight, or innocent, or not-yet-sexual, or otherwise impressionable. That a gay or lesbian teacher might be an *attractive* role model for a queer student, even a lifeline in a heterosexist hostile environment, seems almost beyond the bounds of enunciation, since it raises the tricky specter of transmission.

An exchange in the fictional *Milk* (Gus Van Sant, 2008) that recreates the debate between Harvey Milk (now *sans* Gearhart) and Briggs in Walnut Hills (an affluent suburb of San Francisco) gives an indication of just how difficult it is to apprehend students as either queer or sexual or imitative. It's funny dialogue, historically accurate, but it misses the arena we are most interested in, and now approaching through *Family*, namely a coincidence of a queer teacher and a potentially queer student. Here is the exchange:

> Briggs (Denis O'Hare): They are interested in becoming teachers, because they want to encourage our children to join them.
>
> Milk (Sean Penn): How do you teach homosexuality? Is it like French? I was borne of heterosexual parents, taught by heterosexual teachers, in a fiercely heterosexual society, so why then am I homosexual? And, no offense meant, if it were true that children mimic their teachers, there would be a helluva lot more nuns running around.... [laughs]

What if children mimic their teachers? What if genderqueer could flourish as pedagogy, not in mapping proto-gay into adult gay, but ambient queerness into its messy becoming? Surprisingly, that's what we find in this weird little remnant of television history, an episode of *Family*.

Family

"We Love You, Miss Jessup," episode 6 of *Family*'s third season aired on November 1, 1977, almost exactly a year before the election featuring Proposition 6. This episode was written by Diana Gould, who launched her career writing for television with *Family*, for which she had credits for four episodes over the series' run. Diana Gould now teaches Insight Meditation for the Gay and Lesbian Center, from which we are inferring that she is not unwilling to be identified as or with queer/s.[9] And after earning an master of fine arts in 2004, she published a mystery novel, *Coldwater* (Rare Bird Books, 2013), itself a Hollywood story about a TV writer's redemption. It's a classic lesbian nexus: mystery fiction, new age spiritualism, and lesbian-themed TV.

The episode was one of several that identified a critical relationship between questions of sexuality and the family system. Early in the first of *Family*'s five seasons, the question of the etiology of homosexuality arises.[10] The Lawrences, the family of the title, parents Doug and Kate, children Nancy, Willy, and Buddy, care for Nancy's son, their grandson, and nephew Timmy, born to a brief but troubled marriage whose dissolution anchored the pilot that launched the show. Timmy's parents' divorce sets the scene for the show's almost incessant production of "very special episodes," topical 1970s enquiries into contemporary problems that were characteristic of prime-time shows through the period. The very special episode found fertile ground in *Family*, a show that featured nothing but very special episodes and whose rationale was precisely the representation as intelligible and familiar the kinds of issues that arose to trouble conventional middle-class white families—flirtations with drugs and drinking, sexual initiation, and misrule, "dropping out" of college. By doing so, the Lawrences' travails became a vehicle for charting the inter-implication of intimate and topical forms of knowledge, making intimate revelations and actions in plots ways to rehearse and teach current affairs.

So in the episode titled "Thursday's Child," the prospect of Timmy growing up without a father in situ is raised as a concern when Buddy Lawrence, the young daughter of the family, played by Kristy McNichol, notes that "boys who grow up without fathers can become homosexuals." Buddy offers this commentary as a reason to avoid divorce, but we soon hear a ghostlier echo as we discover that this baby Timmy is named after her brother, a son and sibling, who died five years earlier in a drowning accident. Timmy carries the important charge of continuing the line of the first son of the family, a charge that homosexuality may vitiate. The cross-generational caretaking the Lawrence family performs now has a more complex genealogy; caretaking is a form of grief attenuation or exacerbation, convalescence, or haunting. Substitute a father without a son for a son without a father: cue a grieving mother. Kate Lawrence, the mother of dead Timmy as well as of Nancy, Willie, and Buddy, is the figure around whom the show's family constellates (despite the apparent investment in paternity noted by Buddy), and for her the melancholy is atmospheric and temporally calibrated; in this episode, she notes that she dislikes daylight saving and when asked why she replies "because when it's evening it should be dark."

This observation is appropriately taken for an instruction, directed not only at the characters who populate *Family*'s Pasadena neighborhood and the Lawrence home and adjacent studio, but also at the prime-time television schedule where *Family* was an exceptional show in several ways. Its high seriousness, Sirkian tones and melodramatic pacing, its fascination with static shots of elaborate domestic interiors, its fixation on a family riven by loss (concretely the loss of Timmy but more often something intangible, an incremental deterioration of intimate understanding and social coherence) framed an almost impossible burden of figuring all social malaises either allegorically or corporeally (from hostage-taking to teen alcoholism) while never rocking off its base of steady even quiet composure. Such striking qualities set it against its competition—both in its ABC stable and in its timeslot (*Bionic Woman*, *Donny and Marie*)—in stark ways. *Family*'s five seasons were all in this sense dark, autumnal, informed and invested in televisual history itself.

With its focus on the family home as the space for both liberatory experimentation with lifestyle and ethical instruction, mise-en-scène becomes a dominant signifying system; as Fassbinder remarks of Sirk, "people are always placed in rooms already heavily marked by their social situations. The rooms are incredibly exact."[11] For example, in *Family*, wall furnishings are exactly keyed to social and aesthetic arguments that will be pursued in the diegesis. Nancy lives in a freestanding studio whose walls are adorned with early modern botanical prints and a Hockney print that features the cover of Flaubert's *Sentimental Education*; Willie, aspiring filmmaker, has a poster of *Giant* on his wall; the failed patriarch as queer totem could not be more flagrantly advertised. These images function like the characters who arrive for a story, as apertures to the "real" world, as something more than the usual dressing. Such reliance on props is clear in the credits, after all, where photographs of the family are profusely arranged atop a grand piano.

"Thursday's Child" shares with any typical *Family* episode its structural negotiation of topical content through the show's familiar technique of plotting two separate storylines, one grave, one light-hearted, and locating at their chiastic meeting-place a queer possibility—the complex entanglement of the comic and the tragic. The loss of Timmy and the christening of his erstwhile nephew locates the terms and duration of grief and its ubiquitous presence: one Timmy is gone but another rises in his place, the (homosexual) son without a father metaleptically represented through the figure of the father without his son. A comic plot, the escalating cost and bourgeois embarrassment associated with catering the christening, neatly pairs social and cultural capital as an affectionate but pointed satire of the Lawrence's concern for status but also its predictable collapse in the face of the rigors of social conformity. The Lawrences are unusually and loveably incompetent in these matters: not only in a performative way, where they speak quietly (too quietly), hesitate, stumble, backtrack, flare up and calm down, but in their capacity to care about value systems outside the home.

But whereas the fictional outside-the-home of Pasadena—Buddy's school, Willy's workplace, Nancy's seminar, Doug's law practice—can hardly impose its strictures on them, their robust intimate circle is supported by an attachment to the real that is a televisually mediated one; its symptom the figure of the homosexual son who metonymizes all the way in which a family can go off the rails. As one of us, Amy Villarejo, wrote "television programming in the 1970s relentlessly pursued revisions on and of family life."[12] In its earliest conception *Family* was in fictional dialogue with *An American Family*, the PBS serial documentary of the lives of a real "American family," the Louds, a family touched by divorce *and* the phenomenon of a gay son, Lance Loud.[13] This intersection bears the trace of what Villarejo calls "seriality as queer time" in her meticulous examination of *An American Family* as a "sustained glimpse" occasioned and facilitated by that seriality and by her analysis of "the meshes of the real," "where the indexical traces surface through these ethereal transmissions."(84) This debt is made explicit in the third episode of the second season, "Home Movie," when Willie decides to make a documentary about his family. The episode aligns the otherwise "extractive" logic of *An American Family* with the intimate, hand-held introversion of the family movie, and also acknowledges a sideways genealogy for the series itself as Kate notes of Willie's experiment "He's not the first; there is a precedent. You'll remember the Loud family?"[14]

It's an explicit glimpse of *An American Family* that sees this untimely dead son, Timmy, and his doppelganger cited under the sign of homosexuality and where the queer becomes itself the point of contact between problem plotlines and their comic chords; pairing the social real and highly conventional serial melodrama underwrites a complex negotiation between contemporaneity and the historicized conventions of melodrama reworked for prime time. Like Timmy junior, *Family* is belated: a melodrama sparked by the experimental documentary.

In its vigorous riposte to the homophobia of actions such as the Briggs initiative, *Family* thematized the intersection of staid, bourgeois Pasadena life with a "real world" from which queer subjects arrive to report on their lives. These queer lives are introduced from stage left but come to demonstrate that queer potential has already nestled in its suburban mise-en-scène. *Family* presented two further episodes with queer storylines, episodes where a gay man and a lesbian respectively arrived to trouble the everyday of the Lawrence family. In both cases, queer characters arrive from San Francisco, and in both cases, but especially in the case of Miss Jessup, the question of coming out is presented as an act not of individual consciousness and identification but rather as a social and interpersonal, and pedagogical practice. When Willie's erstwhile best friend Zeke is arrested in a gay bar in Season Two's "Rites of Friendship," Willie's homophobic response is so discordant that it transforms Doug and Kate's bewilderment into a puzzled acceptance. They have known Zeke since he was a child but they wonder—is Zeke still Zeke? Yes he is, though Zeke himself hardly knows it, because he requires of Willie, at least, an acknowledgement of something "new" about him. That secured, rapprochement is reached in the lobby of the Burbank airport and Zeke flies back to San Francisco.

Zeke's coming out is paired with a comic storyline about Buddy's dancing lessons. She asks her sister Nancy to teach her to dance but Nancy neglects her duties and finally Zeke does the honors (to a disco version of "Thanks for the Memories" no less). Contrite, Nancy delivers supplementary dancing lessons amid protestations of loyalty and affiliation. This comic pedagogical subplot choreographs the more serious pedagogy of the episode, which seeks to mitigate the perception of harm posed by the homosexual and even to universalize his predicament when Willie and Doug, father and son, confess to adolescent homosexual crushes in a moment of magnificent complicity, adding that they understood these to be "developmentally appropriate." They had queer feelings because "the book said so," as Zeke later puts it, a further pedagogical moment that ties indexicality to a queer temporality of "development."

Having canvassed the gay as a phenomenon of adolescent development and as a variation elicited by disruptions of the family system, the "teachability" of homosexuality becomes more pronounced in "We Love You, Miss Jessup," where Buddy's high school teacher, fresh from, you guessed it, San Francisco, turns out to be a lesbian and, worse, accused, and only partially acquitted, of an involvement with a student. That Miss Jessup will turn Buddy's world upside down is augured by the episode's opening scene where Buddy, rapt, is walking around the kitchen reading *The Member of the Wedding* – "Miss Jessup's personal copy!"—after already inhaling *The Heart is a Lonely Hunter*—her assigned reading. Buddy's affection for McCullers aligns with other things about Buddy that are inescapable even in the diegesis, such as her resolute tomboyishness. The unlikeable prospect of Buddy wearing a dress, after all, is a standing joke for the series. Miss Jessup semi-confesses and after deliberations by the school, and parents, and the Lawrences themselves, Miss Jessup removes herself from the fray and goes back to San Francisco.

The Pasadena–San Francisco axis offers a west coast topography for television and its queer "real" as it signals the latter city's visibility as a queer community. Buddy's fascination for McCullers, and Miss Jessup, initiates a different version of queer possibility than the etiologies of homosexuality presented in earlier seasons. Although her fascination with McCullers is attributed to Miss Jessup's teaching, Buddy's affiliation with the implicitly queer Frankie of *The Member of the Wedding* has already been intuited by her mother, Kate, who prophesied her love of McCullers prior to Miss Jessup's disruptive literary education. This clarification is critical as it initiates a dialectical argument over the meaning of "influence." In a series of ersatz, legalistic meetings, an unpleasant agitator, Mrs Palmer, denounces Miss Jessup as an "avowed" lesbian. Although Doug Lawrence points out to her that homosexuality "per se" is not illegal, Mrs Palmer avers that it is, *to her*. Thus follows a process of debate during which Kate Lawrence is mazed by the implications of Miss Jessup's sexuality, profession, and proximity to her daughter (perhaps her resemblance *of* her daughter); Mrs Palmer's hyperbolic characterization of the peril posed by Miss Jessup is countered by Doug's precise legalism, and Miss Jessup also defends herself against the insinuation that she is leading Buddy astray. This insinuation becomes overt as Buddy's peers (led by Mrs Palmer's daughter, played by a young Helen Hunt) draw attention to Buddy's queerness, identifying not as much a capacity to be influenced as a vulnerability to be exploited or a nature to be unmasked.

But the episode navigates its audience to a place of empathic identification with Miss Jessup whose persecution, we learn, is serial, and undeserved. How such an empathic pathway arises is limned by Buddy herself, who battles her own negative reaction to the revelation of Miss Jessup's sexuality by citing a phrase drawn from *The Member of the Wedding*, the "we of me." In that novel, the phrase comes to signify the collectivity of any individual bound by familial and affective ties, and in the episode Buddy pronounces herself the "we" of Miss Jessup before declaring "and we love you, Miss Jessup!" Buddy's queerness is by this point almost taken for granted in the episode—acknowledged by her mother when she presses McCullers in her hands, by Miss Jessup in her particular bond with her pupil, and by Buddy herself *precisely* as a pedagogical effect and incitement of desire, where Miss Jessup has created an "appetite" for reading. It is not, however, a case of redefinition of Buddy's tomboy persona as a lesbian, but rather of the plural significance of the "we" Buddy comes to embody in her declaration of affection. Buddy's masculinity, in other words, is not presented as the prelude to a "gay" resolution, and Buddy certainly experiences no homosexual epiphany, no identificatory "aha!" moment—Buddy, in fact, turns away from simple identification with lesbianism. Buddy's "bringing up" is still a matter in process, and the episode settles on identifying Buddy with plural possibilities.

In its fictional refutation of the logic of the Briggs initiative, *Family* performs a series of pluralizing moves. It offers a case study of the effects and implications of the legislative drive behind the Briggs initiative in fictional terms, yet in the context of a series that has already made homosexuality a function of family culture precisely by referring to a "real" family (the Louds). It interposes a literary text whose function is to bridge, not distinguish, family—private—and school, with both parent and teacher espousing a model of empathic identification with difference. Having introduced from its beginning a character, Buddy, redolent of queer potential, it opts to align her with a storyline that neutralizes rather than exacerbates the threat of homosexuality while not taking the route of forming a homosexual identity for Buddy. As such, it teaches queer possibility without subsuming gender identity into a variety of sexual preference.

How to Bring Our Stars Up Gay

It's impossible to close without noting the way in which the show's queer storylines preempted its queer legacies. For example, it's impossible to watch Nancy teaching Buddy to dance, two women dancing, without recalling that Meredith Baxter (then Meredith Baxter Birney) and Kristy McNichol were both associated with queer exposure in later years: Baxter came out on network television after an outing threat and McNichol, earlier, was involved in a palimony suit brought by a former partner.[15] If we have argued that in its plural mode *Family* stimulates rather than resolves a set of queer resonances, we track several other reverberations between the "real world" and the Lawrences' "Pasadena" living room, noting how much damage Hollywood inflicted on these two *Family* members before they were able to discover and disclose their lesbianism.

Carson McCullers is perhaps only the first clue that the asocial tomboy will have a tough journey, and that the tomboy signifies as an invitation to lesbian identification. In her study of another McNichol vehicle, the film *Little Darlings* costarring tomboy Tatum O'Neal, Kristen Hatch observes that just as McCullers' own queerness spilled onto her characters and their avatars, notably Julie Harris, McNichol's star persona likewise congealed as queer:

> McNichol's off-screen identity in the early 1980s was as tomboyish as her on-screen one, if not more so, which worked to reinforce the film's lesbian reading. McNichol rose to stardom through her role as the tomboy, Buddy, on ABC's *Family* (1976–1980), and her publicity tended to play up her status as a tomboy off-screen as well as on. She often appeared in the pages of *Tiger Beat* and *Teen Beat* magazines on a skateboard, dirt bike, or even a speed buggy. While Doris Day's and Sandra Dee's glamorous and feminine star images worked to assure audiences that Calamity Jane and Gidget would eventually succumb to hetero-normative femininity, McNichol's masculinity off-screen suggested the possibility of an adult, butch identity for Angel [McNichol's character in *Little Darlings*].[16]

And a butch identity for McNichol herself: even while Hatch makes the case that the tomboy's masculinity quite often signals her sexual immaturity and even innocent childhood status, McNichol's lesbian significations as she matured into adulthood posed problems her publicity teams could not forestall. After the child star became an adult, she was beset by psychological demons that finally ended her acting career, namely a breakdown that crippled a year-long subsequent shoot and ultimately a diagnosis of bipolar disorder. Are we back to the conjunction of psychic distress and queer emergence that we tracked in Sedgwick's essay? Is "Hollywood" perhaps the very best name for a violent imposition of compulsory heterosexuality under the sign of the nuclear family?

If, as we've argued, the specter of the lost queer son haunts the coherence of the Lawrence unit as a televisual family, Mother Kate Lawrence and Father Doug Lawrence might have been surprised that not just Buddy/McNichol but *both* of their girls grow up to be lesbians! Unlike McNichol's professional difficulties following *Family*, Meredith Baxter of course found spectacular success in her role as Elyse Keaton on the subsequent long-running family television show, the NBC sitcom *Family Ties* (1982–89), and she supplemented that role with a number of acclaimed made-for-TV movie appearances through the 1980s and 1990s. While fans may not have tuned into Baxter's struggles with breast cancer and alcoholism, her coming out on national television (the *Today* show with Matt Lauer on December 2, 2009) made a splash: a TV event for a TV career of "family" melodramas and revelations. We will spare the reader the journey that Baxter charts in her memoir, *Untied: A Journey of Fame, Family, and Floundering*, except to note that she alleges that she was abused in her marriage to David Birney and that the "victim" mentality she developed caused her pain until she became sober and reckoned with her sexuality, culminating in long-term relationship with her now-wife Nancy Locke.

If we have revisited the 1970s and its unruly politics of gender and sexuality, it has been to reassert the wily and non-linear paths of queer kinship and worldmaking that were necessitated by attempts at the violent erasure of queer possibility, in the "real world" and its onscreen inventions. As is the case today, television's circuits of power aren't very queer friendly, but activism in the 2020s already suggests that Hollywood may be better at nurturing its women, its queers, and its BIPOC personnel than it was with McNichol and Baxter. May it be so.

Notes

1 The date for the removal of homosexuality as a diagnosis is often said to be 1973. The work for the DSM-III began in 1974 and culminated in publication in 1980. The term "gender identity disorder" has been replaced, in the DSM-5, by the diagnosis "gender dysphoria," which shifts attention from identity to the experience of distress trans* people may have.
2 https://news.cornell.edu/stories/2010/11/expert-sets-media-straight-gay-youth
3 Grace Lavery, "Egg Theory's Early Style," *Transgender Studies Quarterly* 7, 3 (August 2020): 383.
4 Katherine Bond Stockton, *The Queer Child, or Growing Sideways in the Twentieth Century* (Durham: Duke University Press, 2009), p. 5.
5 Jules Gill-Peterson, *Histories of the Transgender Child* (Minneapolis: University of Minnesota Press, 2018).
6 See Josh Sides, "Sexual Propositions," *Boom: A Journal of California* 1, 3 (August 2011).
7 Sara Smith-Silverman, "Gay Teachers Fight Back," *Journal of the History of Sexuality* 29, 1 (2020), p. 92. Smith-Silverman provides a thorough account of the convergence of gay rights activism with labor struggles through the teacher's unions and their chapters in northern and southern California.
8 "The Briggs Initiative: A Scary Proposition," curated by Sue Englander, Paula Lichtenberg, and Glenne McIlhenney, September 2018 to January 2019.
9 https://insightla.org/teacher/diana-gould/. Accessed March 5, 2021.
10 The first season of *Family* was a short six episodes, in the style of a mini-series.
11 Rainer Werner Fassbinder, "Six Films by Douglas Sirk," *New Left Review* 91 (May/June 1975), p. 97.
12 Amy Villarejo, *Ethereal Queer: Television, Historicity, Desire* (Durham: Duke University Press, 2013), p. 78.
13 Meredith Baxter, *Untied: A Memoir of Family, Fame, and Floundering* (New York: Crown Publishing, 2011), p. 205.
14 Pamela Yates explains the term "extractive" in relation to documentary:

> It struck me that when people come from the outside and "take"—whether it's anthropologists, academics, artists, journalists or filmmakers—and never consider collaborating with the protagonists or replenishing what's been taken, it's exactly

> the same practice as extractive industries (mining, hydroelectric or industrial agriculture)—multinational companies who steal the wealth from below the land, never share the proceeds, and in the process destroy the environment.

"Whose Story? Five Doc-Makers on (Avoiding) Extractive Filmmaking." *Documentary*, Fall 2017. www.documentary.org/feature/whose-story-five-doc-makers-avoiding-extractive-filmmaking?fbclid=IwAR0LwV0Cv2IgsveACMMbwxOAv4JTlp37AkRBliAz5xk1E7hseyAV33pHs5s. Accessed May 7, 2021.

15 Baxter, *Untied*; Matias Viegener discusses Kristy/Buddy as "androgynous" icon subject to a palimony suit in "Kinky Escapades, Bedroom Techniques, Unbridled Passion, and Secret Sex Codes" in David Bergman ed. *Camp Grounds: Style and Homosexuality* (Amherst: The University of Massachusetts Press, 1993): pp. 234–256. The actor who played Miss Jessup, Blair Brown, will eventually appear in the queer-aligned series *Orange is the New Black* as Judy King.

16 Kristen Hatch, "Little Butches: Tomboys in Hollywood Film," in *Mediated Girlhoods: New Explorations of Girls' Media Culture*, edited by Mary Celeste Kearney (New York: Peter Lang, 2011), p. 86.

3

IN THE QUEER-VIEW MIRROR

Looking at 1991

Nick Salvato

Daring to Look

As a number of critics have demonstrated, certain years in the early 1990s—1992, 1993, 1994—could all be understood as breakthrough ones for the queering of North American television (e.g., Becker 2006). Yet how would our television history, as well as our queer theorization of television, shift if we racked focus and paid closer attention to a putatively less promising year for queer TV, 1991? Taking up that question, this essay will also extend and evolve a critical approach, establishing what I call "partial constellations," first developed in my book *Television Scales* (Salvato 2019, 26). In this case, the items constellated together are American media objects produced and distributed in 1991 that simultaneously—and co-constitutively—stake queer ground and make reflexive claims about television as a medium. They include episodic series (*thirtysomething*, *Roc*), a cable special (*Medusa: Dare to Be Truthful*), and a popular mainstream film about television (*Soapdish*). Building on Joe Wlodarz's thoughtful account of cross-serial textuality, I star my partial constellation in the way that I do in order to demonstrate (alongside other critics) that we need, in addition to a method or methods for attending to cross-serial textuality, methodology for understanding textuality—especially queer textuality—cross-*medially*. In other words, comprehending a given moment or era's queer television as capably and capaciously as one ought requires a situating of such television in the larger media ecology of which it forms a part—and where other mediums participate in the construction of the televisual.

In giving this essay its subtitle, "Looking at 1991," I conceive that phrase as alluding to and dialoguing with a similar phrase: *Seeing through the Eighties*, which furnishes Jane Feuer with the title for an important and influential monograph in the history of cultural criticism. If a provisional relay thereby obtains between seeing-through and looking-at, then moving through that relay may disclose the

DOI: 10.4324/9781003109044-5

value of looking-at, as an approach for media studies, that simultaneously owes a debt to and departs from the mode of seeing-through. That is, a critical meditation on looking-at may yield some global insights about method that could have traction beyond the narrower use of looking-at to comprehend the local objects of my attention here. Thus, en route to presenting my objects as imbricated in their queerness and in their meta-televisuality, I offer a brief appraisal of what looking-at is, how it may be deployed, and why that deployment may matter—queerly—at this particular moment in the evolution of the scholarly humanities, contoured as it is by debates about surficial, distant, deep, and other kinds of interpretation (or non-interpretation).

As its punning title indicates, *Seeing through the Eighties* deploys a method that could be nominated as symptomatic interpretation or ideology critique; (pre) supposing that a given cultural artifact (e.g., *Dynasty*) will, whether wittingly or not, manifest a dominant ideology (e.g., Reaganism), Feuer consults those artifacts to discover, in seeing through them, that—lo and behold—they do indeed promote or otherwise participate in said ideology. On the one hand, and as I have argued elsewhere, "what is—usefully—tautological about [this] approach to understanding culture is a necessary part" of the critical landscape, one from which I have learned a great deal (Salvato 2016, 185). On the other hand, the method rests on two allied predicates to which we may generatively, if not pointedly, develop alternatives. First, the critic cherry-picks a case study to make an argument about ideology: in Feuer's example, about Reaganite ideology and television in the 1980s. (What, by contrast to a chapter devoted to ABC's *Dynasty*, would it mean to dwell abidingly with—rather than essentially dismiss in a short paragraph—*Joan Does Dynasty*, an influential feminist video essay by Joan Braderman that aired on PBS? [Feuer 1995, 145].) And second, the critic arrays the case study alongside others (e.g., *thirtysomething*) that shore up what may be taken by a reader as a more or less foregone conclusion about ideology's grip on culture and the objects that symptomatically disclose how tight the grip is.

Regarding the second of these predicates, the critic looking-at would work otherwise and constellate a set of objects more initially eccentric or surprising—though nonetheless sound and justifiable—in order to circumvent conclusions about those objects that might be construed as easy or obvious. (So, collide *thirtysomething* not with *Dynasty* but *Medusa*, et al.) As for the first, the symptomatic interpreter seeing-through can accomplish as much with alacrity; ideology critique sees through things with a penetrating sharpness that is also its penetrating quickness and facility. But to look at things—*really* to look at things—means slowing down and stretching out: a modality that could inhabit the forms of pausing to look lengthily at a frame while taking notes; of rewinding to look-at again; looking at a piece of television multiple times as a way to construe it, and keep construing it, as dimensional and multivalent; moving away from the object, maybe for quite some time, in order to return to it with different eyes. To perform in these ways is to construct a criticism built on patience, doggedness, and generosity toward one's objects, as well as to endeavor to sustain curiosity and openness. In other words, penetrative seeing-through gets to the bottom of things with a force that is, often, blunt and swiftly decisive, whereas looking-at requires ginger, delicate movement, as well as time, to produce its calibrations and their modifications. Certainly not distant or deep, yet also not quite surficial, looking-at may in touching nearness come close—but only close—to what literary critics (used to) call close reading. In its cleaving to yet cleaving from that tendentially decorous and elegant mode of interpretation, looking-at aims for queerer, which is to say (in part) more aslant and excessive, meaning and mattering—say, by pausing on the "wrong" frame, rewinding "too much," moving away for "too long" before coming back. In my effort to model a version of this critical looking-at, I am, that is, yoking fidelity to my objects with promiscuity in my approach to them, while at the same time taking pleasure from the interpretive outputs that can come from intensified descriptive inputs, thickly rather than thinly or crisply elaborated.

Or, in both senses of these words, let's press play.

Opening the Circle

At first blush, 1991 would not appear to be a sanguine or promising year at whose television to look—or, at least, to look at that television for its queerness. In order to understand (partially) why, we may do well to rewind, as it were, from 1991 to 1989, the year in which a gay-themed episode of the ABC dramedy *thirtysomething* caused trouble for the network…and ripple effects well beyond. The episode in question, "Strangers," attracted a substantial amount of journalistic attention in 1989—and relatively numerous, if brief, mentions in later scholarship—for featuring two minor gay characters, Russell (David Marshall Grant) and Peter (Peter Frechette), having a post-coital conversation over cigarettes and next to each other in bed, about queer practices of obituary-reading and about their affective processing of their respective friends' HIV/AIDS-related deaths. What propelled most attention to the episode was not, in fact, its so-called controversial content—which few viewers processed in 1989, because the episode aired on election night and was in many markets delayed until after midnight or preempted altogether—but rather ABC's widely and loudly voiced claims that the network lost over one-and-a-half-million dollars in advertising revenue because of sponsors pulling out of the program, which prompted ABC not to rerun "Strangers" in 1990 for fear of similar losses and, more broad, a retrenchment at all three major networks, in the first three years of the 1990s, from programming that addressed gay lives or the relationship between gay lives and HIV/AIDS (Capsuto 2000, 242–45).

Among myriad critical responses to *thirtysomething*, the only meaningfully developed analysis of "Strangers" as a televisual text, rather than as a footnote in an industrial history, is Joe Wlodarz's penetrating 1994 essay, "Smokin' Tokens: *thirtysomething* and TV's Queer Dilemma." In that piece, Wlodarz makes moves that align with the tendencies of symptomatic reading or ideology critique toward which I have already gestured: he identifies a set of contradictions that together, he claims, contribute to *thirtysomething*'s complicity with a regime of homophobia and compulsory heterosexism. On this reading, convincingly and indeed passionately unfolded by Wlodarz, the episode is disturbing because its gay representations are normalizing, but also because those representations are spectacularizing. Equally disturbing is the manner in which the gay characters' sexuality is derealized—at the same time that the characters are over- or hypersexualized. In a different vein, Wlodarz puts pressure on the way in which, in his interpretation, the recurring gay characters' scenes are structurally subordinate to scenes featuring straight series regulars, a structural feature that works in the service of the containment of gay representation. This account is driven by an understandable and righteous indignation about what Wlodarz is not seeing or can't find in *thirtysomething*—implicitly, a nuanced, sustained representation of politicized and sexually oppositional, provocative gayness (Wlodarz 1994, 192–211). Yet it's possible, if one were to build on this kind of symptomatic reading or ideology critique and, in so building, to move away from a thoroughgoing hermeneutic of suspicion, to come to a different set of conclusions about the series.

One route for such criticism would find its way through a counter-reading in response to Wlodarz's close analysis of "Strangers"; that counter-reading could take up his own claim that contamination provides a lens through which gayness appears in *thirtysomething* in order to demonstrate how everything ostensibly straight and straitening about "Strangers" is, in fact, contaminated or spoiled—that is, made deliciously *queer*—by contact, in the forms of continuity or contiguity, with a gayness that is thus not merely "contained." In this context, I only gesture to and suspend such a potential counter-reading in order, rather, to maintain a focus on the "1991-ness" of 1991 television programming. Indeed, pivoting forward from 1989 to 1991 enables a continued, if differently inflected, attention to *thirtysomething*'s representations of gayness and HIV/AIDS; for the 1991 episode, "Closing the Circle," one of the last in the four-season series, was, like "Strangers," driven by the work of openly gay series writer/director Richard Kramer and, like "Strangers," features Frechette in the role of Peter. In so re-centering Peter, the episode (to which Wlodarz only has brief space to attend in "Smokin' Tokens") gives one charged meaning, among others, to its title, which indicates a would-be knotting of the vexed and vexing gay loops opened up by "Strangers."

Alongside a more dramatically meta-televisual moment that Wlodarz identifies (in which we may read Peter's critique of his workplace as allegorizing a critique of *thirtysomething* itself [Wlodarz 1994, 203]), the very opening dialogue of the episode could be construed as meta-televisual—and reflexively gay-coded. Like Michael and colleague Peter at their ad agency, trying to save yet "another account," the makers of *thirtysomething* are producing this episode in the face of potential cancellation; and like the proposal he has packaged for their client, Peter is a "tastefully neutral" gay character—at this point. But shortly thereafter, Peter's somber, troubled face in close-up, as wistful music plays, ends a scene about his recent erratic behavior—and telegraphs, before any further dialogic or narrative work needs to be accomplished, that he has received "the" bad news of a positive HIV test (Figure 3.1).

FIGURE 3.1 Peter looks troubled in *thirtysomething*.

Screen capture from "Closing the Circle" by author.

It's true that network television is operating on the loaded logic that this version of bad news is the only imaginable one to assign to a gay character in 1991; but it's also true that once we discern, before Michael, what's shaken Peter, a principle of *virality* gets activated, contra ideology critique's insistence on containment as the rule that governs (for instance) gay representation in heterosexist and heteronormative contexts.

Peter may be a marginal character representing a marginalized community, but his diagnosis comes to touch and even to suffuse elements of the episode with which it would seem to have no truck or traffic. Michael tries to sort out the status of Gary's life insurance—and an agent wonders aloud whether "friend" is a euphemism and whether Gary and Michael lived together (in an era of epidemic, he is seeing, he explains, a lot of situations like the one he initially imagines Michael inhabiting). Gary's ghost appears to Michael in a night vision—and we cannot help but think, again, of Peter, as both characters are established in the episode as overly fond of literary and cinematic quotation. And then, in the highly overdetermined bathroom scene in which Peter discloses his positive test result to Michael, unusual shots and reverse shots, in each one of which the camera pushes slowly closer and closer to the two figures, we grasp not their equivalence but their strong parallelism. We learn in the prior scene with Gary that Michael is not taking care of himself and needs to; so, too, Peter, who has avoided the HIV test until now but who, like Michael, "feels old" in 1991 (in a way, we may infer, that neither character did in 1989).

Among other effects, this eking of a parallelism subtends the episode's subtle critique of Michael's paternalistic and often presumptuous impulse to take care of others, including Gary's feminist-identified widow Susannah and Peter himself. Coming full circle, that critique is hitched back to the meta-televisual impulse with which the episode began, as ghostly Gary appears for a second time and dubs Michael and Hope "Ozzie and Harriet." But coming full circle is not the same as "Closing the Circle." Though Gary must, the episode insists, be let go, the energies unleashed in this open-ended serial melodrama need not—indeed, cannot—and they include the queer ones, which will pass subtly from Peter to series regular Melissa in the last pivotal episode, also highly meta-televisual, that foregrounds her, "Melissa in Wonderland" (wonderland being—where else?—Hollywood).

At the top of this essay section, we glimpsed one snapshot of the ways in which the still-dominant American television networks of the early 1990s—that is, the "Big Three"—exerted a great deal of power over circulating images of gay subjectivity and HIV/AIDS and, more pointedly, over the suppression and lack of such images (through kowtowing to skittish advertisers, but also through the procedures of their Standards and Practices divisions, through capitulation to rightist activist groups like the American Family Association, and more). Yet another network—of writers, directors, actors, and others, equally worthy of our attention—offset suppression and lack by working within *and against* the constraints of different media, including but not limited to television, as they developed a body of work about gay lives and lives touched by HIV/AIDS.[1] That network includes, of course, Richard Kramer, who may have felt emboldened to risk reanimating Peter in the moment that ABC was already and otherwise contemplating—and would soon be calling—*thirtysomething*'s cancellation; Frechette, who appeared in a 1990 episode of *Law and Order*, "The Reaper's Helper," as a gay activist who assists the suicides of other gay men with HIV/AIDS; and Grant, who played Joe Pitt in the first Broadway production of *Angels in America* in 1993. (Clearly, early 1990s casting directors looked again and again—because they had precious little alternative—to the slender pool of actors, gay and straight alike, willing to brave "playing gay" for more or less mainstream audiences.)

Yet this second, alternative network could and should be peopled to connect these artists to a number of less obvious others besides, including (as we shall see in the next section of this essay) those working at television locations aside from the Big Three, such as FOX, MTV, and Showtime. And, not incidentally, it's Wlodarz himself, writing 15 years after the appearance of "Smokin' Tokens," who paves the way for exactly this sort of connective critical work when he theorizes cross-serial textuality—a phrase through which he indexes the meanings that obtain *across* many different strands of a given era's television programming and through the braiding together of those strands—and claims that attending to cross-textual seriality is the only sensible way to understand such an era's gay or queer televisuality (Wlodarz 2009, 88–107). In tandem, and as I indicated in this essay's introduction, I move not just cross-serially but cross-medially in order to star a constellation with works by creators who took a multi-*platform* approach to the cultivation of queer art and commerce in their particular historical moment, 1991. In other words, get ready both for *Roc* and *Medusa: Dare to Be Truthful and* for *Soapdish*.

"Don't You Ever Watch Oprah?"

Though *thirtysomething* features deliberately as the biggest star in this essay's partial constellation, its other objects shine all the same (and, like most shiny things, they are a pleasure to play with). One of the shinier aspects of the FOX sitcom *Roc*, a series that "sought to reimagine monolithic formulations of the black family, home, and community" (Zook 1998, 87), is its more specific claim to fame as the narrative television series that features, in an episode penned by gay staff writer Jeffrey Duteil, the medium's first-ever depiction of a same-sex wedding; it is an interracial one, to boot, complicating the prevalent wisdom (as do projects like *The Women of Brewster Place*) that gay and queer television representations are whiter...before they aren't. Regarding this wedding not just for its examination of sexuality, sociality, and kinship but also for its meta-televisuality, I find the latter—unlike the dialogically allegorical and referential work in *thirtysomething*—lodged primarily in the register of allusive and haunted *casting*. One of the grooms in question, an uncle of eponymous Roc and brother to crusty Andrew, is Russell, played by *Shaft* icon Richard Roundtree. Roundtree's indelible association with the role of Shaft is dually televisual because of his career-foiling migration into the tepid 1970s television adaptation of the legendary blaxploitation film *and* because of the demographically amplified sense of the film's legendariness as it circulated regularly in cable syndication in the 1980s (Briggs 2003, 28–29).

It can only ever be an understatement to note the irony, shading into dissonant complexity, of having an actor inescapably associated with hypersexualized masculinity and aggression play a gentle, gay, sitcom uncle. Yet beyond—and more interesting than—its irony, the casting choice could be comprehended as instantiating a significant repetition with a difference, as Roundtree is once again playing a character whose sexuality (his gentleness notwithstanding) is perceived as charged and dangerous (Figure 3.2).

FIGURE 3.2 Andrew is disruptive in *Roc*.

Screen capture from "Can't Help Loving That Man" by author.

What's more, this repetition with a difference is just one among a conspicuous number on whose intrication the gay-wedding episode is built: repetitions of the men in the family retreating from the living room into the kitchen each time a further disclosure from Russell (not just gay but wedding, not just wedding but wedding a white man) makes them yet more uncomfortable; of the words that they fumble and stammer in a set of expressions of their discomfort; of bathrobe-clad Andrew's disruptive and protesting movements through the living room when it has been repurposed as the space for the wedding; of Roc's brother Joey's comically improvisatory noodling at the family piano on the wedding day; and, perhaps most telling, of meta-televisual jokes about watching *The Oprah Winfrey Show* and *The Sally Jessy Raphael Show*, the Emerson family's main source of information about gayness and its potential acceptance (and, indeed, as Joshua Gamson demonstrates in *Freaks Talk Back*, the impact of the ambivalent appearances of sexual minorities in American talk shows was very high, bordering on outsize, in the 1980s and 1990s [Gamson 1998]). These formal devices, enacted in tandem with one another, accomplish a series of key *modulations* and thereby underscore the poignant point toward which the episode is driving: Andrew can modulate his homophobic take on his brother's revelations even if he cannot wholly accept them right away—a "message" that is itself a repetition with a difference, ringing a change on the canned sitcom principle that an episode's problems must be tidily, which usually means ham-fistedly, resolved by the half-hour's end.

To think in this way about a television genre and the complicating of its predicates, as *Roc* invites us to do, accrues yet further meaning and value when the genre in question is situated on a spectrum with its others. To slide, for instance, to a near elsewhere in 1991, we see that no such confining generic constraint, specific to the sitcom, needs to be escaped by Julie Brown when she is given premium cable-level license at Showtime to create her musical comedy-cum-mockumentary special, *Medusa: Dare to Be Truthful*. Co-written by Brown with Charlie Coffey, her gay best friend and collaborator on her contemporaneous MTV variety series, *Just Say Julie*, the special comes fast on the heels of—and works as a meticulously close, blow-by-blow parody of—*Madonna: Truth or Dare*, released cinematically earlier in 1991. In my view, the special's most striking quality inheres in its tonal strangeness: more nearly, its tonal hybridity, as it oscillates between—or sometimes, weirdly, enacts at once—juvenile goofiness and withering takedown. Perhaps nowhere does this quality manifest more delightfully than in the simultaneously silly and acid musical number, "Vague," a parody of "Vogue." Like the other numbers in the special, the music pastiches the Madonna hit that inspires it; by contrast, the lyrics pointedly depart from and comically critique their progenitor. Where Madonna's song is a paean, in list form, to the glamorous—and glaringly white—film celebrities of Hollywood's bygone Golden Age (a troubling litany in a piece that also appropriates voguing from Harlem's black and brown queer ballroom scene), Brown, in a 180-degree turn, recites the names of contemporary *television* personalities indicted for their various forms of boringness, blandness, vacancy, and vacuity; her roster of the cornfed and moronic is also super-white, a reflexive choice that indicates how cringeworthily easy it is in the 1980s and 1990s for the underwhelming Vanna Whites and Ed McMahons of the small screen, precisely because their whiteness opens doors for them, to waste our time. Just as important, the lyrics also directly and indirectly indict Madonna for her own putative stupidity, as for instance Medusa opens the number with the assertion, "I'm not thinkin' nothin'," or as the inversions, "Dawber, Pam" and "Brosnan, Pierce," so facilely yet savagely echo one of the worst contrivances in "Vogue" ("Harlow, Jean" enables a rhyme with "picture of a beauty queen," a sloppy penning that could have been avoided in dozens of possible, alternative ways).

To encounter and ruminate on this mockery is delicious fun! Yet more than making fun, more than simply mocking Madonna, Brown is implicitly pleading with her to engage in self-reflection—a capacity for which scant evidence is available in *Truth or Dare*'s narcissistic endeavor—in the pivot from cinema to television. Responding to Madonna's effort, with the documentary, to earn cinematic respect after a series of Hollywood film flops, Brown's subtextual invitation in "Vague" could be textually rendered as, "Please accept that the phenomenon that is 'Madonna' is thoroughgoingly a television phenomenon!" After all, where would Madonna be without MTV, the network where Brown toils more modestly (and where, as well as at VH1, *Medusa* would appear regularly in syndication throughout the 1990s)? If this meta-televisual maneuver is also a queer one, then its queerness accrues in gesture and movement, as Brown in her persona as Medusa and her (like Madonna's, gay-presenting and bra-wearing) backup dancers substitute for the fashion-, martial arts-, and breakdance-inspired moves of voguing a series of camp alternatives: exaggerated coverings of eyes to throw shade at television's clueless class, sleazy scissoring of arms to jibe with the bitchy intonation of "Nicollette Sheri-DAN" (rhymes with "McMahon"), semi-bizarre rotating of pinky by ear and mouth to signify at once, it would seem, the use of a microphone headset...and the clearing of wax from the ears of the thick (Figure 3.3).

Medusa encourages a "leap," though only a modest one, from television to cinema, given the acid way in which it parses and skewers Madonna's movements between the mediums. And where better to leap in a reckoning with 1991 than to *Soapdish*, precisely because similar forms of camp exaggeration and bitchiness animate that film, the daytime-serial/backstage comedy conceived and co-written by gay playwright turned screenwriter Robert Harling, shortly after the runaway cinematic success of his *Steel Magnolias* adaptation. Given the blatant phobia with which it treats trans character Montana Morehouse, one could easily consign *Soapdish* to the dustbin of pop culture's history; yet without taking an unjustifiably reparative approach to the film, I do wish briefly and en route to closing to highlight one of its worthily reconsidered features, its odd marriage of satire and realism. The charm of *Soapdish* is predicated on its invitation to audiences to indulge in the close correspondence between ludicrous characterizations and narratives within the diegesis of a fictional serial, *The Sun Also Sets*, and the equally ludicrous shenanigans and schemes of the serial's on- and off-screen personnel. The sharp comic appraisal of these interleaved vices and follies should, we may think, land us squarely and solely

FIGURE 3.3 Medusa and her dancers perform "Vague."

Screen capture from *Medusa: Dare to Be Truthful* by author.

FIGURE 3.4 The style of *Soapdish* is garish.

Screen capture from *Soapdish* by author.

in the realm of satire…except that anyone, ranging from fans to journalists to television scholars, who knows anything about daytime serials will *also* see in *Soapdish*'s satirical provisions its simultaneous—and really genuine—hewing to realism, because the behind-the-scenes worlds of daytime serial production, as attested in a variety of popular and academic accounts, have been marked by its denizens' truly bizarre and antic behavior. That satire and realism should so nearly and uncannily coincide is a queer business; moreover, that queer business extends to and runs through the audiovisual style of the film (Figure 3.4).

One could see the flamboyant costuming choices of *Sun*'s wardrobe department and the over-the-top decisions of its sound stage's designers and setters as mocking (as Janet Maslin wrote in a *New York Times* review of the film, "[costume designer Nolan] Miller and Eugenio Zanetti, the production designer, give the film a loud, happily preposterous look that amounts to a satirical edge" [Maslin 1991, C10]). Yet, at the same time, those of us who have watched the visual train wreckage of soap opera know the precision and fidelity, wholly imbricated with ridicule, with which *Soapdish*'s makers have rendered *Sun*'s palette. And we are likely to experience a giddily queer pleasure in savoring that overlay.

Coda: Partial Conclusions

As a stifling-schoolroom sufferer in the 1980s, I scoured and devoured the pages of magazine *Soap Opera Digest*, with a cloaking math workbook providing literal cover. Eight years ago, I assiduously rewatched *thirtysomething* and took copious notes, while not knowing for long thereafter (save a couple of one-off conference presentations) what to do with them. A year ago, I watched the cheering "Vague" clip from *Medusa* for almost every day of ten forlorn weeks in Berlin. And in weird pandemic summer of 2020, I enjoyed settling down, and in, with my consoling, bootleg DVDs of the commercially unavailable *Roc*. I couldn't know in advance what this before-and-behind activity would yield once I followed it by making this essay's partial constellations. Now, having made them, I find provisional value in some partial conclusions that the essay's arraying suggests.

Virality operates as a structuring force not just in "Closing the Circle" but in my other case studies, too. (Ambivalent talk about Russell's gayness seeps from the Emerson household to the neighborhood bar in *Roc*. *Medusa* plays with *Truth or Dare*'s fixation on the paparazzi's role in abetting Madonna's virality. And gossip's viral power motors the social and (un)professional relations in *Soapdish*'s world.) Similarly, the workings of repetition with a difference, located above in *Roc*, animate each of the other representations under consideration here. ("Closing the Circle" repeats the problems of "Strangers" with different accents and emphases—and with the aim to (re)solve them. And what better rhetoric than repetition with a difference to describe formal parodies that work in the service of cultural satire, such as *Medusa* and *Soapdish*?) Tonal hybridity, a distinguishing feature of *Medusa*, also emerges in quintessential 1980s/1990s dramedies like *thirtysomething*; sitcoms with serious ethical and political ambitions like *Roc*; and in the co-written *Soapdish*, where, as Maslin observes, Harling manifests deep-seated melodramatic inclinations, leavened by co-writer Andrew Bergman's swerves into the terrain of the screwball and the zinger (Maslin 1991, ibid.).

Finally, if the queer intersection of satire and realism in *Soapdish* makes it worth revisiting, then at the same time this rhetoric could extend its reach to disclose that *queer intersection* may metaphorize generatively how we think of the 1991 media streetscape where these four objects come together—and where others could join them in an elaboration upon my current thinking and writing. To scale this partial constellation otherwise, adding further objects to its arrangement, would mean not only to make a bigger construction but also, inevitably, to shift the keywords and phrases that cross in the queer intersection. Thus, for instance, if *L.A. Law*, *Northern Exposure*, and *Roseanne* were to join the mix, so, too, might the respective notions of witnessing and testifying, of the alibi of quirkiness, and of avuncularity (hi, Leon) become more prominent conceptual motifs.[2]

1991 may not have been the most watershed year for queer televisuality, but it was nonetheless a year in which a viewer could tune in to Indigo Girls performing "Watershed" in an episode of *The Tonight Show*. Their queer appearance in the ether could invite yet more constellating as speculating; for now, I am content to watch the clip at YouTube and to hit pause after the intonation of the lyrics, "There's always retrospect (when you're looking back) / To light a clearer path."

Notes

1 In similar language regarding networks of one sort versus another, I elsewhere make a likewise similar, though more general, point about mainstream television images of Left subjects and issues in the 1970s and 1980s. See Salvato, *Knots Landing* (Detroit, MI: Wayne State University Press, 2015), 23.

2 I refer here to the gay series regular in *Roseanne*, played by Martin Mull.

Works Cited

Becker, Ron. 2006. *Gay TV and Straight America*. Rutgers, NJ: Rutgers University Press.

Briggs, Joe Bob. 2003. "Who Dat Man? *Shaft* and the Blaxploitation Genre." *Cineaste* 28:2. 28–29.

Brown, Julie and Charlie Coffey. *Medusa: Dare to Be Truthful*. Showtime. Aired December 1, 1991.

Capsuto, Steven. 2000. Alternate Channels: The Uncensored Story of Gay and Lesbian Images on Radio and Television, 1930s to the Present. New York: Ballantine Books.

Duteil, Jeffrey. "Can't Help Loving That Man." *Roc*. FOX. Aired October 20, 1991.

Feuer, Jane. 1995. Seeing through the Eighties: Television and Reaganism. Durham, NC: Duke University Press.

Gamson, Joshua. 1998. *Freaks Talk Back: Tabloid Talk Shows and Sexual Nonconformity*. Chicago, IL: University of Chicago Press.

Harling, Robert and Andrew Bergman. *Soapdish*. Paramount Pictures. Released May 31, 1991.

Kramer, Richard. "Strangers." *thirtysomething*. ABC. Aired November 7, 1989.

Kramer, Richard and Paul Monette. "Closing the Circle." *thirtysomething*. ABC. Aired April 16, 1991.

Maslin, Janet. "Gossip as Juicy off the Soap Opera Set as on It." *The New York Times*. May 31, 1991. Section C, Page 10.

MISCchout. "Indigo Girls – Watershed on The Tonight Show 1991." *YouTube* video. 6:35. November 9, 2008. www.youtube.com/watch?v=oWNhpTfQ9lU

Salvato, Nick. 2015. *Knots Landing*. Detroit, MI: Wayne State University Press.

_____. 2016. *Obstruction*. Durham, NC: Duke University Press.

_____. 2019. *Television Scales*. Brooklyn, NY: punctum books.

Wlodarz, Joe. 1994. "Smokin' Tokens: *thirtysomething* and TV's Queer Dilemma." *Camera Obscura* 11:3. 192–211.

______. 2009. "'We're Not All So Obvious': Masculinity and Queer (In)Visibility in American Network Television of the 1970s." *Queer TV: Theories, Histories, Politics*. Ed. Glyn Davis and Gary Needham. New York: Routledge, 2009. 88–107.

Zook, Kristal Brent. 1998. Color by Fox: The Fox Network and the Revolution in Black Television. New York: Oxford University Press.

4

LIKE LIVING IN A DIFFERENT TIME ZONE

SBS's Queer Orientations

Robert Payne

"Was 2020 the gayest year for TV ever?!" With this clickbaity question posted to their Instagram account at the end of 2020, British monthly magazine *Attitude* announced its "must-watch" round-up of the year's "LGBTQ-inclusive" television shows (Attitude 2020). It may not come as a surprise that the list imagines television to mean only English-language content from North America and Britain and mostly series available on digital streaming platforms. Equally notable is that the list singles out representation and visibility as its main criteria: here, it is characters and storylines that determine how to identify LGBTQ television. Beyond these limitations (and leaving aside whether *Attitude* means to use "gay" and "LGBTQ" interchangeably), more telling is the accumulation implied by the superlative "gayest" in the opening line. Implicit is the idea that television's gayness has built up progressively with every year until the present.

Popular journalism is by no means alone in this making this reflex. Amy Villarejo (2014, 3) notes a similar tendency in some critical accounts, too, which presume "some narrative of homosexual televisual evolution whereby the clandestine has yielded to the overt" and "the retrogressive has ceded to pride". Ever since *Queer as Folk*, *Will & Grace*, *The L Word*, and *Queer Eye for the Straight Guy* ushered in the current century, television (and very often American television) has been applauded by some for its role in the development of a progressive queer politics. According to this narrative, a broader range of programming and a braver repertoire of representations correspond to a new baseline of respect for queer lives, desires, and bodies. In turn, this representational progress can supposedly be mapped on to a new terrain of civil and political rights for queer people in many parts of the world. The recent development of wider and easier global access to media content through digital networks seems to slot into this argument. If the enthusiasm of my own students is any measure, it would seem that a whole generation of young people has come to accept diverse queerness on their screens and in their daily lives

DOI: 10.4324/9781003109044-6

as unremarkable. At the same time, an older generation of queers—including many of these students' professors—seems to be confronting the fading force, if not the obsolescence, of their own youthful struggles for recognition during times of seemingly scarcer queer television.

Putting reductive generational characterizations aside, this chapter is motivated by the problem of what to do with a feeling of nostalgia for a media past which conventional wisdom would regard as having been less sustaining of queer lives than the present. Are there are ways of taking this feeling seriously without stoking intergenerational rivalry over the question of which queer experiences are most authentic? My discussion aims to explore temporal alternatives to narratives of "homosexual televisual evolution" and their interpretation as an index of queer life affirmation. It asks what a televisual version of the "stubborn lingering of pastness", which Elizabeth Freeman (2010, 8) identifies as "a hallmark of queer affect", can contribute to the future of queer media studies. And it proposes that a generative queer politics might be enriched by ambivalent attachments to moments in television history with harder-to-recognize queer resources.

We need to think differently about queer televisual history, but we also need to think more widely about where that history has taken place. A too-frequent focus on American examples, including the usual suspects noted above, downplays the importance of media cultures in other geographical and cultural locations (and let's not forget that the US *Queer as Folk* was a remake of an edgier British original). This focus risks leaving assumptions of an American brand of global gay hegemony unquestioned. To offer one alternative historical and geographical focus, this chapter will be primarily concerned with Australian television of the 1980s and 1990s, in particular the state-run channel SBS-TV, which was launched in 1980 with an official mandate to be the country's 'multicultural' broadcaster. Woven into this fabric of multiculturalism were rich queer resources for a generation of viewers—not just representationally, even though SBS was about the only television channel where queer content could be found at the time, but also phenomenologically in terms of orientations to discourses of home, family, and nation. I will argue that the experience of geographical positioning among other spatiotemporal orientations were key factors contributing to SBS's queer potential.

As Villarejo (2014, 6–7) also insists, rethinking the history of queer television means looking beyond images to account for how the televisual apparatus organizes time and space and does so in fundamentally gendered and sexualized ways. Accordingly, this discussion will consider television as infrastructure. This term is useful for highlighting the distributive functions of television as a life-sustaining presence in people's lives. Distributive functions include both the technical and sociopolitical means through which television delivers content and, in many cases, a nationalist imaginary.[1] From this materialist perspective, I propose to think about queerness as a lived relation to infrastructures, or an affective orientation to technical and sociopolitical systems that are designed to deliver normative futures. In distributing resources and values to a selectively imagined population, infrastructures constitute a kind of promise of how things will be (Larkin 2013; Anand, Gupta and

Appel 2018). Implicitly, this promise is also a prescription of how things should *feel* as a citizen making use of those resources and values. Such projections are often made without considering the viability of queer lives, given that queerness has historically been only marginal to or fully erased by many societies' dominant visions of their civil economic, and political well-being. Nonetheless, how infrastructures are designed and constructed does not completely determine how they evolve and are put to use, so it is important to recognize the negotiated and improvised quality of how people live with them—perhaps queer people in particular. Some uses and experiences of infrastructures exceed and subvert the normative futures their designs imagine. Unplanned intimacies can emerge from our encounters with infrastructures, raising questions about how completely they embody political and economic authority (Wilson 2016).

What follows is an attempt to register the ongoing affective resonance of television's complicated queer history. Focusing on a specific place and time, I attend to enduring personal traces of how television felt as an infrastructure which aimed to distribute a national self-image based in norms of domesticity and relations to the other. In addition to traces of my own experience, I analyze the responses of a small sample of other gay- and queer-identifying Australians for whom SBS-TV had a significant presence in their adolescent home life precisely because it felt differently from other television channels.[2] While this sample is in no way representative, responses are included here to provide glimpses of singular lived experiences. My hope is that this approach may contribute to a living archive of queer encounters with the materiality of television and other media, one which embraces the subjective, the heterogeneous, and the ambivalent.

Bringing the World Back Home

If you ask queer Australians who were adolescents in the 1980s and 1990s which queer cultural resources were available to them at that time, many would name SBS-TV. Queer content was not, however, the stated purview of this Australian television channel, and nor did it form a very large proportion of programming. But the queer content that was broadcast, most often to be found in European films and late at night, set SBS very much apart from the other television channels. These programming decisions contributed to SBS's double-edged reputation. For some, it was suspect, irrelevant, or laughable. For others, like me and many of my generation, it was a vital haven where one could begin to enter other worlds—notably, worlds of homoerotic possibility. As one respondent Douglas expressed: "It felt like a different world – literally a world, where mainstream TV was white, straight, perky."

The Special Broadcasting Service (SBS) was first launched by the Australian federal government as a radio network in the mid-1970s and expanded into television in 1980. Both state-run services were established with a mandate to provide a wide range of content in languages other than English to the "multicultural" nation, that is a nation which had significantly increased its intake of migrants during the decades after World War II. New residents came initially, during this period, from countries across southern Europe, and later from countries in Asia and the Middle East, going on to establish rich local communities across Australia in subsequent generations. By the 1970s the former British colony, which had long held to the overtly racist White Australia Policy, was now officially embracing the reality of a multiethnic society and the ideal of a multicultural national identity. A decade later, SBS-TV became one of the most prominent manifestations of this recent governmental vision—though not without controversy and opposition.

In their history of SBS-TV, Ien Ang, Gay Hawkins and Lamia Dabboussy (2008, 3) recognize misconceptions that dogged the broadcaster from the start, notably that its offering of content from various cultural and linguistic contexts made it "simply a niche broadcaster servicing discrete ethnic communities". Instead, they insist, "SBS [was] a *public* broadcaster" which made "cultural diversity a matter of public representation, public interest and public conversation". The public that its content aimed to reflect and worked to construct was characterized by a fundamental plurality, that is by multiple forms of sociocultural difference. For a national broadcaster to begin with such heterogeneity in how it imagined and communicated with its audience is a challenging brief. To meet the challenge, SBS had "to develop an on-air look and sound that distinguished it from the cosy culture of whiteness" established by Australia's existing television channels, which included three commercial channels plus the ABC, the primary government-run broadcaster (Ang, Hawkins and Dabboussy 2008, 12). If SBS's overarching mandate was one of nation-building, according to which the nation was to see, hear, and otherwise sense itself as culturally diverse, then its task was also to generate a new medium for affective citizenship. In Carol Johnson's (2010, 496) use of the term, affective citizenship designates "which intimate emotional relationships between citizens are endorsed and recognized by governments in personal life" as well as "how citizens are encouraged to feel about others and themselves in broader, more public domains". As a distinct national broadcaster reaching into private homes, SBS was to transmit ways for citizens to *feel* in themselves and in relation to one another. This broadcasting model confirms the home as metonym for the nation and the location from which to develop an affective orientation to others. The home is therefore both private and public: the privacy of domestic relations (of gender, sex, and kinship, in particular) is framed by an ever-present and shared sense of the public that is the nation.

Three years after SBS began broadcasting on television, it adopted the slogan "Bringing the World Back Home" (SBS 2020). This slogan figures SBS in the active role of delivering the world, and the home that is the nation is imagined as hosting the world. Here, SBS signals its delivery function and therefore highlights its role as infrastructure, defined by anthropologist Brian Larkin (2013, 328) as "built networks that facilitate the flow of goods, people, or ideas and allow for their exchange over space". Given their role in the provisioning of everyday life, infrastructures must also be recognized for how they "enable or hinder intimacy" in ways that reveal concrete forms of power (Wilson 2016, 2). When the national home hosts the world, a fantasy of intimacy is enabled in which the domestic space welcomes its new proximity with the global elsewhere. Of course, a new domestic intimacy is one of the main promises that always distinguished television as a medium. However, to bring the world *back* home implies it already belonged there, which is surely a way of gesturing to Australia's history of immigration as well as its imagined future as worldly or cosmopolitan. So the channel's infrastructural or distributive function extends beyond sociotechnical capacities (transmitting televisual signals to deliver images of the rest of the world) into the realm of the political. As a political infrastructure, SBS's aim was to transmit a worldview: to reinforce a selective account of the nation's orientation to the world, at once cosmopolitan and domestically contained, and to usher in future generations of citizens who would share the feeling of this orientation.

Given the channel's reputation for unusually erotic programming, as we'll see, I am tempted to suggest that the slogan "Bringing the World Back Home" also implies the pleasures and value of sexual promiscuity. The worldly viewer is figured as one who hooks up with a diverse assortment of racy international items and brings them home for intimate encounters. This intimation significantly complicates the traditional discourses of home and nation that television history helped to construct. Feminist media scholars (such as Spigel 1992) have richly theorized how television was always closely involved in assigning normative gender and sexual roles in the domestic realm, especially through the ways that programming, scheduling, and advertising contribute to the organization of the time and space of the heteronormative family and reinforce divisions of labor and patterns of leisure and consumption. In the case of SBS, we can infer a curious tension in the kind of national cosmopolitan values it was mandated to deliver. Bringing the multiplicity of the world into new proximity with the national domestic, which SBS understood to be richly heterogeneous, opens the door to all kinds of intimacy that might take place there beyond the channel's technical or sociopolitical infrastructural purview. In this sense, the broad but somewhat regulated discourse of cosmopolitanism translates into a surprisingly permissive scope of possibilities for domestic life, which exceed conventional gender and sexual norms established by commercial television and traditional narratives of the nation.

One of the most effective ways SBS enabled new domestic intimacies with the world was through regular programming of international films in a variety of languages. Films were initially selected to fulfill the channel's "multicultural" requirements rather than on the basis of quality. Later, more emphasis was placed on programming culturally significant "world cinema" to help generate the channel's "cosmopolitan multicultural sensibility" (Ang, Hawkins and Dabboussy 2008, 103). This move aimed to shift SBS from a service channel to a destination channel, and whether viewers went looking for this content or stumbled upon it SBS became known for out-of-the-ordinary programming that was not available elsewhere on television. Respondent Paul recalls:

> I started reading the TV guide from the paper each week and looking for the film descriptions for Friday or Saturday night, which, if home, I could watch. This is how I discovered art house cinema.

For Andrew, discovery of some out-of-the-ordinary programming was serendipitous:

> I guess, also, if you stayed up late enough you'd see some Italian movies with some hairy, naked men romping around, but that was rare.

Central to its exceptional status was the fact that SBS remained for its first decade unfettered by the commercial interests that constrained programming and scheduling on other channels. Compared to them, SBS felt bold, sometimes obscure, often exciting. Respondent Benedict describes this feeling at length:

> I also remember watching foreign films first for their adult content and then, as I became aware of my own sexuality as a gay teenager, of films depicting gay people. In the 90s these were still fringe and hard to find, so it felt elicit and edgy to watch them, as well as educational. (…) For the stranger content or the gay-themed movies, I would watch these in my room secretly as I was not out. For this reason SBS also seemed edgier or "cooler" because it featured content about subcultures and non-ethnic minorities. As I mentioned, it squared in perfectly with my feelings of being alternative or counter-cultural.

Feeling "elicit," "edgy," "alternative," or "counter-cultural" suggests SBS benefited from the opportunity of not being caught in a conventional frame of televisual capitalism. We see that Benedict made the most of SBS's recognition of the heterogeneity of its audience, in contrast with how commercial channels tended to construct audience around tightly imagined consumer profiles. Moreover, Benedict's access to feeling countercultural was spatialized ("in my room"), suggesting that SBS's freedom from commercial imperatives fragmented the home into distinct affective zones rather than containing it in a singular domestic fantasy of family members and citizen-families all aligned with each other and "facing the right way" (Ahmed 2010, 37).

Films broadcast at night and especially after primetime appeared to be uncensored, though they were still subject to government classifications like AO (Adults Only) or later MA (Mature Audiences). In practice, these codes functioned to signal to viewers when they could expect to see more sex and nudity than was usual on television, and the strong likelihood of homoerotic images and themes. Whether by design or not, the result of this programming was that Australian television was made more visibly queer than it had ever been—but significantly, it did so under the tasteful cloak of cosmopolitanism.[3] For respondent Eddy, the queer and the cosmopolitan merged in the feeling of watching SBS:

> I felt like it was exciting, like my first memories of horror films on VHS alone without the adults. The difference being that with SBS I believed I was learning something about "the world outside" (about how to move around in a non-heteronormative way [perhaps]).

Here, "the world outside" is not so much an objective reality to be learned about through the delivery of content, as if looking through a window, but something made available as an affective orientation of the body. Eddy describes a kind of mobility ("how to move around") which watching SBS allowed him to try out, and the feeling of this mobility recalls early glimpses of independence. Crucially, this feeling was qualitatively different from prior domestic experience (perhaps "non-heteronormative"), and thus the images Eddy consumed served to construct a future world he could move into inhabiting rather than just to calibrate his orientation to an existing world.

Meanwhile on commercial television, just as SBS was closing out its first decade, a sketch-comedy show called *Fast Forward* was becoming one of the most popular programs in the history of Australian television. Running from 1989 to 1992, several of its performers would become household names. *Fast Forward*'s winning formula was to offer a recurring roster of keenly observed character studies alongside somewhat silly parodies of other programs and personalities from Australia's collective televisual consciousness. These included locally produced favorites as well as American and British programs that were permanent fixtures of the afternoon re-run schedule. Each episode of *Fast Forward* was structured by the device of channel-surfing to produce a self-reflexive simulation of an evening's television viewing: the nation watches itself watching, but through a humorously distorted lens. Looking back, it's striking how many sketches based their humor on the exaggeration of supposed deviations from normative identity categories and, at face value, crude stereotyping of ethnic, sexual, or linguistic difference.

Among these sketches was "SBS Woman", one of *Fast Forward*'s signature characters. The deadly serious, unblinking, and mysteriously accented parody of an SBS presenter offered fictitious highlights of a typical evening's viewing on SBS. With a mounting laugh track behind her, SBS Woman would deadpan her way through teasers for ridiculous documentaries from Eastern Europe or unlikely sex-romps from Scandinavia. I'd argue that it is here, in both the relentless parody of the perceived absurdity and obscurity of public "multicultural" broadcasting and in the suggestive representation of "ordinary" television viewer reaction, that we can find evidence of the widely acknowledged "truth" of SBS's queerness. An example from 1991 serves to illustrate. Having previewed a Turkish film which tells "the heart-breaking story of a boy who befriends an orphaned weevil, only to have it cruelly snatched from him by the secret police" followed by "a mesmerising tour of the hairdressing appliances of Budapest," SBS Woman announces the inauguration of advertising on SBS—a form of which did, in fact, begin at this time—and promises it will "comply with our policy of artistic excellence and tastefulness" (*Fast Forward* 1991). And so we cut to a pre-recorded studio shot of SBS Woman in equally deadpan infomercial mode (Figure 4.1):

> Now from Holland via SBS Marketing, we applaud the arrival of a new and exciting, nutritious, low-calorie snack food product with an unmistakable taste that will linger for hours. [*lifts product*] Yes, it's Dyke Fingers. And not

FIGURE 4.1 Dyke Fingers point to the 'truth' of SBS's queerness. YouTube screen capture.

"SBS Woman," Ted Emery, *Fast Forward*, season 3, episode 14, 1991.

> only are Dyke Fingers the perfect accompaniment for a steaming bowl of *rookworst* or *snert*, they're useful for day-to-day plumbing disasters around the home. Just pop a Dyke Finger in the offending hole and your hun is your uncle. Dyke Fingers. Personally I couldn't go a day without one. Available in either dry or soggy biscuits.
>
> *Fast Forward 1991*

Needless to say, this sketch is puerile and unfunny. But it is instructive in that the joke behind its premise depends on the self-evidence of a conflation of foreignness with queerness. It naturalizes the connotative slippage between unfamiliar European delicacies and implied queer sexual practices, and in turn draws a direct line between the latter and butch domestic competence.

It would be too easy to read the Dyke Fingers sketch as no more than the normative other to the queerness of SBS—as a metonym for the homophobic, commercial backdrop against which SBS offered itself as queer accent. To put this a little differently, let's not be too quick to brand Dyke Fingers a *bad* representation of queerness in contrast to the *good* representations seen on the real SBS. For one thing, there is no easy distinction between commercial and queer; in fact, the sketch depends on the premise that even commercial breaks on SBS will not be able to contain the channel's signature queerness. As Hollis Griffin (2016) has shown, it may well be that the normativity of much commercial television is exactly what generates its "affective value" for queer viewers, partly because it activates a fantasy of belonging extended to all viewers. Griffin (2016) distinguishes affective value from other ways that television is appraised, such as critical reputation, aesthetic and ideological evaluations, and industry measures of financial viability.

Like much comedy, the affective value of SBS Woman can be measured by how its humor—crass as it is—invites a feeling of inclusion among viewers. Laughter registers recognition of the cultural references at play and the version of normative national-cultural imaginary that undergirds the sketch's parody. But at the same time, the collective safety of laughter offers an alibi for the parody's dual function of emphasizing queerness; after all, parody involves an intimate knowingness and a performative logic of imitation, which invite a second degree of recognition among viewers so attuned. To the queer adolescent viewer, for instance, scouring the screen eagle-eyed for *anything* erotically sustaining in a desert of overtly queer images, even ridicule and stereotype may point in the right direction. In the end, the commercial crassness of SBS Woman may be one of the unlikely affective vectors through which the queerness of SBS circulates.

Out of Time and Out of Place

Sara Ahmed (2004, 148) has proposed that the sensorial experience of queerness can be measured by how comfortably the queer body fits into material environments that have been systematically constructed as heteronormative. A heteronormative space extends comfort only to certain bodies because it allows them to feel that they fit in: the space has "already taken their shape". Queer theory also teaches us that the feeling of fitting in is experienced as a bodily relation to the normative organization of time, including the schedules by which successful family life and the relations that comprise it are measured. As a result, argues Freeman (2010, 172), "not fitting in often feels both like having the wrong body and like living in a different time zone".

Queer spatial and temporal orientations emerge strongly in respondents' memories of their adolescent SBS viewing practices. Benedict's viewing of some programs, noted above, took place "in my room secretly as I was not out" and "at night". Here the secluded space of the bedroom literalizes the metaphor of the closet, from which he had not yet come "out", and nocturnal viewing confirms his distance from family schedules. Similarly, a practice of safety can be inferred in Paul's negotiation of the parameters of domestic space and parental authority:

> Until I was 15 we had only had a B&W television in the garage, on which we were allowed to watch the ABC news. After this we got colour TVs in two loungerooms at home so on the weekends I would go to the empty or most distant loungeroom and watch TV, knowing I probably wouldn't be disturbed.

While Paul reports the relative freedom of more than one potential viewing space, Douglas recalls SBS being limited to his grandmother's house next-door because television was not normally allowed in his parents' house:

> TV was very much associated with my gran and so a little furtive or illicit. Not related to home life much at all as I rarely if ever did it either in the home or with immediate family. It was solitary, night-time, my own thing.

Separated in space and time from immediate family, SBS felt "furtive or illicit". Solitude and night-time viewing are also reported by Andrew, as is a distance from family which he implies to be a question of taste rather than space:

> I was the only one watching SBS [whereas] the local TV station was more of a family affair. I never discussed any of the programmes with my family, and would have to stay up late, happily, on my own to wait for what I wanted to come on.

In his geographical location, Andrew reports that SBS was the only alternative to "the local TV station," which he equates with family. The combined parameters of infrastructural provisioning and family scheduling required him to separate himself in space and time, but he experienced this obligation "happily". Across these memories, we can interpret how modes of improvisation and ingenuity in the face of normative domestic parameters generated positive affective states both as the result of viewing and in some cases for their own sake.

I also came of age with SBS-TV. By the time it was hitting its stride as a viable alternative broadcaster in the mid-to-late 1980s, I was a queer teenager struggling increasingly to feel at home in the normative discourses of family and nation that surrounded me in suburban Australia. Even though as a white, middle-class male I had every reason to feel that my environment had been structured around the priority of bodies like mine, I felt nonetheless pushed out because of my burgeoning homoerotic desires, my gravitation toward "feminine" interests and toward Europe, and by the fact of being recognized as smart. Throughout high school and even into adulthood, these distinct dispositions seemed to merge interchangeably and conveniently in a powerful discourse of "how not to be Australian". I, too, began to accept them as evidence of not belonging, of being a queer fit.

Watching SBS during this period is how I discovered queer European film. Three films stand out most strongly in my memory of this time: Patrice Chéreau's *L'Homme blessé* (*The Wounded Man*, 1983); Pedro Almodóvar's *La ley del deseo* (*Law of Desire*, 1987), and Derek Jarman's *Caravaggio* (1986). They were all broadcast late at night and I watched them alone and in secret, having calculated a high probability for homoerotic content from the briefest synopses in the television listing. The only television set in my family home was in the living room, so viewing missions involved sitting close enough to the screen that I could turn it off if I heard my parents coming. The experience felt thrilling and dangerous—and, as it turns out, unrepeatable. For when I found and watched these films again years later, I was slightly disappointed. Something was missing, even though my skills of appreciation and evaluation had increased. What was missing, I came to realize, was a particular affective quality that distinguished the first encounters. Beyond their particular images, the intensity of these films' ongoing resonance in me was flamed by the awkwardness of the conditions in which I first encountered them. The specific material configuration of these encounters—the coming together of bodies and objects, schedules and spatial arrangements, discourses of family and home and nation made material—impressed itself into how I experienced queerness on the screen.

The sensorial quality of this experience was also generated by certain technical components of the material configuration. These films were shot on celluloid in wide-screen format and transferred to the small screen of television, so their transfer inevitably caused significant loss in image definition and sound quality. In addition, SBS had an infamously poor signal. As respondent Francesca phrased it, SBS was "the channel where people had actual sex and you had to struggle through the poor reception to make it out!" Technical glitches remind us of the presence of infrastructures behind the screen that make the television image possible but tend to remain beyond viewers' unconscious. They burst into the room with us and literally make their presence felt, giving rise to unplanned but very real affective events. So just as my queer adolescent body did not extend comfortably into the domestic space that was not designed for it, I think of these film telecasts as a queer fit, too. They had been reformatted for technical and cultural protocols different from their own. They, too, were out of time and out of place.

Conclusion

This chapter has proposed that if we look beyond television's images to its materialities, queerness might also be found in the orientations it generates in viewers. This does not mean that television turns viewers queer, as if queerness were an effect of watching television (if only!). Rather, queerness might help to name the bodily sensations and dispositions that characterize some viewers' relations to television as a medium and as an infrastructure. As the case of SBS-TV Australia demonstrates, television inhabits everyday lives as a sociopolitical infrastructure that works in parallel (if not always fully in synch) with the technical infrastructures that make television viewing possible. The quality and feel of viewing experiences may differ according to the specific configuration of technical components like cables, antennas, and formats. At the same time the sociopolitics of television distribution, such as a channel's mandate, its programming policies, and broader discourses of home and nation, work to articulate an audience. By articulation, I mean both how the audience is constructed by these policies and discourses and the degree to which the audience feels it fits into this construction.

The initial anecdotal evidence presented above suggests that SBS participated in a queer reorientation of the normative scene of late twentieth-century Australian domesticity, but it did so through the nationalist multicultural imaginary that it was mandated to deliver. Looking back at this moment has not been intended to secure the foundations of queer identity in some mythic historical hardship; as Heather Love (2007, 6) has argued, such a move risks equating queerness with backwardness. My purpose has been to offer one modest corrective to accounts of media which insist on the forward drive of queerness. New categories of queer backwardness are arguably being generated by recent accounts of queer politics which maintain that the failure to make ourselves visible and available to network circulation equals the denial of our value, if not of our very social existence. I have hoped to show that paying attention to our own lingering resonances of media's complicated materialities might help to "resist the commodity-time of speedy manufacture and planned obsolescence" (Freeman 2010, 9) whose current force risks normalizing queer media as little more than algorithmically calculated playlists and curated social media feeds.

Notes

1 For a detailed historical and infrastructural analysis of 'ethnic media' in Canada, see Hayward (2019).
2 Written responses to a short series of open-ended questions were gathered via email in November and December 2020. Questions invited respondents to describe in their own words their personal experiences of SBS-TV as adolescents growing up in Australia. All respondents were born between 1971 and 1980, gave permission for their responses to be quoted here, and were given a pseudonym.
3 Ron Becker (2006, 81) argues that American television networks began to incorporate "gay and lesbian material" into prime-time programming in the 1990s as a way to target "upscale" audiences and thereby alleviate steady declines in ratings. See also Griffin (2016, 115–116).

References

Ahmed, S. 2004. *The Cultural Politics of Emotion*. London: Routledge, 2004.

Ahmed, S. 2010. Happy Objects. In *The Affect Theory Reader*, ed. M. Gregg and G. J. Seigworth, 29–51. Durham: Duke University Press.

Anand, N., A. Gupta and H. Appel, ed. 2018. *The Promise of Infrastructure*. Durham: Duke University Press.

Ang, I., G. Hawkins and L. Dabboussy. 2008. *The SBS Story: The Challenge of Cultural Diversity*. Sydney: University of New South Wales Press.

Attitude (@attitudemag). 2020. "Was 2020 the gayest year for TV ever?!" Instagram post, December 26. www.instagram.com/p/CJRf1f7jbW2/?igshid=1n3ydojdx04go

Becker, R. 2006. *Gay TV and Straight America*. New Brunswick: Rutgers University Press.

Fast Forward. 1991. Season 3, episode 14. Directed by Ted Emery, performed by Marg Downey. July 11. Seven Network. www.youtube.com/watch?v=n2Sp6MRhjb4

Freeman, E. 2010. *Time Binds: Queer Temporalities, Queer Histories*. Durham: Duke University Press.

Griffin, F. H. 2016. *Feeling Normal: Sexuality and Media Criticism in the Digital Age*. Bloomington: Indiana University Press.

Hayward, M. 2019. *Identity and Industry: Making Media Multicultural*. Montreal: McGill-Queen's University Press.

Johnson, C. The politics of affective citizenship: from Blair to Obama. *Citizenship Studies* 14, no. 5: 495–509.

Larkin, B. 2013. The Politics and Poetics of Infrastructure. *Annual Review of Anthropology* 42: 327–43.

Love, H. 2007. *Feeling Backward: Loss and the Politics of Queer History*. Cambridge: Harvard University Press.

SBS. 2020. Our History. www.sbs.com.au/aboutus/our-history (accessed December 20, 2020).
Spigel, L. 1992. *Make Room for TV: Television and the Family Ideal in Postwar America.* Chicago: University of Chicago Press.
Villarejo, A. 2014. *Ethereal Queer: Television, Historicity, Desire.* Durham: Duke University Press.
Wilson, A. 2016. The Infrastructure of Intimacy. *Signs* 41, no. 2 (Winter): 1–34.

PART II

Temporal Play

Queer Histories and Possibilities

5

MAKING THINGS PERFECTLY SKETCH

Reflexive Queer and Trans Themes in Sketch Comedy

Candace Moore

Given sketch comedy's reliance on intertextuality and tendency to construct parodies and satirical bits around popular culture and televised celebrities, sketch shows themselves, at their most canny, critique and even historicize queer and trans media representations. At their worst, sketches may end up reiterating homophobic and transphobic tropes in comedians' quick attempts to riff on cultural themes. Current debates in queer and trans communities abound about the purview of comedy, especially jokes focused on sexuality, gender, and race—namely, what's considered respectfully edgy and what's cancel-worthy? Sketch comedy, as a form, tends to focus its barbs on whatever's fresh or notable in the ever-swiftly-passing "moment-we're-in." Because sketches, packed with topical and contextual references, bear so many markers of the times when they're crafted, with rare exceptions, whole episodes of sketch TV tend not to be replayed much past original release. Made of quicksilver, sketch comedy maintains some immunity to cultural cancellation, as the form does not especially aim to assume a place in the cultural archive. In his book *Sketch Comedy*, Nick Marx correctly diagnoses that the genre's power-punch of timeliness is the same factor that ushers particular sketches so quickly out of collective memory and into the metaphorical dustbin.[1] But precisely because of the critical and interpretive work such shows do to throw their respective "nows" into relief, sketch comedy begs a rewatch for understanding the representational politics of the near present. In what follows, I revisit touchstone sketches in queer- and trans-themed sketch comedy on post-network television, analyzing the role humor plays in destabilizing LGBTQ stereotypes and reframing TV's tokenized characters. I consider how sketch shows seeking to conscientiously reflect queer and trans culture reinterpret the TV texts they mimic and implicitly compare their own interventions in representation to the very scenes they replay and rethink.

DOI: 10.4324/9781003109044-8

Sketch Politics

After over 46 years in production, *Saturday Night Live* (*SNL*; NBC, 1975–) maintains an iconic role as NBC's longstanding sketch comedy hit. Any up-and-coming sketch show produced in an American context relies upon *SNL* as a reference model—whether comics actively aim to break from its improvisational character-driven style or directly emulate it. Although *SNL*'s sketches certainly take on sensitive issues and make plays for relevance, its producers, stars, critics, and fans consistently remark upon *SNL*'s profound political ambiguity. *Paste*'s Garrett Martin coined this tendency as "bothsidesism," suggesting that one of *SNL*'s head writers, Colin Jost, who co-hosts the current "Weekend Update" segment, takes center stage as "the defacto face of its very white, very bourgeoisie brand of apoliticism."[2] This correlates to *SNL*'s historical role in representational politics, which Nick Marx brands as operating on an "egotistical aesthetic" that privileges white masculinities at the same time that *SNL* sketches leave room to both enunciate and lampoon the diverse identities and perspectives of its cast members and guests. In his examination of network-era *SNL*, Marx finds that "[a]lthough sketches based in transgressive racial politics would seem to have bolstered SNL's edgy aesthetic early on, the show marginalized black identities by privileging those of white men."[3] Today, in television's post-network era, since viewers more often consume the production piecemeal through isolated clips that go viral, *SNL* content gets remotivated through social media distribution to further support a variety of perspectives—thus, this baked-in political ambiguity serves the program within the streaming television landscape nearly as well now as it did during the 1970s network television model.

Taken to task in the mid-1990s by cast members like Janeane Garofalo for a swell of homophobic content, *SNL* has been panned of late for its lack of sensitivity about trans issues[4]—and not just for its notorious ridiculing of Julia Sweeney's androgynous character Pat back in the 1980s—but for "Weekend Update" barbs made as recently as 2021. In February 2021, Michael Che seemingly doubled down on his much criticized schtick from 2019, which intentionally misgendered and dead-named Caitlyn Jenner. He referred to President Biden's reversal of the military's transgender ban as "Don't Ask, Don't Tuck"— clearly refusing to cease making genitalia the center of any trans-related joke. Che's in-poor-taste pronouncements follow Jost's illogical suggestion on "Weekend Update" in 2016 that trans and other gender-expansive individuals, emblematized by the app Tinder's recent inclusion of 37 gender options for users, "lost [the election]" to Trump, implying that recognizing the self-determination of trans and non-binary individuals was somehow un-American or deserving of ridicule. *SNL* sketches from the 2010s and early 2020s infamously, and seemingly intentionally, fumble queer and trans content, renewing the perception that despite cycles of diversifying its cast and claims to political "neutrality," *SNL* continues to prioritize white straight cis male worldviews.

In contrast, two comedy series intentionally focused on representing and serving specific communities, *The Big Gay Sketch Show* (LOGO, 2007–2010) and *A Black*

Lady Sketch Show (HBO, 2019) [hereafter, abbreviated as *BGSS* and *BLSS*, respectively], tend to foreground progressive politics. Gleefully queering and genderqueering classic characters, while drawing attention to intersectional considerations of race, class, gender, and sexuality, *BGSS* offers subtextual re-readings of the very television landscape that cable network Logo hoped to transform in the mid-aughts. If *BGSS* offers something of a creative historiography project, consciously diversifying TV's past in terms of LGBTQ representations, *BLSS* centers multiply minoritized subjects—black women: queer and straight, trans and cis—in the present and speculatively imagined into a post-apocalyptic future. *BLSS* produces bold send-ups of popular culture's appropriative and reductive practices when it comes to depicting black social worlds. Among their explorations of LGBTQ themes, sketches in both shows figure, if briefly, black trans femininity within their reflexive projects on television's representation of race, gender, and sexuality. Produced at different historical moments, each show engages different intersectional foci. *BGSS*, made in the mid-aughts, implicitly centers white gay and lesbian culture, with queer Black, Indigenous and people of color (BIPOC), bi+, and trans individuals and cultures largely left at the margins. *BLSS*, launched at the end of the Trump era, implicitly centers black cis feminist cultures, both straight and queer, while gesturing at trans experiences or perspectives.

Sketchwork

In their parodies of television source material and incorporation of guest stars famous for television roles, *BGSS* and *BLSS* actively perform a kind of intertextual *sketchwork*. This sketchwork makes pointed revisions that criticize, historicize, and speculate. In *Satire TV: Politics and Comedy in the Post Network Era,* Jonathan Gray, Jeffrey P. Jones, and Ethan Thompson suggest that specific forms of humor, though they may lack "clear-cut or easily digestible meanings," not only do critical work but also occasion interpretive work on the part of audiences—they can "be 'work'" as well.[5] Of these forms, Gray, Jones, and Thompson find that parody, with its superimposition of new material on older texts, "offers 'new' ways to make sense of 'old' texts or genres."[6] Parodies such as those on *BGSS* and *BLSS* model and demand participation in cultural criticism, calling attention to television's style and production of meanings while reflecting on the past, near and distant, through a lens presented as "current."

However, neither *BGSS* or *BLSS* produce parodic sketches that are simply affirming or uncontroversial. This reflects how comedy, whether socially progressive or otherwise, theoretically operates: it produces byproduct discomfort alongside chuckles as it pokes at multiple perspectives and makes taken-for-granted logics strange. In their introduction to *Critical Inquiry*'s special issue on comedy, "Comedy Has Issues," Lauren Berlant and Sianne Ngai argue that the genre of comedy isn't "just a field of narrative expectation punctuated by the surprise of laughter or vertiginous enjoyment. It is also epistemologically troubling, drawing insecure boundaries..."[7] The work of comedy, in as much as it stretches, explores, plays with, and often inadvertently reestablishes categories and boundaries, is always political. The interpreted significance of and audience response to a particular comedic expression (whether a joke lands or tanks, for example) shift depending on the framework from which the comedic text is received. Context and venue matter, as do tone of delivery and timing. In their introduction to a *Cinema Journal* special issue on "Comedy and Humor Studies," Maggie Hennefeld, Annie Berke, and Michael Rennet concur with Berlant and Ngai's declaration that "Comedy Has Issues"; they make explicit that just because comedy itself problematizes culture, that doesn't mean it gets a free pass from criticism.[8] What happens when comedy content in a show we broadly regard as aligned with socially progressive politics maintains a certain absurd inscrutability? Or when it becomes uncomfortably difficult to draw clear distinctions between those bits disingenuously framed as apolitical on *SNL* and those made by queer and BIPOC comics that similarly engender a twinge of cringe?

Gay Historicizing Sketch

The PR discourse around the 2006 launch of Logo, Viacom's LGBTQ-focused channel, proposed that the basic cable network finally addressed a specific, "underserved" niche. As openly gay Brian Graden, entertainment president of Logo and MTV, declared: "If you're gay and lesbian you have seen yourself represented on television for the last 20 years but you've never had a home."[9] One of Logo's first original programs, *The Big Gay Sketch Show* exhibited self-historicizing tendencies within its sketches, implicitly setting itself and the emerging LGBTQ network it represented in contrast to network era broadcast television. Self-congratulatory, these sketches worked to reinforce the notion of a discrete divide between television's pre- and post-gay visibility periods, yet they also provided transgressive, and occasionally troubling, readings of pre-1980s sitcoms already full of contestatory potential during their original air dates.

BGSS provides savvy parodies of vintage TV, positioning its own project as historically distinctive (a "first") at the same time as it historicizes television comedy past as always already queer. Executive-produced by out daytime talk sensation Rosie O'Donnell and modeled after late night network shows *Saturday Night Live* and *Mad TV*, the half-hour sketch comedy program premiered in April 2007. In its first two installments, *BGSS* parodies famous episodes of sitcoms *The Honeymooners* and *All in the Family*. The show traces a lineage from which an "out" comedy production is both a frank departure and an explicit, in group-authorized display of often poached queer cultural traditions of camp, drag, butch, femme. *BGSS* either revises television texts by imposing queer and transgender characters where there were previously none or scant few, or makes the sexuality of connoted queer characters blatant. The act of queering becomes, for *BGSS*, a variant of the act of parody.

Marked by inter-titles that proclaim "Logo at Nite Presents Another Gay TV Classic," *BGSS's* spoofs on classic TV are put into dialogue with the show's lampoons of then-contemporary cable fare, like Bravo's *Project Runway* and *Queer Eye for the Straight Guy*, delivering digs at a trend of "taste-maker" queers on reality-style shows. Consider the choice of classic TV sources and how they relate, metaphorically, to Logo's entry into cable's spectrum and distinction from other networks: the major topics covered in the original episodes include integrating a discriminated-against household onto the block (*All in the Family*) and questioning TV's purpose in the home and the increasing taste segregation of viewers (*Honeymooners*).

One of the first television shows of the early 1970s to explicitly deal with the issue of homophobia, *All in the Family* included one-off episodes about homosexual characters, beginning with its sixth episode, "Judging Books by Covers" (CBS, 2/9/71). By choosing instead, however, to spoof the sitcom's first season finale "The First and Last Supper" (4/6/71) an episode that openly airs and ostensibly critiques racism, the producers of *BGSS* rely on a minority-based model of apprehending queer difference to position Logo's LGBTQ content in conversation with a larger history of minority representation on television, suggesting false equivalencies between TV's negotiations of sexuality and race. "The First and Last Supper," a follow-up to the earlier episode "Lionel Moves into the Neighborhood," concerns a black family's entrance into the Bunker family's all-white suburb and home despite clear lack of genuine welcome. This sendup of executive producer Norman Lear's 1970s classic, which appeared in *BGSS's* second episode, asks, "What if television's infamous sitcom bigot, Archie Bunker, were gay?" Changing out lyrics from "Those Were the Days," the show's opening song, creates an alternate anthem to queer culture, pre-AIDS: "Oh, the way Sylvester plays…songs that make the gay parade…We can use a man like Harvey Milk again/didn't need no condoms then/54 was always in/no one went to the gym/those were the days…" This sketch imagines Archie, replete with potbelly and cigar, as part of an extravagantly queer household, where Edith is replaced by "queer as a four dollar bill" Eddie, and Gloria and Michael (a.k.a. Meathead), with Gloria and Michelle (a.k.a. Tofu-head). During the camera's sweep of the neighborhood, consistent with *All in the Family's* opening credits, we're offered shots instead of the intersection of New York's Christopher and Gay streets. Eddie observes that "Arch hasn't left the neighborhood since the Stonewall rebellion of '69" and Archie reminisces how "Eddie fought those cops at Stonewall like a dingbat outta hell."

Archie's vast bigotry, in this version, is completely directed at straight people. The sketch culminates in an argument about whether or not to let George and Louise Jefferson, invited guests to dinner, into the house, switching out Archie's blatant white supremacy for a strong bias against straight folks. Archie declares that he "ain't having no breeders up in this here house." His daughter gently corrects his "slur": "Dad, they're called heterosexuals," while Michelle, playing Michael's role, tries to educate this throwback: "kids our generation have lots of heterosexual friends, Archie, don't be so heterophobic." But when the Jeffersons finally do arrive, Archie cheers right up, welcoming them with open arms: "Wait! They're black! Well, come on in!" By having its Bunker refuse dinner with the Jeffersons because they are heterosexuals and then accepting them immediately upon learning the color of their skin, this sketch simultaneously barbs the conservative discourse of "reverse discrimination" and mocks forms of othering that liberal whites produce despite performing wokeness. The sketchwork shows the absolute absurdity of swapping white supremacy with so-called heterophobia, as if these two differently weighted separatisms could be equated within a structurally racist, historically hetero-centric culture. Through the foil of a queer Archie Bunker, the sketch demonstrates that those who experience discrimination based on certain aspects of their identities may experience social privileges based on other aspects, or in certain contexts, and that experiencing discrimination oneself does not make one in any way immune from potentially disenfranchising or dismissing others.

The Honeymooners' infamous episode "TV or Not TV" (CBS, 10/1/55) revolves around whether or not the Kramdens will purchase the relatively new technology of the television set; when they do, TV splinters the Kramdens and their neighbor Ed into differing audience segments as they bicker about what to watch. The sketch afforded the most airtime during *BGSS*'s premiere willfully queers *The Honeymooners*, replacing the sitcom's heteronormative 1950s couple with butch and femme lesbians. Presented in black and white to match the show, the sketch is introduced first by a Logo@Nite frame and secondly by a parody on a sponsor's ad: over a display of a Chesterfield cigarettes pack, a male announcer bellows that the brand "won't give you cancer in forty years." Given that conglomerate Viacom owned both Nickelodeon and Logo, Logo's network-specific play on the "Nick at Nite" slogan functioned as a cross-platform wink to a sister station. The first frame suggests retroactively viewing the sitcom through a cable intermediary, while the commercial segment that follows suggests seeing the episode during its original airing or as an archival document, with advertisements intact.

The *Honeymooners* parody re-imagines Jackie Gleason's Ralph Kramden as "bull dagger" Rhonda (played by Julie Goldman), who swaggers home in her tie, bus driver's cap, and work jacket to a discontented Alice (Nicol Paone). Alice begs her "secret homosexual lifetime commitment partner," as she calls Rhonda, for a "black and white TV set with rabbit ears," because she wants to watch "Liberace on TV," a reference that sounds like a queering of the script to insert a gay icon, yet obtains added humor when reviewing *The Honeymooners'* pilot "To TV or Not TV." In the original source, first broadcast October 1st, 1955, Alice Kramden mentions wanting to use television not only to escape the claustrophobic sight of "that icebox, that stove, and these four walls," but precisely because she wants to "look at Liberace." In the updated version, the writers toy with Alice's "four walls" diatribe; she additionally threatens: "If these walls could talk, too!" tossing in a reference to the popular lesbian-themed triptych of short films from the 1990s. Where Ralph patronizingly wondered out loud "whatever happened to the sweet unspoiled girl I married?" Rhonda muses "whatever happened to the sweet girl I met at the Patricia Highsmith book club?" *The Big Gay Sketch Show*'s allusion to Highsmith, who penned the lesbian-themed novel *The Price of Salt* in 1951 under pseudonym

Claire Morgan, pleases those with the cultural capital to get the reference and simultaneously recalls a lesbian culture during the 1950s to which the mystery writer belonged, a culture left largely unimaged by classic television.

By queering one of the most emblematic sitcom examples of a husband who attempts to keep his stay-at-home wife under his thumb, *BGSS*'s comedy troupe highlight gendered forms of inequity instead through butch and femme lesbians. When Rhonda threatens Alice with Ralph's characteristic raised fist at bay and the expressions "Pow, right in the kisser!" or "Straight to the moon!" queer Alice dryly retaliates. "Spousal abuse," she says with flat affect, "that's some fun stuff." *BGSS*'s Rhonda capitulates, selling her bowling ball to bring home what she thinks Alice wants: a black transvestite in a white dress wearing white bunny ears. Despite the fact that Rhonda brought the wrong sort of "TV," Alice is grateful for the gesture and effuses: "Even though you're sweaty, you threaten me with domestic violence, and never allow me to leave the apartment, I love ya!"

In the original *Honeymooners,* Ralph purchases the television set presumably to keep his wife company while he is away at work, yet it is Ralph and his neighbor Ed who become so fascinated with television that they eat across from it and sleep next to it, neglecting their wives at night. Television becomes a more enticing stand-in for their respective spouses as Ralph and Ed produce a domestic scene where two men dine by flickering light, bicker, and fall asleep together. *The Big Gay Sketch Show* presents, in lieu of this triangulation between Ralph, Ed, and the television set, a trans person as the "commodity" Rhonda and Ed become enamored with, trading on stereotypes as it links trans bodies, and black trans feminine bodies specifically, to sex work. This look back at how *The Honeymooners* figures television as a force capable of rechanneling desire and reorganizing married life suggests an introspective look *at* the challenges facing a channel like Logo. For Logo attempts to balance producing an identity-based product for capitalistic profit—presenting queerness or transness for consumption—with cultural and iconic promises made to its viewers: the fantasy of a cable channel capable of providing a site for coalitional community building or presenting LGBTQ referents unproblematically. The substitution of a transfeminine sex worker for a television set reveals Rhonda's (and Ed's) underlying desire to objectify black trans women, but acts as more than a play on abbreviations. The sketch injects a black, trans character into a white working-class comedy as exoticized other, while highlighting the white-washed landscape, not-so-subtle misogyny, and precarious compulsory heteronormativity of fifties television. While one read of this sketch might therefore argue that *BGSS*'s sketchwork personifies television as black and trans to editorialize on how television constructs categories of gender, sexuality, and race in particular ways in order to commodify them, another might be disappointed to recognize trans femininity posed once again, through *BGSS*, as a punchline, plain and simple. Clearly there are no guarantees that gay sketch evolves or becomes vastly less problematic just because it's gay and lesbian comics now setting up the jokes. Perhaps gay comedy still has issues?

Sketching the Basic, Bad, and Ratchet

The first episode of *Black Lady Sketch Show* appeared only nine years after BGSS's run ended, but by then, politics in America had drastically changed and cable seemed old school, if not obsolete, when compared to subscription streaming services and digital apps. *Black Lady Sketch Show's* parodic scenes mine media discussions on social networks like Twitter, while commenting on the insularity and precarity of life during and after the Trump presidency. The polarizing effects of the Trump era were arguably emergent during his primary run, as gaslighting techniques and fearmongering became frequent headline news fodder. Under Trump, the public sphere, especially the internet, surged with highly visible, mainstreamed bigotry and hate speech. Yet the late 2010s also saw increased social diversity represented within popular culture (compared to previous decades) as digital media somewhat democratized production and distribution, and larger media outlets mimicked independent influencers' inclusive creative projects and production practices.

Issa Rae, executive producer of *A Black Lady Sketch Show* and *Insecure,* is a perfect example of a Hollywood creative who was "found" on YouTube by HBO, following buzz around her web series *The Misadventures of Awkward Black Girl.* Rae lends her name to *BLSS,* helped set up the show's all black women's writers' room, and also guest stars. Stand-up comedian Robin Thede co-executive produces the series and acts as lead writer and a primary cast member alongside Ashley Nicole Black, Quinta Brunson, and Gabrielle Dennis. Within its first two episodes, *BLSS* not only delivers original sketch comedy made by and about black women, but also features the black queer and trans community, setting sketches in a queer dance club full of lesbian exes (infiltrated by an alien stealing everyone's dance moves) and at a ballroom event where un-glamorousness is in vogue. *BLSS* hosts guest stars most known for their LGBTQ roles on TV, such as Laverne Cox (*Orange is the New Black*) and Caldwell Tidicue, best known as Bob the Drag Queen (*RuPaul's Drag Race, Tales of the City*), to star in sketches involving fierce femmes in a "Bad Bitch Support Group" or imagining "Basic" as a runway category in a nod to FX's TV series about the ballroom community, *Pose* (2018–).

In his ethnography *Butch Queens Up in Pumps: Gender, Performance, and Ballroom Culture in Detroit*, Marlon Bailey describes the roles of houses and balls in the ballroom scene, a longstanding primarily black and LGBTQ kinship and performance culture, as family-like structures named after aspirational commodities and ideals, whose members compete in dazzling theatrical showcases of performative gender and sexual identities.[10] As Bailey and Judith Butler and others have clarified, the standards that inspire ball categories are not simply ideologically reinforced through mimesis. Ball participants transform the cultural models they reference as a crucial element of their "performance labor," according to Bailey.[11] Ball contestants stage critiques and cultural recalibrations through striking poses—their citations of standards re-signify these scripts with differences, remapping them onto the bodies of individuals who are often trans, queer, non-white, or economically or otherwise disenfranchised. Reframing and augmenting in order to carve out fresh resonances, ballroom works much the way sketch comedy parodies do, though without humor as its central aim.

BLSS's parody of *Pose* imagines a ballroom runway where the houses and categories encapsulate the "basic" in lieu of the glamorous. Wearing a yellow formal tie repurposed into a plump bow ("executive realness" restyled), Caldwell Tidicue guest stars as MC of *BLSS*'s "Basic Ball," whose performers represent categories such as "Mother Exhausted from the House of Tired" or "Eternal Children from the House of Forever 21" and together "bring" audiences the category "Clinical Depression," as the announcer celebrates: "For all my children serving chemical imbalance realness… I'm looking for sadness, I'm looking for Eeyore in Dior!" One contestant vogues into "deep REM sleep on the floor." Further "Basic Ball" categories consist of "BBQ daddies," who serve up "arguments about which route to take to work," the realness of "Running Errands," along with the Grand Finale, "Just Awkward in the Body." *BLSS* imagines what would happen if ballroom performances actually theatricalized *norms* of gender, in the first dictionary definition, common denominator sense of the word—as in commonplace, typical productions (i.e. the basic), rather than reworking, as they often do, elite, fashionable cultural fantasies or *ideals* of gender—inherently impossible standards to live up to for anyone.[12] Actual norms are pedestrian, depressing, uncomfortable, uneventful, everyday—and in American dominant culture, they often emerge from white culture.

The running commentary, delivered with sarcastic aplomb by Tidicue, thus explores what has become culturally ordinary. These "basic" categories confront harsh lived realities and struggles with mental health; disappointing or dull masculinities; how the self-awareness of second guessing oneself gets read, through the prism of gender, as lack of self-esteem; and how awkward gaffs that result from trying to communicate tend to be socially punished, specifically in folks who are feminine presenting. The categories the sketch imagines are "basic" norms inasmuch as they represent unacknowledged but familiar affective forms of emotional paralysis and endemic boredom—the feelings and positions late capitalism repeatedly cues. This BLSS sketch underscores how the categories textually poached at balls not only often relate to the performance of class (and through class, to constructions of race) but to the trappings of the confident, the fulfilled, the recognized, the appropriate—and moreover that antiblackness, misogyny, and other shame mechanics greatly underwrite and guide these codes. BLSS's sketchwork hints at the critical and radical pleasures produced within ballroom culture's pointedly recast idealizations, yet renders the essence of these pleasures palpable in absentia, staging in its place an all-too-familiarized form of negative space: the basic.

In "Basic Ball," Tidicue's drag-fame and his/her own non-binary gender expression lend authority to the send-up of ballroom culture, launching the sketch from an insider's perspective. Given Tidicue's influencer cred, he/she doubles as the master of ceremonies not just for the fictional ball but for the sketchwork itself as it roasts rituals of taste and style arbitration, while simultaneously imagining how significantly less fun a "basic" ball might be. The cameo functions to mark this new program as worthy via the television celebrity's borrowed presence. In choosing known queer and trans black television personalities as well as longstanding black feminist icons to offer cameo appearances, *BLSS* banks on a very specific kind of credit, working both camp and honorific angles, and displaying broader proof of LGBTQ+ allyship to complement the fact that one of its four main black female co-stars, Ashley Nicole Black, identifies as queer.[13] The sketchwork folds in intertextuality not through mere parody or topical cultural references, but through cameos as iconic star signs.

One of the most star-powered sketches of *BLSS*'s premiere episode imagines the confessions and crosstalk taking place in a "Bad Bitch Support Group." Guest starring Angela Bassett and Laverne Cox as top bitches within the group's share circle, this sketch not only got featured in HBO's trailer for the show, but resulted in an Emmy nomination for Bassett for her role as the arch high femme Mo, who leads and massages the group's discussions. Scientists (also black women) testing the experimental drug Foxycodone have access to Mo's earpiece and observe the self-proclaimed "bad bitches" from behind a glass wall, as one BB Mya (Gabrielle Dennis) shyly admits that sometimes she wishes she was "just an okay bitch." Mo gently coerces Mya back to the group's fold, first affirming her feelings: "Well there's nothing wrong with being an okay bitch, as long as you're not a basic bitch." Appalled, Kiana (played by Cox) makes an audible exclamation of horror as Mya describes wanting to wear "normal house slippers, not three inch heel house shoes" or sometimes wanting to "sit down for a moment before wearing a waist trainer." "Breathe when you die, henny, okay!" Kiana asserts. Behind the fake wall, the two observing researchers discuss whether or not they should double Subject Four's (Mya's) dose: "If women start rejecting impossible beauty standards, we'll all go out of business!"

Given her role as a hard-liner protecting the honor of bad bitchery, expressed through her exaggerated protestations at Mya's slippage toward the "basic," Laverne Cox's character, Kiana, comes to represent the peer enforcer of "impossible beauty standards," alongside the pharmaceutical company plant Mo. Because Cox is known for her trans activism as well as her acting, the producers of *BLSS*'s choice to incorporate Cox's cameo in this particular sketch, which employs ratchet-style caricatures of black femininity, and in this specific role (as a rigid devotee of "bad bitch" standards) might easily come under fire for floating a trans exclusionary radical feminist (TERF) thesis about trans women as the ultimate upholders of gender norms. That said, such a misreading would only gloss the outlines of *BLSS*'s sketchwork and importantly miss that since Kiana is nowhere enunciated as trans, the character likely is cis. Contrast, for instance, this "Bad Bitch Support Group" sketch with *BGSS*'s *Honeymooners* parody, which in the process of deftly queering 1950s domesticity, presents a cis black male company member (Dion Flynn) cross-dressed in a white gown as a sight gag-pun on "purchasing a black-and-white TV." Meanwhile, the voices of trans feminine comics do not contribute to *BGSS*'s joke-writing or telling. *BLSS* refuses to make trans femininity the butt of the joke—rather, a trans actress participates as an invited collaborator in a black feminist sketch poking fun at the hegemonic reinforcement of gender and beauty standards. The comedy also functions without flatly disavowing, in the process, the prowess of the "ratchet" or the "bad bitch."

Important for understanding BLSS's work and play with the vexed figure of the "bitch"—bad or basic—is its celebration and exploration of blackness as polysemic, its refusal of a logic of "respectability," and its use of a subjunctive stance and near-future setting for many of its scenes to reflect on black women's agency and self-determination even in the face of worst-case scenarios. *BLSS*'s sketch recognizes the "bad bitch" at once as an enviable and vaunted category and as demeaned as "ratchet" by a popular culture that attempts to assimilate her power and incorporate her image.[14] For Kristen Warner, as "a modality characterized by how it reflexively exceeds normative bounds of acceptability,"[15] ratchetness is "performative in nature. It largely functions as something done by the individual, an action that always demonstrates a measure of reflexivity—an awareness that one actively puts on this hyperexcessive performance. Perhaps most important, ratchetness occupies a space within black identity politics."[16] Within the support group, some of the members clearly perceive the label as an "honor" or associate feeling the "baddest" (in a good way) with being "worshiped"; others experience the maintenance of the bad bitch persona as related, in a pressured way, to feminized labor, and influenced by the fashion, beauty, and pharmaceutical industries.

Cox's perfectly exasperated, better-than-thou delivery of the line "Breathe when you die, henny, okay!" was meme-ified, celebrated, and circulated on social media—the scene and its meme encapsulating expressive ratchetness as pushing back against respectability politics. If Bassett's character represents the "baddest bitch" as the episode title proclaims, Cox's character maintains the "ratchet bitch," leaning into this stereotype which paints black women as too brash, too loud, too much, as outside of "polite society" (code for outside of white cultural norms). *BLSS*'s and Cox's semiotic strategy of "leaning in" resembles the approach Racquel J. Gates describes in her book *Double Negative: The Black Image and Popular Culture,* when she considers "the possibility of using the trope of negativity in ways that demonstrate self-awareness, agency, and even subversion."[17] What's radical about the sketchwork is that it traces not (or not only) the pratfalls of misogyny bound up in these constructions, but the antiblackness of only interpreting "bad bitches" through a single-framework form of feminism. Furthermore, in choosing Cox as a collaborator, BLSS expresses its understanding of intersectional feminism as trans-inclusive.

Both *Big Gay Sketch Show* and *Black Lady Sketch Show* end up using the form of parody to formulate "What If?" questions about LGBTQ and BIPOC representations in television, posing relationships between their own projects and the cultural artifacts and categories they trouble and tweak. These socially progressive, post-network sketch shows emerged out of two very different political, social, and technological eras, if only a decade or so apart. Their approaches differ most in the degree of either presentism expressed in looking back, as *BGSS* predicts "progress ahead" through its revisionary queer television histories, or cynicism about a projected future in which today's problems only get magnified or exacerbated, as *BLSS* scours the defunct 'now' in the midst of the #MeToo and Black Lives

Matter movements' struggles for justice, and imagines our next fresh hell with aliens, end days, and drug shills, drawing on absurd humor as a form of resilience and recalibration. In their intricate sketchworks, both comedy shows question respectability politics and heteronormative structures, resist grasping for the alibi of the "apolitical" to excuse complicated representations, and try to make us laugh in a way that extends some grace.

Notes

1 Marx, Nick. 2019. *Sketch Comedy*. Bloomington: Indiana University Press, 4–5.
2 Martin, Garrett. 2019. "SNL's Blatant Bothsidesism Makes Its Political Comedy Worse Than Ever." *Paste*, December 16, 2019. www.pastemagazine.com/comedy/saturday-night-live/snl-politics-bothsidesism
3 Marx, 68.
4 Marx, 79.
5 Gray, Jonathan, Jeffrey P. Jones, and Ethan Thompson. 2009. *Satire TV: Politics and Comedy in the Post Network Era*. New York: NYU Press, 15.
6 Gray et al., 18.
7 Berlant, Lauren and Sianne Ngai. 2017. "Comedy Has Issues." *Critical Inquiry* 43 (Winter): 235.
8 Hennefeld, Maggie, Annie Berke, and Michael Rennet. 2019. Introduction to "What's So Funny about Comedy and Humor Studies." *Cinema Journal* 58, no. 3 (Spring): 137–142.
9 Salamon, Julie. 2005. "Logo, a New Gay Channel, Looks 'Beyond Sexuality.'" *New York Times*, June 28, 2005, E1.
10 Bailey, Marlon. 2013. *Butch Queens Up in Pumps: Gender, Performance, and Ballroom Culture in Detroit*. Ann Arbor: University of Michigan Press, 5.
11 Bailey, 18.
12 See Butler, Judith. 1993. "Critically Queer." *GLQ* 1, 17–32.
13 Phillips, Carmen. 2019. "'A Black Lady Sketch Show' is Queer, Brilliant, and Ridiculously Funny." *Autostraddle,* August 14, 2019. www.autostraddle.com/a-black-lady-sketch-show-is-queer-brilliant-and-ridiculously-funny
14 Warner, Kristen J. 2015. "They Gon' Think You Loud Regardless: Ratchetness, Reality Television, and Black Womanhood." *Camera Obscura* 88, vol. 30, no. 1: 129–153.
15 Warner, 140.
16 Ibid, 130.
17 Gates, Racquel J. 2018. *Double Negative: The Black Image and Popular Culture*. Durham: Duke University Press, 11.

6

REALIZING UNREALIZABLE JOY

Forming Queer Utopia in *The Fathers Project*

Hunter Hargraves

Imagine a world without AIDS. For many queer audiences, the act of imagining a world without AIDS or HIV—two terms I use rather interchangeably throughout this chapter—is an act heard only in trite marketing campaigns to raise awareness about an NGO or initiative, an anticipatory challenge designed to incite present-day action. But the call to imagine a world without AIDS also summons the radical question of an alternate history. *What if the virus never happened in the first place?* Asking this question risks offending those dead at the hands of the epidemic, as well as those that formed communities of care and activism, drawing from their impassioned grief and rage to demand rights for sexual minorities. Within the many texts that have chronicled questions of gay male legacy, after the worst of the epidemic, AIDS appears to overdetermine representational scope and scale; literalized, for example, in Matthew Lopez's 2018 play *The Inheritance*, in which the ghosts of the epidemic, as one character explains, form "a necessary haunting."[1] Like its generational antecedent *Angels in America*, any movement toward a queer future is riddled with ghosts, angels, and spirits, fantastical tropes that formally allow for queer characters to confront and reflect on the past in the hopes of a better future—perhaps in order to imagine a future without AIDS. This framing enables an intimate spectatorship that is reverent yet distant, or what Christopher Castiglia and Christopher Reed call a process of "de-generational unremembering," a strategy by which popular memory is acknowledged and exploited in the service of a teleological narrative of progress and assimilation.[2]

This question—*what if the virus never happened in the first place?*—explodes the question of historical legacy and popular memory in radically speculative terms. *The Fathers Project* (2018–2020), a web series conceived by artist and filmmaker Leo Herrera, takes such a provocation as its concept by avoiding visual and narrative tropes of popular queer media such as ballroom scenes or coming out. In five episodes, Herrera envisions a history in which AIDS does not claim the life of

DOI: 10.4324/9781003109044-9

any queer subject: progressive queer communes pop up all over rural America and queerness—amorphously defined yet aesthetically associated with Radical Faerie and leather/BDSM subcultures—has been declared a religion by the Supreme Court, allowing queers to amass as much political power as evangelical Christians. As a web series that traverses generic boundaries of documentary and pornography (and that required multiple distribution platforms for the series' sexually explicit fourth episode), *Fathers* invites unremembering in reverse, using the signifiers of the past in the service of a fantasy that is as temporally confusing as it is aesthetically rich. My goal in this chapter is to use the web series as a way to think about the mediation of queer utopia, the AIDS epidemic, and radical sexuality, all themes that television has either historically ignored or sensationalized in the service of an assimilatory politics. As television encompasses new modes of distribution that in turn solicit new stories from underrepresented groups, it must contend with the often-uncomfortable political formations that arise from more radical and provocative expressions of queer experience. *Fathers* approximates these gestures of queer utopia through its explicit sexual politics, but these are constrained by its televisual and documentarian engagements, which scramble the already unstable theoretical and affective milieus necessary to imagine a world without AIDS. Yet this instrumentally shapes the capacity for stories of queer utopia to be told *in the present*: that is to say, suspended between the ghosts of the pasts and the desires for a future while reinforcing the importance of fantasy as a constitutive fulcrum for making sense of collective queer history.

Separating *Fathers*

While I will discuss *The Fathers Project*'s unique form and mode of distribution, a cursory summary may provide a useful orientation to understanding its provocations. *Fathers* consists of five episodes, each focused around a particular queer subcultural expression: queer separatism, nightlife, elder care, leather sex, and spirituality.[3] Weaving together footage of queer gatherings predominantly populated by cisgender men with some staged events, *Fathers* conjures a noble separatist utopia built on sexual liberation and religious freedom, granting life and future accomplishment to gay heroes who died of AIDS: in this timeline activist Vito Russo won the White House in 2020, artist Robert Mapplethorpe is the most-followed person on Instagram, and Roxana Hernandez runs a sanctuary in which queer migrants are reunited with their families. (In reality, Hernandez was an undocumented trans woman who died of AIDS complications in 2018 under Immigrations and Customs Enforcement custody while awaiting deportation.)

Fathers uses a fictional documentary setup to explore these historical hypotheses, but the series lacks the diegetic sound found in narrative dialogue, instead setting its lush visuals to ambient music (the beats of a nightclub, for example). This has the effect of privileging the neutral voice of the fictional documentary and situating the viewer as a witness to a live event, rather than the consumer of a media text. Yet it also has the effect of subsuming individual voice, since there is only one real narrative character in *Fathers*: the Stonewall Colonies, the group of queer separatist collectives that have sprung up across the United States in a surprising display of political and cultural power. While the web series reanimates victims of AIDS such as Russo and Mapplethorpe, these individuals are not given any interiority as characters and are reduced to their symbolic potentiality. The Colonies function as the kind of utopic community found in other queer speculative fictions, such as the Dump in Samuel Delany's *Through the Valley of the Nest of Spiders*, in which a semi-autonomous queer separatist community provides free health care for its members and housing for its elders; Herrera's alternate timeline implies that without AIDS, we might not have neoliberal capitalism and its attending cult of the individual, either.

Fathers' language of separative speculation relies on acts of re-signification, in which symbols of queer culture evolve without the historical impact of AIDS. The series charts the narrative history of the Colonies through a number of interconnected advances in technology and to public services. For example, in the second episode, "The Colonies at Night," we learn that prophylactic poppers were pumped into nightclubs during the late 1990s to curb the spread of common sexually transmitted infections, with Rush™ poppers being advertised to housewives on daytime television during that same decade. This is told to the audience through parodies of conventional TV forms such as the commercial, which becomes a stand-in for straight culture's consumer appropriation of queer objects. This strict demarcation between the mediated mass culture of heteronormativity and the performative culture of the queer underground represents a curious artistic choice for a text that claims to be, on one level, television. If web series articulate a desire to be free from the corporate strictures of legacy television, *Fathers* projects a fantasy of anti-capitalist queerness that attempts to distance itself affectively from television itself. Indeed, its formal negotiation of the televisual becomes key to understanding the contradictions about AIDS and queer utopia present within its rich fantasies.

Queer Fantasies of Television Past

Queerness, it might be said, relies on affective structures of fantasy in order to exist: to be divorced fully from normative ideologies and identity formations requires reimagining relations of kinship, of habit, and of sexual behavior, even and especially before one assumes a legibly queer identity. Given the traumas that have historically structured daily queer life—the closet, excommunication from biological family, AIDS, a historical lack of rights, and literal and figural criminalization throughout many ideological state apparatuses—fantasy represents an extraordinarily important tool of survival for queer populations as they attempt to construct counterpublics and find joy in worlds often hostile to them. As Lauren Berlant and Michael Warner persuasively argued in "Sex in Public," the art of queer world-making "is dispersed through incommensurate registers, by definition *unrealizable* as community or identity," and it is through these "unrealizations" that the transformative work of queer resilience emerges.[4] This is especially evident in media representations of queer experience on television, which frequently draws from the dialectic of queer fantasy and trauma in order to represent, however imperfectly, these incommensurate registers. Television's deep investment in fantasy as one of its primary modes of address structure these representations; after all, the medium was originally used to sell household products to housewives through the fantasy of ameliorated domestic labor. A foundation of fantasy is even said to be a primary motivation for viewing television; most viewers, we are told, watch to escape their own mundane realities, through either glancing as a distraction from the drudgery of housework or gazing immersively at elaborately constructed worlds of dragons, superheroes, or melodramatic love triangles.

Yet queerness has also historically been thought of as "unrealizable" outside of a narrow range of images deemed acceptable by the networks and corporate advertisers that have controlled televisual programming, and thus queer audiences have turned to a variety of interpretative strategies in order to forge identifications with the screen. Part of this involves the work of subtext, as in Quinlan Miller's innovative analysis of camp sitcoms, which examines how comedy writers fused witty wordplay with physical direction in order to imbue the formal techniques of comedy with subversive challenges to established gender norms.[5] Locating a multiply genderqueerness within classic sitcoms similarly dovetails with studies of 1960s sitcoms, which read the deployment of fantastic characters such as witches and talking cars as coded references to the turbulent social changes of the decade, cracks within the façade of stable white middle-class heteropatriarchy.[6] These incisive historical framings illuminate the ways in which camp aesthetics and the fantastic worked together to reveal television's obvious *gayness*, but these readings of queerness are not radical insofar as they are formally governed by the logic of the closet; given mid-century America's refusal to acknowledge homosexuals in empowering terms, their political effects might be best encapsulated through Eve Sedgwick's famous quip "kinda subversive, kinda hegemonic."[7]

Early television's intertwining of queer subtexts with fantastic narrative tropes created what Lynne Joyrich has identified as an epistemic double-bind: industrial prohibitions and cultural norms relegated sexuality on television in ambivalent terms, seemingly everywhere without being explicitly announced as such. In the "epistemology of the console," Joyrich writes, "some things are apparently better not really apprehended even as this ignorance is maintained and betrayed by an attitude of smug knowingness about things supposedly beyond our need to fully comprehend."[8] One prominent example this is the sitcom *Ellen* (ABC, 1994–1998), known within the annals of television history for the coming-out of its star, Ellen DeGeneres, in a 1997 two-part episode; though, as Joyrich points out, the series managed this revelation through a series of running gags and humorous mismatches across the entire season. Similarly, Anna McCarthy's own reading of *Ellen* uses the series' epistemological problems to advance a historiographical argument, particularly through an analysis of the last-season episode "Ellen: A Hollywood Tribute," which re-situated title character Ellen Morgan within the annals of television history in a parody of television's own documentary history programs such as *E! True*

Hollywood Story and A&E's *Biography*. The episode plays with older ideas of "queer television as an interruption" in projecting Ellen into key diegetic worlds of famous sitcoms such as *I Love Lucy* and *All in the Family* while also somewhat revising the history of Ellen's own sexual narrative, as the character/star downplays her coming-out on national television by claiming that "twenty years from now it's going to be one fat 'so what.'" In reading scenes like this, McCarthy advances the idea that fantasy (here read as intertextual parody) can be used to accent the formal limitations of the sitcom to represent queerness:

> The incoherence of *Ellen*'s double-voiced representational politics, relying on and disavowing identity analogies as the basis of future network policy, suggests that queer network television appears more readily through practices of reading the television past, like camp, or the familiar "between-the-lines" stance of the queer reader than through official moments, like the manufactured interruptions of media events. Does this mean that cable television, the nation's television attic, is some kind of homo heaven?[9]

Importantly, McCarthy locates the resistant potential of televised queerness, however double-voiced, in its ability to disrupt the medium's own intertextual commentaries on form and genre. Yet equally as important is that this occurs through a formal renegotiation with TV history itself, one mediated through the fantasy of alternate histories. In this sense, "Ellen: A Hollywood Tribute" not only re-situated its star as a crucial figure within television history, but it also accurately predicted the future trajectory of its star as a celebrity that eventually transcended identity politics, with DeGeneres becoming a successful mainstream daytime talk show host as a symbolic proxy for the increased assimilation of LGBT people into American culture, though she has also come under recent scrutiny for allegedly fostering a toxic workplace culture: kinda subversive, kinda hegemonic indeed.

Inconsistently Queer Forms, Inconsistently Queer Futures

Yet despite the fact that *Ellen*'s "so what" moment rings so accurately decades later, the basis of McCarthy's question is still worth revisiting: might less hegemonic forms of television offer richer opportunities for rewriting queer history, or at least an articulation of a less-ambivalently queer politics? To some extent, these arguments about television's regulation of sexual knowledges reproduce similar ones made about queer media images more broadly: *Ellen* leverages the formal techniques of cable celebrity documentaries to renarrate Ellen's own queerness as incidental, diagramming a system in which unusual form becomes the vehicle for expressing the contradictions of queer representation. This is a queerness gleaned from formal technique that "acquires all the transgressive fascination of homosexuality, while homosexuality is consigned to the status of a dry technical detail," in the words of D.A. Miller.[10] While Miller's thesis applies to a specific text (the use of the single-take in Alfred Hitchcock's 1948 film *Rope*) made under the Hays Code, it advanced the idea, widely taken for granted by many queer media scholars, of the potential for formally uncommon techniques to represent queerness, even when that queerness is explicitly endorsed by the events within the narrative and treated with more complexity than "a dry technical detail." *The Fathers Project* invites a reconsideration of queer form through its complex episodic structure and inconsistent modes of distribution, which it uses to acclimate its audience to its radical rewriting of history.

Fathers was released in five episodes, but then later recut as a single 45-minute edit divided into five "parts," each with a similar narrative structure. Testimonials from real-life survivors open each episode, making clear the historical devastation of the epidemic on gay social life—what *happened*—before pivoting to the speculative history—what *could have happened*. This is told through a similar framing device as "Ellen: A Hollywood Tribute," the fictional documentary. Yet unlike *Ellen*, the conceit here is neither parodic nor the framing device immediately encountered by viewers. In fact, the precise and soothing tones of a vaguely British female narrator enable the fictional documentary a certain degree of aesthetic legitimacy, making it easier to digest as history. Of course, the testimonials from survivors that open each episode already function as a documentary, and the slippage between these two registers, however pronounced, helps manage the viewers' ability to suspend their disbelief and entertain the notion of a world without AIDS.

Fathers' fictional documentary consistently refers to events from the 1980s to the 2020s, dating itself as from the future (perhaps in 2030 or 2040), which further increases this sense of objectivity through its condensation of historical events and use of visuals. Voiceover narration mediates between a variety of sources, in the process emphasizing the importance of gathering and sharing space as a necessarily queer tactic of community-building. Completely absent from *Fathers*, however, are any technological devices such as the personal computer or the mobile smartphone, which allows the documentary to move between different historical registers freely and to reappropriate footage shot from real-life events such as Folsom Street Fair in San Francisco or Mardi Gras in New Orleans as part of the alternate historical record. Each episode then closes with titles announcing real-life historical facts about the disease and its victims. *Fathers* bookends its fictional history with montages alluding to real-life historical events and people partly as a sign of respect for both those who have died from AIDS and those who lived through the worst of the epidemic, facilitating entry for the latter category into the narrative's radical premise on empathetic terms. Yet in so doing it also habituates the viewer into a discordant time loop that reinstates the problems of the present into its speculative future, which has the effect of making education about the epidemic a form of political action in and of itself (an endorsement of ACT-UP's important reminder that silence equals death) that could one day lead to other, more imaginative political futures.

Fathers' history of distribution echoes this queerly inconsistent temporality, illuminating the struggles of queer storytelling in a digitized television landscape. Herrera released the first three episodes on platforms such as Vimeo and YouTube, focusing on an episodic distribution model like many other web series creators in order to generate buzz for the project and thus secure funding for future episodes. Aymar Christian has written extensively about the open TV market, referring to the ways in which "television has been an object of both desire and abjection for those seeking to reinvent it online."[11] This is especially true of *Fathers*' fourth episode, "Creep City," which reanimates Robert Mapplethorpe (who died in 1989) as a powerfully influential artist. In speculating as to Mapplethorpe's future oeuvre, *Fathers* finds the celebrated photographer documenting the feats of "sexual gladiators" in underground arenas like abandoned military bases. Key to this sequence are the gladiators, who are shown in an exquisitely filmed orgy of anal fisting. This sequence prevented Herrera from using open-distribution platforms for the episode's release, as it would obviously violate those platforms' terms of service agreements that prohibit pornographic images. Instead, Herrera partnered with fetish pornography website Kink.com to host "Creep City," marketing the episode's release as part of the service's annual Pride display as a commentary on the increased censorship of artistic nudity on social media. This censorship extends to the reassembled version of *Fathers* released in 2020; viewers watching on a smart television, for example, can find a censored version of the recut series with the sex scene removed on YouTube.

The multiple versions of the text required to accommodate these platforms' terms of service agreements challenge an idealistic faith in media convergence to increase the overall accessibility of a text, although these complications of distribution may have revealed new audiences and thus potential revenue for future episodes. "Television" here is reified through industrial functions of censorship, functions that Silicon Valley has often parroted from Hollywood even as they brand themselves as committed to ideals of open-access and user privacy. These reiterations of standards and practices also then indirectly attempt to regulate generic framings of the web series as it crosses the boundary into the pornographic. *Fathers* links together speculative fiction, documentary, and pornography, though the way in which it bridges all of these genres destabilizes viewers' investment in affect. Frequently found within both web series and so-called prestige television, generic hybridity is a synonym for creativity and formal innovation within the competitive landscape of peak TV. This is in part because, as Kim Akass and Janet McCabe argue, "the generic hybrid functions to exploit repetition and regulate difference in the same product around audience pleasures and industrial expediency."[12] *Fathers*, however, must also wrestle with the generic affects of AIDS, such as the anxiety provoked by the diseased body and the grief that follows death. These affects somewhat contain the impulse of pornography to incite erotic arousal within its viewer automatically; despite the erotically charged cinematography, it is hard to jerk off in a club full of ghosts. This inevitably may disrupt the repetitive affective flows of *Fathers*' episodic structure, yet the web series' embrace of unconventional generic hybridizations also reaffirms the experience of seroconversion, insofar as the HIV-positive person's body rearranges the boundaries of the body through the changed function of the individual's immune system.[13] While I am hesitant to ascribe to *Fathers* the formal structure of a retrovirus—*qua* D.A. Miller, an exemplary epistemological gimmick—the web series evokes a similar array of discursive instabilities surrounding the audience's ability to understand itself within larger histories of AIDS cinema or pornography. These instabilities may point to the impossibility of speculative fiction to erase AIDS entirely from the historical record, but this merely enhances the authenticity with which *Fathers* can resignify history, functioning as what Adam Zmith calls a "love letter to our queer elders."[14]

Fisting Utopia

Fathers imagines queer political formations unencumbered by homonormative desires for marriage and recognition by state capitalism, in part because of the political mobilization of a robust leather and BDSM community. One of the consequences of the AIDS epidemic, the web series claims, are prohibitions on sexual expression, and hence sexual politics comes to define politics at large within the Stonewall Colonies. This fantastic figuration of the political has much in common with José Muñoz's foundational writings on queer utopia, a vein of queer theory that has recuperated affects of joy in opposition to the anti-social turn within the field.[15] In *Cruising Utopia*, Muñoz outlines a performative repertoire of collective moments that express futurity in the present. Drawing from the logic of cruising—the practices by which gay men have historically sought sex with each other—Muñoz expands the concept to document the ephemeral ways in which queers comprehend the "anticipatory illumination of the utopian": how social milieus of the present can function as a vibrant repository of possibility that satisfy short-term desires while investing in larger, more long-term networks of care and community.[16] *Fathers*' Stonewall Colonies replicates much of this queer promise through its explicit exhibition of sexual politics, giving life to Muñoz's notion of the "ghosts of public sex" that haunt most queer spaces, in part because of AIDS. This ghosting becomes literalized through *Fathers*' reanimation of otherwise departed artists and activists, but also through how it situates live social performance—dancing and nightlife, sex parties, bonfires, and other rituals—as the primary sites of queer self-expression, forms of nourishment for a queer ethos that is as political as it is erotic (*CU*, pp. 46–48).

This is most easily apparent in the example of the fisting orgy documented by Mapplethorpe in "Creep City," which lasts for not quite ninety seconds. The action takes place at the Mineshaft, a series of rotating underground venues modeled after the legendary Manhattan leather bar, of which in real-life Mapplethorpe was reportedly and unofficially the "official" photographer. The voiceover narration sutures the spectator into the position of privileged witness: "The only camera allowed is Robert Mapplethorpe's, but we have been granted unprecedented access," she says, although the audience remains unaware as to who "she" is throughout *Fathers*, abstracting the voice of the documentary onto the gaze of Mapplethorpe's own camera, a camera that is actually Herrera's, the primary witness to this semipublic sex act. Indeed, unable to find the words to describe the sexual activities in front of the camera, the narrator's voice (and thus the documentary's omniscient point of view) drops from the orgy scene, which is set instead to the sensual rap track "Demi Monde" by the queer Chicago collective Banjee Report. At this point, the fictional documentary reads more as an artistic pornographic film, in line with visual signifiers often attributed to Mapplethorpe (a single overhead light illuminates the scene in the gladiator pit, which is presented in black and white). Flashbulbs, presumably from Mapplethorpe's camera, document the ritual of extreme fisting from a variety of angles, and the composition of these shots emphasize the sublime call-and-response between the gladiators, who move with effortless intuition.

Obvious comparisons can be made here to a scene in William Friedkin's *Cruising* (1980)—a film initially protested by gay activists only to be reclaimed by gay audiences—in which the undercover detective Steve (Al Pacino) witnesses a man fisting another man in the basement, only to be distracted by an emerging fist-fight between two other patrons.[17] Fisting in both *Cruising* and *Fathers* is figured by the text as authentic, through filming in real-life locations and utilizing non-professional actors (in *Fathers*, many pornographic actors can be spotted among the group, though they were not compensated by Herrera for appearing in the film; the fisting in *Fathers* is also more stylized and explicit). But whereas Steve, a straight man playing gay, mediates between these two violent fists, Mapplethorpe becomes the triangulator between the documentary's presumed audience and the gladiators, displacing the scene's mystique and rendering it within more familiar cinematographic lexicons of montage. In *Cruising*, Steve was merely a witness; in *Fathers*, Mapplethorpe is a participant of sorts, serving not only to archive as the Mineshaft's "official" photographer but also to mediate these intense acts of anal penetration. The flashes of his camera set against these acts is evocative of what Deleuze identified as visibilities: "not forms of objects, nor even forms that would show up under light, but rather forms of luminosity which are created by the light itself and allow a thing or object to exist only as a flash, sparkle or shimmer."[18]

But at this point, what is the spectator watching—is it a documentary from the future, or stylized hardcore pornography? To be sure, it is both of these, but there is Herrera's own positionality behind the camera to account for as well, which scaffolds the framing device of Mapplethorpe's camera. Herrera used footage shot at an unnamed underground leather nightlife event for this sequence and could only gain access to it through a personal relationship with the venue and the promoters. This belies the rhetorics of trust implicit in documentary filmmaking—and implicit in fisting, too—but also exceeds these boundaries: unlike in *Cruising*, Herrera did not direct the orgy, and in fact had to think very strategically in selecting a small camera setup as not to be too intrusive on the scene. The sequence thus serves as an archive of a present including AIDS just as much as a future without AIDS, with the totalizing vision of documentary consistently destabilized through and against itself, much like in the HIV-positive body's own misrecognition of its compromised immune system. And upon the scene's conclusion, repetition is exploited once more, as the robotic British voice snaps back on to remind the audience that "these freedoms did not come without a price," as news footage of a burning building (presumably one of the Mineshaft locations) and a homophobic mob appears. The fluctuating documentarian impulses in the sequence and throughout *Fathers* more broadly challenge Muñoz's insistence on queer utopia's ephemerality and fragmentation; their desire to be archived and mediated through a shifting relationship to documentary form complicates Muñoz's already destabilized nature of utopian longing, in which the fragments of such cannot be glimpsed as a coherent whole (*CU*, p. 51).

Lighting the Ghosts of a Future Utopia

The Fathers Project uses its sexual politics to conjure a future without AIDS in a present with AIDS, engaging in historical speculation that becomes narratively overdetermined by its ultimate fragmentation. This occurs through its negotiation with the formal conventions of television and documentary film, which simultaneously create and undo not just a future of the present but also one that enforces a certain historical distance to the actual past. In this sense, it also mediates a post-AIDS relationship as well; perhaps AIDS can be so easily erased from the realm of queer possibility because in certain contexts it already has been, made manageable by a viciously effective array of antiretroviral medication that now can even prevent HIV-negative men from becoming infected. But pharmaceutical innovation does not preclude the possibility of imagining a world sans the virus. In an eerily parallel register, *Fathers* ends with the same Oscar Wilde quotation with which Muñoz opens *Cruising Utopia*: "A map of the world that does not include utopia is not worth glancing at…" This quotation has significant cultural capital as a respective bookend for these two approaches to queer utopia. Muñoz notes that "Wilde's sentence, when properly broken down and appreciated for its stylized precision, makes explicit the connection between queerness, utopia, and world-making," drawing a line between the cartographical metaphors invoked by Wilde and the economy of looking central to gay male cruising practices (*CU*, p. 40).

This also animates the quotation's appearance at the end of *Fathers*. In the final episode, the Wilde quotation appears as the camera pans around a burning bonfire, structured and contained by a pyramid of stacked wood. In explaining the ways in which radical queerness became discursively and legally categorized as a religion, the faux-documentary educates its audience to the Stonewall Colonies' repertoire of ritual and ceremony: during the evening of the holy day of December 1, "flaming triangle sculptures light the night sky, meant to illuminate the path for spirits to find their way home." This is set to cuts between footage of various queer altars—featuring the thick prayer candles common in celebrations of Día de los Muertos—and footage of a lone Sister of Perpetual Indulgence kissing a rock in the San Francisco AIDS Memorial Grove. The light emitted from the burning pyramids symbolizes the network of queer colonies while creating the visual effect of a population-density map of a queer utopia that also serves as a "path for spirits to find their way home," thus yoking together the project of queer world-making with queer spirituality. This is the spiritually dissociative power of a radical queerness without AIDS: its ability to allow its subject the privilege to detach from oneself not out of self-shattering desire, but as interpellated into a structure of feeling that goes beyond localized expressions of sexual community or political action. It is a spiritual moment grounded, in the words of Alexis Pauline Gumbs, in learning "how to see the invisible...the unborn, the unremembered, the discounted, ourselves," to see oneself in those thick descriptions and relations.[19] Yet even this signaling to the ancestors incorporates the hauntological temporality of AIDS: the pyres burn on December 1, or what has been "celebrated" as World AIDS Day in the real calendar since 1988. The web series thus shines a clear light on the ghosts of all queers—those who have passed of AIDS and those who have not—while also using fire as a cleansing tool through which to assert affects of a spiritually queer separatism. Through this complex circuit of ghosting and lighting, *Fathers* places a remarkable faith in the spectator's ability to pay reverence to the past while creating glimpses of an unrealizably defiant future. Herrera had only heard, but had not read, *Cruising Utopia* while making the web series, and perhaps in his world without AIDS, the ghost of Muñoz, who passed heartbreakingly and unexpectedly in 2013 (though not of the virus), would be hovering near a bonfire, an intense luminosity that helps others queerly shimmer.

Notes

1 Matthew Lopez, *The Inheritance* (New York: Faber & Faber, 2018), 287.
2 Writing in 2012, Castiglia and Reed claim as a consequence of this unremembering "the insistent invisibility of AIDS or sexual liberation in popular media," an effect that this chapter complicates somewhat. Christopher Castiglia and Christopher Reed, *If Memory Serves: Gay Men, AIDS, and the Promise of the Queer Past* (Minneapolis: University of Minnesota Press, 2012), 9.
3 The series can be viewed at www.iftheylived.org/
4 Lauren Berlant and Michael Warner, "Sex in Public," *Critical Inquiry* 24.2 (1998): 558.
5 Quinlan Miller, *Camp TV: Trans Gender Queer Sitcom History* (Durham: Duke University Press, 2019).
6 The most notable of these engagements with 1960s sitcoms include Lynn Spigel, "From Domestic Space to Outer Space: the 1960s Fantastic Family Sitcom," in *Close Encounters: Film, Feminism, and Science Fiction*, ed. Constance Penley (Minneapolis: University of Minnesota Press, 1991), pp. 205–235, and Patricia White, *Uninvited: Classical Hollywood Cinema and Lesbian Respectability* (Bloomington: Indiana University Press, 2000), pp. 192–193.
7 Eve Sedgwick, "Queer Performativity: Henry James's *The Art of the Novel*," *GLQ* 1.1 (1993): 15.
8 Lynne Joyrich, "Epistemology of the Console," *Critical Inquiry* 27 (Spring 2001): 449.
9 Anna McCarthy, "*Ellen*: Making Queer Television History," *GLQ* 7.4 (2001): 615.
10 D.A. Miller, "Anal Rope," *Representations* 32 (1990): 117.
11 Aymar Jean Christian, *Open TV: Innovation Beyond Hollywood and the Rise of Web Television* (New York: NYU Press, 2018), 57.
12 Kim Akass and Janet McCabe, "Analyzing Fictional Television Genres," in *Media Studies: Key Issues and Debates*, ed. Eoin Devereux (London: Sage, 2007), 291.

13 On this rearranging of the HIV-positive body's boundaries, see Emily Martin, *Flexible Bodies: The Role of Immunity in American Culture from the Days of Polio to the Age of AIDS* (Boston: Beacon Press, 1994).

14 Adam Zmith, *Deep Sniff: A History of Poppers and Queer Futures* (London: Repeater, 2021), 166. For Zmith, however, the web series' focus on history overprivileges cisgender gay men and prevents it from achieving a fully inclusive utopia.

15 One interesting commonality throughout queer theory's generational iterations, found in work both supportive and skeptical of its anti-relational thesis, might be an unstated belief in the power and prevalence of the fantastic as a way to represent, even if antithetically, notions of loss, absence, and historical memory that often appear to structure queer identity and affect.

16 José Esteban Muñoz, *Cruising Utopia: The Then and There of Queer Futurity* (New York: NYU Press, 2009), 18. Hereafter *CU*.

17 D.A. Miller has emphasized within this semiotic juxtaposition Steve's longing and curious gaze, indicative of "his identification with both 'victim' and 'attacker' [that] is buried alive in the self-ignorant relation of a fascination with the Other." See Miller, "*Cruising*," *Film Quarterly* 61.2 (2007): 73.

18 Gilles Deleuze, *Foucault* (Minneapolis: University of Minnesota Press, 1988), 52. More recently, Pooja Rangan has extracted from this concept the idea of audibilities, ways of listening that "call into being a mode of relation or resonance—a "shared world"—between these felt but often unspoken forms of speaking and listening." These have the effect of dislodging conventional ways of figuring "voice" within the documentary as a metaphorical or textual signifier. *Fathers* replicates this logic only insofar it replaces the voice of its omniscient narrator (stylized already with British accent and the cadence of technological voice assistants) with a high degree of visual and sonic stylization; setting the sexual activities to music thus deprives the spectator of listening to the gladiators' apparent pleasure, which can be located only through visual signifiers such as open mouths and physical contact between flesh. Of course, since *Fathers* is formally a fictional documentary, its verisimilitude easily accommodates such a slippage in stylization. See Rangan, "Audibilities: Voice and Listening in the Penumbra of Documentary: An Introduction," *Discourse* 39.3 (2017): 282.

19 Alexis Pauline Gumbs, *Dub: Finding Ceremony* (Durham: Duke University Press, 2020), 212.

7

MURDERING OUR QUEER PAST

Bridget Kies

In an idyllic Cotswolds village in the 1950s, the Anglicans and Catholics organize a joint picnic to celebrate the Anglican church's new bells. Given Britain's bloody history between these two Christian sects, this moment shows that after facing bigger enemies like the Nazis, internal squabbles can be put aside for the sake of gentility. With the war over, life in rural England is restored to a perpetual springtime harmony…until a dead body is discovered.

So begins "The Hammer of God," the first episode of BBC One's *Father Brown* (2013–). As the title character investigates the murder, he learns the victim, Norman, was the Anglican priest's brother and was being blackmailed for his relationship with another man. Since only one person—a man named Philip—attended Norman's funeral, Father Brown assumes Philip was the lover. At this point in the investigation, afficionados of murder mysteries may expect to learn that Norman ended the affair, prompting Philip to murder him in revenge. According to the logic of earlier murder mysteries, that is what homosexuals do, isn't it?[1] They can't be trusted.

Instead, in this twenty-first century story, Philip is at first reluctant to admit to the affair because he would face "arrest and chemical treatments."[2] When Father Brown pledges that he will not expose him, Philip confesses he was in love with Norman. This confession leads Father Brown to believe him to be innocent of the murder. Instead, Norman was murdered by his own brother, the Anglican priest, who had seen Norman and Philip together and was driven to kill out of belief that God would want them dead for their abominable actions. Father Brown lashes out at what he sees as a perversion of Christian doctrine: "God is not your scapegoat!"

"The Hammer of God" is based on a 1911 short story by G.K. Chesterton that did not include any homosexual subplot. Neither did its previous ITV television adaptation in 1974 or its radio adaptation for BBC Radio 4 in 1984. In the original story and previous adaptations, the murder was motivated by Norman's general sinning, rather than any specific "ungodly" sex action. Series creators and

DOI: 10.4324/9781003109044-10

writers Rachel Flowerday and Tahsin Guner explain that they took liberties with Chesterton's story because of the difficulties of translating written prose to a visual storytelling medium.[3] Nonetheless, it is clear that while this episode—like *Father Brown* more generally—is supposed to be "nostalgically reassuring fiction," it is also supposed to speak to contemporary values.[4]

This example demonstrates how contemporarily made but historically set murder mysteries tend to treat LGBTQ themes. On the whole the "good guys" are sympathetic, as in the case of Father Brown promising not to put Philip at risk of arrest. In reality the Catholic church considered homosexuality a mortal sin in the 1950s, and it would be 19 years until the first LGBTQ-supportive Catholic organizations were formed.[5] In many historically set murder mysteries, non-heterosexuality is portrayed as harmless, and the main characters protect, defend, and help acquit vulnerable LGBTQ people from unjust laws and social mores. By depicting cis heterosexual characters as empathetic to queer people's social and political struggles, these series project dominant social values of today onto the past. This is not to say that queer history can be reduced to past as bad and present as good, since throughout the twentieth and twenty-first centuries there have been activist organizations and campaigns for social change existing in tension with homophobic and transphobic movements. However, twenty-first century television's accounting of early twentieth century queer life often erases important realities in favor of flattened depictions of diversity, tolerance, and acceptance.

One strain of activism in the present is to seek more recognition for LGBTQ history, often by advocating for its inclusion in school curricula. California became the first U.S. state to mandate inclusion of LGBTQ history in all public schools in 2011, and by 2020, five other states had similar educational standards.[6] In 2021, Scotland became the first nation in the world to require inclusion of LGBTQ content in its public schools after polls indicated that nearly 70% of British people aged 16–24 supported such a measure.[7] These efforts to make LGBTQ history better known are concomitant with historically set murder mysteries that depict cozy tranquility in which queer people are embraced, thus ignoring the same history.

As the plot to any murder mystery is driven by whodunnit and why, tropes about villainous and immoral queer people persisted through much of film and television history, especially in the pre-Stonewall era. Today's historically set murder mysteries therefore not only rewrite queer history but also queer media history in their revisionist depictions of early twentieth-century life.

Murder Mysteries in the Pre-Stonewall Era

Murder mysteries with historical settings offer the thrill of investigation before digital technologies and modern forensics reshaped detective work. In series produced in Australia, Canada, and the United Kingdom, for broadcast around the world, investigators solve crimes using their ingenuity and understanding of human nature. The historical setting also allows for the exploration of social conventions now considered antiquated to the modern audience. While many of these conventions are viewed as charming and idyllic, some, such casual everyday racism and misogyny, are treated as more horrifying. Secondary characters may serve as mouthpieces for dominant social values at the time, but the detective or sleuth is usually driven by a transgression of social norms.

One of the social conventions often explored is the mistreatment and ostracism of queer people. Series like *Poirot* (1989–2013), *The Mrs. Bradley Mysteries* (1998–2000), *Marple* (2004–13), *Murdoch Mysteries* (2008–), *Miss Fisher's Murder Mysteries* (2012–15), *Father Brown*, and *Frankie Drake Mysteries* (2017–) depict queerness with some frequency and always with sympathy. The historical setting for these series, between the 1890s and 1960s, was characterized by a tension between growing LGBTQ subcultures and conservative social norms and laws that attempted to eradicate or at least limit the growth of these subcultures.[8]

In the twenty-first century, historically set drama series (or costume dramas) have experienced a renaissance. Numerous series have been created as transnational productions shared between the United States and the United Kingdom and broadcast in the United States on cable and premium cable channels where explicit violence and sex is permitted. Fictional accounts of famous ruling families (*The Tudors* [2007–10], *The Borgias* [2011–13], *The Crown* [2016–], *Versailles* [2015–18], *Medici* [2016–19]), as well as societies of fascination (*Knightfall* [2017–19], *Vikings* (2013–20), *The Last Kingdom* [2015–], *Downton Abbey* [2010–15], *Outlander* [2014–]) offer viewers the chance to see history through stylized characters and storylines.

These series wrangle verisimilitude with contemporary values. The historical setting allows viewers to "indulge a fantasy of experiencing the mores of the past and comparing them to their current circumstances."[9] In the name of historical accuracy, queer characters are shunned, beaten, and sometimes killed for their identities. As Thomas West argues, these series have developed "a specific set of rules of engagement" with queer history in which death or tragedy can be avoided through passing as cis and straight.[10] Thus, the experience of watching can give the viewer reassurance that we live in more progressive and more tolerant times. In other words, it gets better.

Whether this is a good or bad approach to historical fiction is complicated. Seeing queer characters suffer may help the audience understand the reality that for much of human history queer people have been oppressed, particularly when that history is often left out of formal education. At the same time, depictions of violence and death, even when framed as "historically accurate," perpetuate harmful media conventions. Studying contemporary trans representation, Cael Keegan finds that what is regarded as "good" is "authentic, progressive, and diverse" and makes trans people "visible, but in the right ways."[11] Keegan notes that increased "good" representation doesn't equate to improved real-life conditions, and increased exposure in media may even result in a decline in real-life conditions. As Keegan puts it, "of what value is cultural recognition, when it can so easily be weaponized against us?"[12]

The weaponization of cultural recognition has plagued murder mysteries characters in the past. Exposure often resulted in death or was the impetus for killing, and secret, unnamed queerness was often a safer alternative. My study uses historically set murder mysteries, rather than the broader category of costume dramas, because of the imperative of the genre. In murder mystery television series, there is always one murder in the first act, often in the teaser before the opening credits; a second murder occurs as the detective gets closer to the solution; and the episode's conclusion always definitively names the killer, who then confesses. This resolution reassures the audience that good has triumphed over evil, and the social order has been restored.

Among the most popular series are cozy mysteries. In literature, the label "cozy" came into popularity in the late 1980s because of these books' emphasis on domestic life and tranquility. The hard-boiled detective novels popular during the 1930s and 1940s—the books of Raymond Chandler and Dashiell Hammett—feature sex, violence, and grit in a morally dark world where crime and dishonesty prevail. In screen media, the hard-boiled detective novel lends itself to film noir.[13] In contrast, the cozy mystery has "nonthreatening content and nonviolent characters" in a world that is morally just.[14] The murder is an "irruption in an otherwise trouble-free world."[15] Cozy mysteries work well on episodic television, where the emphasis on domesticity means the same cast of characters can be recycled each week. Each episode resets to tranquility as the murderer is found and taken by the police.

Many cozy mystery novels hearken back to the "golden age of detective novels," usually dated to the 1920s and 1930s. Like cozies, the mysteries of the golden age often took place in sprawling country houses, among wealthy, genteel characters.[16] The murder disrupts the genteel façade, but finding the killer restores it.

Despite the cozy feel to these stories, it cannot be forgotten that gruesome murders occur in every episode. Though gore and bloodshed are minimally portrayed, the audience is supposed to be horrified at the idea of a human life being taken. In the golden age of detective fiction and pre-Stonewall film and television, murders were often motivated by rejection from a beloved, blackmail, or betrayal—all situations queer people might find themselves in because of their perceived immorality and weakness or the necessary secrecy of their queerness.

Queer People in Film and Television History

In the film *Rope* (1948), roommates Brandon and Phillip commit murder as a demonstration of their intellectual superiority. Although the Hays Code in effect at the time prohibited explicit homosexuality, Brandon and Phillip are queerly read. As Tyler Coates notes, the "simple suggestion of homosexuality was enough to create unease" for the audience, which he views as part of Alfred Hitchcock's talent "as a director and provocateur."[17] But that same unease is what makes Brandon and Phillip such callous murderers; their amorality manifests in their sex lives and their murderous impulses.

This is just one of many examples entangling queerness and villainy in film and media history. Television historians have noted that from the earliest days of television until the late 1960s or 1970s, explicitly LGBTQ characters were largely absent from fictional series. There has always been queer representation on television, which historians categorize in two ways: the character whose sexuality was never explicitly identified but was understood through coded language and gesture (as in films made during the Code era) and the explicitly identified but pathologized homosexual who was the subject of news reports, talk shows, and special investigations.[18] According to Stephen Tropiano, the earliest explicit discussions of homosexuality were on talk shows in the mid-1950s that "debated if and how the homosexual poses a threat to American society."[19] By the early 1970s, fictional primetime series featured LGBTQ-identified characters in situations posing moral dilemmas. A 1973 episode of *Marcus Welby, M.D.* (1969–76) involves a man who suffers from depression resulting from his belief he is homosexual. The title doctor believes the depression can be cured if the man overcomes his homosexual impulses to live a "normal" life.

With greater quantitative representation on television in recent decades came a broader range of representation, moving beyond the simple "queer villain" or "queer problem" mode. Yet even some recent television history falls into the trap of portraying queerness as a problem leading to other moral shortcomings. In a 2004 episode of *Law & Order: SVU* (1999–), a man kills his secret lover after finding out he has contracted HIV from him. The murderer, Andy, a career man with a wife and children, has been involved in a sex circle for men who sleep with men "on the down low." Queerness is framed as the problem, but not because Andy and the other men on the down low are inherently evil as a result of having gay sex. Instead, the problem is their unwillingness to name their homosexuality. (Bisexuality is never mentioned as possible identity.) The episode concludes with the idea that if Andy and the others had been open about their desires for other men, they could have avoided the spread of HIV and a murder. Ron Becker finds the episode to be an example of television in what he terms "post-closet TV," in which a gay man's need to stay in the closet is the problem, rather than the queerness itself.[20]

In the cases of *Rope* and *Law & Order: SVU*, (queer) men have committed murder, somehow related to their queerness. In the Code era, the shadow life of Brandon and Phillip is emblematic of the darker secrets they keep. In contemporary television, the dominant social value is that gay is okay. By maintaining queerness as a secret when it need not be, Andy has been forced to murder. Although attitudes about whether queerness should be a secret have radically changed, queer villains and queerness as villainy connect these temporally distant examples.

Two Kinds of Queerness in Murder Mysteries

Within historically set murder mysteries, queer villainy is far rarer than in the literature from which some series are adapted or the media made in the time period when these series are set. In general, there are two modes of queerness in historically set murder mysteries. Characters may have been queer coded in the original literature or source, but due to legal restrictions, the publisher's in-house standards, or the author's vision, these characters are never explicitly named as queer. In the twenty-first century television adaptations, queerness can be and often is named—or, at least, is coded and interpreted with greater conviction. The second mode is when queerness is added by contemporary writers and producers to stories that did not originally feature it. The addition of queerness seems to speak to a recognized need that twenty-first century television feature diverse racial, sexual, and gender identities more prominently.

When queerly interpreted characters are openly identified, the series acknowledges to the contemporary audience that LGBTQ identities are valid, have long existed, and deserve recognition. Since murder mysteries operate on secrets, this often means the queer characters aren't the killers. Viewer responses to this explicitness vary. Purists' love for the original source material often leads to negative reactions while many popular critical and fan responses praise the series for contributing to greater LGBTQ representation in the present moment.

One example are the lesbians Miss Hinchcliffe and Miss Murgatroyd in "A Murder Is Announced," a 2005 episode of the ITV series *Marple*. In the 1950 novel by Agatha Christie, Hinchcliffe wears pants, is gruff, and is protective of her more feminine housemate, Murgatroyd. Thus, the women may be read as queer through the stereotype of the butch and femme. In the 1985 BBC adaptation as well as the 2005 version, viewers and critics did not hesitate to label the women as a lesbian couple. Writer Carolyn Gage, for instance, praises the media depictions of Hinchcliffe and Murgatroyd for presenting a complex, realistic long-term relationship in which "each partner has gained a monopoly over the areas in which she possesses the greater strengths, ceding to her partner the territory to which she holds the lesser claim."[21] For others, the more explicit depiction, compared to the subtlety of Christie's novel in which the characters might be understood as either lesbians or mere companions, is an example of a progressive agenda set by contemporary television producers and writers. In a blog post, self-identified Catholic writer "Mrs. Darwin" describes the characters as a "dowdy old pair of friends, with nary a whiff of sexuality about them," though her individual descriptions draw heavily on butch and femme stereotypes.[22] An anonymous commenter agrees that "these women were not sexually involved, simply because they denied and despised sex."[23] Perhaps most amusingly, one commenter claims that as originally written in the novel, Hinchcliffe and Murgatroyd "are lesbians, but that Agatha Christie was unaware of that!"[24] The commenter argues that Christie based the characters on two women she knew in real life, and thus the women were likely secretly a couple, but Christie perhaps did not even know lesbianism existed. This claim provoked mocking reactions on social media. @felicitydisco calls Murgatroyd and Hinchcliffe "the least subtle couple of all time."[25] @NicolaMDavidson tweeted that she would "laugh forever over the notion of accidentally writing lesbians."[26]

Arguments over whether Hinchcliffe and Murgatroyd are "accidental lesbians," a cogently written pair of long-term lovers, or only lesbians in the media adaptations call attention to the difficulties with historical settings and adaptations. If the women could not openly identify as lesbians in a small English village in 1950, can they in a 2005 story set in 1950? But despite the dominant social sanctions against queerness in the post-war United Kingdom, there were open lesbians. Though more judgmental than tolerant, there were even news stories about their relationships.[27] Some of the comments assume lesbianism was not described in literature in the 1950s, though of course lesbian pulp novels flourished at the time. In general, the debate about Hinchcliffe and Murgatroyd seems to hinge upon popular conception that openly LGBTQ-identified people could not exist prior to the late 1960s.

It is true that the late 1960s served as one turning point in LGBTQ rights in the United States, United Kingdom, and Canada. In 1967, the Sexual Offences Act decriminalized sex between men over the age of 21 in England. (Sex between women was never formally criminalized.) Advocates felt that prosecuting consenting adults over their private sex lives was not the business of the state and that homosexuals should be "pitied, not prosecuted."[28] The law's passing did not necessarily reflect a sea change in dominant social attitudes toward homosexuality, which British human rights advocate Peter Tatchell says "alternated between vicious homophobia on one side and patronising, apologetic tolerance on the other."[29] The penalty for gross indecency (sex acts not including penetrative anal sex) was actually increased in an attempt to ensure that men would carry out their sexual relationships in the privacy of their homes. While the 1967 act left much to be desired, it was an important step in changing the daily lives and safety of gay male couples, who could now openly acknowledge their relationships. It inspired an equivalent reform to Canada's criminal code, in which homosexuality was removed as a felony in 1968–69. In the United States in 1969, several days of protests after a raid on the Stonewall Inn, a bar frequented by the queer community on Christopher Street in New York, became known as the Stonewall riots or Stonewall uprising. The event is remembered in popular history as a turning point in the modern gay rights movement in the United States as activist groups coalesced around the idea of demanding gay liberation, rather than seeking tolerance.

Because of these developments in the late 1960s, common misunderstandings that Stonewall was the first LGBTQ protest or that all people lived in secrecy and fear prior to this time have arisen. While many did—and I do not want to negate those experiences—historians have found plenty of evidence of queer communities and queer life in the pre-Stonewall era. In New York, queer people gathered in clubs, dining halls, and balls that existed outside mainstream society and always faced the risk of exposure and closure under vice laws.[30] Between World War II and the late 1960s, the United States was rife with gay and lesbian activism, including organizations like the Mattachine Society that formalized demands for social acceptance for LGBTQ people.[31] Likewise, despite the pathologizing of what we today term being transgender from the late nineteenth to mid-twentieth centuries, trans movements formed, and some trans people lived visible lives.[32] Prior to the 1970s, queer-associated activities such as cross-dressing, engaging in sodomy, even dancing with a same-sex partner were illegal in many places, but while there was discrimination, there was also a thriving underground—and sometimes aboveground—life. Thus, the notion that characters in pre-Stonewall narratives must be secretive or shameful neglects the complexity of history.

In the second mode, queer characters and storylines that are not present in the original literary source are added. This is the case with the "Hammer of God" episode of *Father Brown*. By making Norman's sexuality the reason his brother, the Anglican priest, took his life, and by allowing Father Brown to lash out at the other priest, the series immediately establishes that its main character understands and reflects contemporary social values.

In a few of the episodes I studied, the addition of LGBTQ characters and subplots to existing source material was done purely for shock and scandal, in a return to villainous queer tropes. In *Marple* "A Body in the Library" (2005), two women have committed murder, so they can be together. In the original novel, this was not the solution to the murder, and the characters were not romantically involved. Their secrecy and murderous impulses are reminiscent of media made in the pre-Stonewall era.

The 2006 *Poirot* episode "Cards on the Table" is based on Christie's 1936 novel with the same title. In the television adaptation, J.C. Bernthal notes that "the only improprieties are sexual, and the only kind of sexual impropriety is homosexual."[33] The murderer, Dr. Roberts, has killed twice to the protect the secret of his love affair with another man. Once was his lover's wife, and the second was a man who blackmailed him with photographs of the affair. When another man tells Poirot he was also in a male–male love affair, Poirot tells him his behavior is "up to him" but cautions him not to be photographed. Poirot's ambivalence is in line with the tolerance exhibited by Father Brown, Miss Marple, and the other twenty-first century sleuths studied here. Homosexuality itself is not the problem; its possible exposure, however, is. This homosexual subplot is a departure from Christie's novel, leaving some viewers frustrated with the series' agenda of "political correctness." Writer Peter Majda dismisses the idea: "To say these depictions of homosexuals are archaic would be an understatement."[34] While he likewise finds the introduction of queer content misguided, it is not because it is politically correct but rather homophobic. These conflicting responses echo reactions to Hinchcliffe and Murgatroyd from "A Murder Is Announced": the feeling that the text is stuck between twenty-first century treatment of LGBTQ themes and some kind of historical accuracy.

The Quasi-Educational Function of the Historical Setting

"Cards on the Table" might have been intended as a way to remind viewers about the difficulties queer people experienced in a less tolerant age. This leads to my final observation about historically set murder mysteries: the quasi-educational function of the time period. One of the tenets of gender and sexuality studies is that these concepts are not transhistorical, and a historically set narrative can offer a way to understand how LGBTQ identities were understood and labeled in other periods.

When a murder victim's body is examined in a 2008 episode of *Murdoch Mysteries*, the coroner, Julia, discovers he was recently the receiving partner in anal sex. Because there are no cuts or tears, she assumes the act was consensual. This leads the detective, Murdoch, to infiltrate an underground society to find his lover, the presumed murderer. Murdoch must "pass" (an inversion of the usual meaning), so he is given a mauve velvet suit and a purple pansy for his lapel, which the police chief, Brackenreid, explains is "the symbol of fairies the world over." At this point, the episode has shown underground societies existed in 1895, the symbols that helped queer men identify each other, and, sadly, a litany of period-specific slurs. Murdoch initially refers to the victim as a "sodomite," but the better educated Julia tells him the current term is "homosexual."[35] Brackenreid, who has led raids on the society before, calls its members mandrakes, shirt-lifters, mollies, benders, left-footers, and worse.

The solution to the murder is only tangentially related to the victim's sexuality and has nothing to do with his lover. The episode serves as a journey to enlightenment for Murdoch, a staunch Catholic who regrets that the police have driven the lover to suicide. Brackenreid and Julia voice opposing viewpoints that help Murdoch understand his values. While he turns a blind eye when Brackenreid beats a man from the society for information, he also listens to Julia when she insists homosexuality is natural. In its final quasi-educational function, the episode reminds viewers how much life for queer people has improved in the twenty-first century, with all the characters commenting that someday, hopefully, things might change.

Conclusion

Historically set murder mysteries reinterpret and recontextualize the queer past. Rather than echoing the values of the pre-Stonewall era, most of the episodes within these series reflect and allegorize today's debates for LGBTQ rights. The overall effect is a strange retelling of history. Queer representation in historically set murder mysteries celebrates a marginalized and underrepresented group, making them innocents and sometimes heroes rather than the murderous villains they have historically been portrayed as. But these examples also negate a tragic past by showing point-of-view characters as sympathetic, rather than the more historically accurate reality that queer people in the early part of the twentieth century were often social and legal outsiders. While increased queer content in these series contributes to improved statistics in contemporary media, the historical setting elides previous media history in which industry practices and social conventions obscured, negated, or villainized queerness. As these series circulate transnationally on streaming platforms as well as terrestrial networks, they have reshaped the cozy mystery and the way we regard queerness in the twentieth century.

Notes

1 This was also the logic of real-world events. During the "Lavender Scare" in U.S. federal workplaces in the 1950s, anyone with homosexual experiences was fired out of fear these employees' moral weakness meant they could be blackmailed or turned into double agents for the Soviet Union. A similar fear pervaded government offices in the U.K. at the time. See David K. Johnson, *The Lavender Scare* (Chicago: University of Chicago Press, 2004).

2 The chemical treatment to which Philip refers was likely estrogen "therapy" given to known homosexual men to reduce the effects of their testosterone and, by consequence, their sex drive. Also known as chemical castration, this was done in real life to mathematician Alan Turing after his conviction for gross indecency in 1952. He died by suicide in 1954, and some have attributed his death to the physical and psychological effects of the attempted "cure" for homosexuality. See Andrew Hodges, *Alan Turing: The Enigma* (New York: Simon and Schuster, 1983). The 2014 film *The Imitation Game* was based loosely on the book.
3 Rachel Flowerday and Tahsin Guner, "Developing *Father Brown* for BBC One," BBC Writer's Room, January 14, 2013. www.bbc.co.U.K./blogs/writersroom/entries/f4668ac0-53db-36a3-a9d2-4265bd2635f; "'It Was Fun to Find a Reason for Him to Throw Soup at the Wall': An Interview with the Creators of the BBC's *Father Brown*," PastOffences.com, February 24, 2014. https://pastoffences.wordpress.com/2014/02/24/it-was-fun-to-find-a-reason-for-him-to-throw-soup-at-the-wall-an-interview-with-the-creators-of-the-bbcs-father-brown/
4 Mark Lawson, "*Blandings* and *Father Brown*: TV Nostalgia at Its Best," *The Guardian*, January 11, 2013. www.theguardian.com/tv-and-radio/tvandradioblog/2013/jan/11/blandings-father-brown-nostalgia
5 Dignity USA, for example, was founded in 1969. It is a support group and ministry for LGBTQ Catholics. At the time of writing, the Catholic church's official doctrine remains that homosexual impulses should be avoided and same-sex marriage should not be sanctioned, even as Pope Francis has publicly stated support for civil unions and encouraged empathy, rather than condemnation, for LGBTQ people.
6 Olivia B. Waxman, "As More States Require Schools to Teach LGBTQ History, Resources for Teachers Expand," *Time*, December 13, 2019. https://time.com/5747670/lgbtq-history-resources/
7 Sam Damshenas, "Scotland Will Become the First Country in the World to Add LGBTQ+ History to School Curriculum," *Gay Times*. Accessed January 18, 2021. www.gaytimes.co.U.K./life/scotland-will-become-the-first-country-in-the-world-to-add-lgbtq-history-to-school-curriculum/
8 John D'Emilio, *Sexual Politics, Sexual Communities* (Chicago: University of Chicago Press, 1983).
9 J.C. Bernthal, *Queering Agatha Christie* (London: Palgrave Macmillan, 2016), 219.
10 Thomas J. West III, "Brothers in Arms: Spartacus, Historical Television, and the Celebration of Queer Masculinity," in *Queer TV in the 21st Century*, edited by Kylo-Patrick R. Hart (Jefferson, NC: McFarland, 2016), 143–144.
11 Cael Keegan, "In Praise of the Bad Transgender Object: *Rocky Horror*," *Flow*, November 28, 2019. www.flowjournal.org/2019/11/in-praise-of-the-bad/
12 Keegan, "In Praise of the Bad Transgender Object."
13 Homer B. Petty, "Hard-Boiled Tradition and Early Film Noir," in *Film Noir*, edited by Homer B. Pettey and R. Barton Palmer (Edinburgh: Edinburgh University Press, 2014), 58–79.
14 Marilyn Stasio, "Murder Least Foul: The Cozy, Soft-Boiled Mystery," *New York Times*, October 18, 1992, section 7, 42.
15 Larry Landrum, *American Mystery and Detective Novels* (Westport: Greenwood Press, 1999), 17.
16 Lucy Worsley, *The Art of the English Murder* (New York: Pegasus, 2015).
17 Tyler Coates, "When Hitchcock Went Gay: 'Strangers on a Train' and 'Rope,'" Decider.com, August 11, 2014. https://decider.com/2014/08/11/alfred-hitchcock-gay-strangers-on-a-train-and-rope/

18 Joshua Gamson, "Publicity Traps: Television Talk Shows and Lesbian, Gay, Bisexual, and Transgender Visibility," *Sexualities* 1, no. 1 (1998): 11–41.
19 Stephen Tropiano, *Prime Time Closet* (New York: Applause Theatre and Cinema Books, 2002), 3.
20 Ron Becker, "Guy Love: A Queer Straight Masculinity for the Post-Closet Era?" in *Queer TV*, edited by Glyn Davis and Gary Needham (New York: Routledge, 2009), 127.
21 Carolyn Gage, "The Case of the Missing Older Lesbians," CarolynGageWeebly.com, February 6, 2013. https://carolyngage.weebly.com/blog/the-case-of-the-missing-older-lesbians
22 Mrs. Darwin, "Miss Marple and the Case of the Superfluous Lesbians," Darwin Catholic, August 23, 2005. http://darwincatholic.blogspot.com/2005/08/miss-marple-and-case-of-superfluous.html
23 Anonymous comment dated August 11, 2007. http://darwincatholic.blogspot.com/2005/08/miss-marple-and-case-of-superfluous.html
24 Anonymous comment dated August 10, 2006. http://darwincatholic.blogspot.com/2005/08/miss-marple-and-case-of-superfluous.html
25 @Felicitydisco, December 1, 2020. https://twitter.com/FelicityDisco/status/1333859265195421698
26 @NicolaMDavidson, December 1, 2020. https://twitter.com/NicolaMDavidson/status/1333862368435077122
27 Alison Oram, "Love 'Off the Rails' or 'Over the Teacups'? Lesbian Desire and Female Sexualities in the 1950s British Popular Press," in *Queer 1950s*, edited by Heike Bauer and Matt Cook (London: Palgrave Macmillan, 2012), 41–57.
28 Florence Sutcliffe-Braithwaite, "The 1967 Sexual Offences Act: A Landmark Moment in the History of British Homosexuality," *BBC History*, July 2017. www.historyextra.com/period/modern/the-1967-sexual-offences-act-a-landmark-moment-in-the-history-of-british-homosexuality/
29 Peter Tatchell, as quoted in Geraldine Bedell, "Coming Out of the Dark Ages," *The Guardian*, June 24, 2007. www.theguardian.com/society/2007/jun/24/communities.gayrights
30 George Chauncey, *Gay New York* (New York: Basic Books, 1995). Although Chauncey writes about New York exclusively, archival evidence has shown similar conditions existed in all major cities in the United States, United Kingdom, Canada, and Australia.
31 John D'Emilio, *Sexual Politics, Sexual Communities* (Chicago: University of Chicago Press, 1983).
32 Susan Stryker, *Transgender History*, 2nd ed. (New York: Seal Press, 2017), 45–78.
33 Bernthal, *Queering Agatha Christie*, 230.
34 Peter Majda, "Agatha Christie's Poirot: 'Cards on the Table' – A Critical Look at Homophobia in an Adaptation," An American in London, April 8, 2012. https://anamericanexpatinlondon.wordpress.com/2012/04/08/agatha-christies-poirot-cards-on-the-table-a-critical-look-at-homophobia-in-an-adaptation/
35 At the time the episode is set, sexologists, scientists who studied the new field of human sexuality, sought to identify the origins of sexual desire "inverted" toward members of the same sex. Richard von Krafft-Ebing described this inversion as "homo-sexual" (drawing on the Greek word *homos* for "same") in his 1886 book *Psychopathia Sexualis*.

8

OBSCURE TEMPORALITIES

Dark and the Queering of Time Travel

Michael DeAngelis

Midway through the first season of the Netflix series *Dark* (2017–2020), the exasperated teenager Jonas Kahnwald (Louis Hofmann), plagued by the senselessness of his father's recent suicide, the summer he has just spent recuperating as an inpatient at a mental health facility, and the inexplicable disappearance of his ex-girlfriend Martha's younger brother Mikkel near the entrance to an elaborate network of caves in a rural German village marked by the looming presence of a nuclear power plant, bemoans the tragic yet absurd set of family connections that have gradually surfaced in the course of his recent time travel across a number of 33-year cycle. "Now I have another grandma and she's the principal of my school!" he exclaims. "Her husband, who's fucking my mom, is looking for his son who is my father! A few days ago I kissed my aunt." Jonas's convoluted lineage derives from a world that has dismantled the conventions of time order while challenging its audiences' capacity to remain oriented. The phrase "Everything is connected" is repeated across *Dark*'s three seasons, but rather than signaling a model of human interaction that is comprehensible as a linear narrative, the series disrupts the normative division of time into past, present, and future. As a result, characters inhabiting time periods decades apart interact within arms-length of one another, and the matter of discrete identity is discounted as Jonas and his fellow Windenites interact and converse with younger and older versions of themselves.

Unfolding over the course of 36 hour-long episodes, delivered in doses of eight-to-ten-episode seasons released a year or more apart, and embedded with family trees and split-screen sequences to help keep its characters "straight,"[1] *Dark* requires its viewers to gradually acclimate to the terms of a narrative that disengages time from its normative progression. Although the series' homosexual themes and representations certainly contribute to its "queerness" through the markings of incest, abuse, and even homosexual desire, here I will argue that an even more potentially subversive queerness emerges from the unique experience of time that

DOI: 10.4324/9781003109044-11

the narrative constructs. Just as the demonstration of queer sexuality heightens our awareness of the unstable foundation upon which heteronormativity has established itself as a cultural default or a "given," narratives that intentionally disrupt the seeming integrity of hetero-"normative" time elucidate the largely arbitrary nature of the time structures that undergird everyday life. Undermining our adherence to the temporal experience that is aligned with this heteronormative configuration, the project of critically de-throning such normative structures becomes a queer intervention, one that strives to expose, interrogate, and disrupt the ideological conditions that dictate how we structure our lives; which goals we should establish (and when); what constitutes success, qualifies as "home," and counts as an acceptable notion of "family." The journey ultimately foregrounds the ways that we are invited to conceptualize the past and present in relation to the future. In *Dark*, this de-throning becomes analogous to the phenomenon of reverse culture shock, where the extended immersion in a non-native, foreign culture is followed by a return to a "home" culture that now resonates as strange and unnatural despite its familiarity.

For the benefit of those who are unfamiliar with the series (and those in need of a refresher), the following study begins with an overview of the series' plot and structure, and it continues with a brief overview of theoretical perspectives on queer temporality that aim to distinguish heteronormative from queer time. The analysis subsequently proceeds to a discussion of *Dark*'s queer revision of three phenomena that have been established as formative life events under heteronormativity: birth, death, and reproduction. The scope of the analysis then broadens to examine *Dark*'s queer response to several other aspects of the "normative," linear life progression that *Dark* reworks: the "directional" aspect of time, the derivation of lineage and heritage, the notion of future-facing progress, the manifestations of nostalgia that anchor us to the past through the process of yearning, and the configuration of the concept of home. The study concludes with a treatment of the "queer utopia" that the narrative assembles with a marked temporal shift in the series' final two episodes.

The Plot of *Dark*

Dark is set in the small, rural German village of Winden, whose distinctive feature is the looming presence of a nuclear power plant, still active yet scheduled for closure. The first season introduces the personal and professional interconnections among four Windenite families: Hannah and Michael Kahnwald, and their only child Jonas; high school principal Katarina Nielsen, her adulterous husband Ulrich, and their three children Magnus, Martha, and Mikkel; police commissioner Charlotte Doppler, her husband Peter, and daughters Franziska and the deaf-mute Elizabeth; and hotel manager Regina Tiedeman, her husband Aleksandr, who manages the operations of the power plant, and their son Bartosz. Martha Nielsen and Jonas Kahnwald had dated before his father's suicide, but after Jonas was sent to recover at a psychiatric institution for the summer, Martha has begun a relationship with

Bartosz. Unbeknownst to Katarina, her husband Ulrich is having an affair with Hannah Kahnwald. Charlotte and Peter's relationship has been strained by sexual attraction to Benni, a transgender sex worker.

The series begins in the current day with two seemingly unrelated occurrences that establish the basis for the narrative's investigative trajectory: the unexplained suicide by hanging of Michael Kahnwald, and the sudden, mysterious disappearance of Mikkel Nielsen outside the entrance to a nearby cave on Halloween night. We soon learn that the two incidents are connected by a wormhole in the village's underground network of caves, resulting from an accident at the nuclear power plant that has enabled time travel to the past and future. The young Mikkel Nielsen who disappears on Halloween night 2019 travels through this wormhole to the village of Winden in 1986, within the previous 33-year cycle.[2] He has remained there indefinitely, following a timeline that ultimately connects him to the present-day cycle in the form of Michael Kahnwald, Jonas's suicidal father! We are also introduced to the mysterious priest Noah who, with the aid of Helge Tiedeman, conducts failed time travel experiments on young boys, none of whom survives the ordeal, their corpses dispersed and then discovered in other time zones like so much transgenerational waste. The season later introduces us to past and future iterations of the 33-year cycle, with developments in 1953 and 2053, where we witness the barren, post-apocalyptic landscape to which Jonas has been relegated. Season 1 also introduces us to a character known as The Stranger, a "version" of Jonas 33 years older than the teenager who is coping with his father's suicide and who has returned to Winden intent upon destroying the wormhole.

The second season brings additional time cycles into the mix. In 1921, Jonas meets Adam, the leader in the cult known as *Sic Mundus* and, we soon learn, yet another, even older version of Jonas. Adam aims to ensure that an anticipated apocalypse prompted by nuclear explosion actually occurs so that the cycles of time will no longer perpetuate; in this endeavor his efforts are opposed by Regina's mother Claudia Tiedemann, newly appointed chief of the nuclear power plant intent upon ensuring that the apocalypse never happens. Ulrich's search for his son Mikkel first takes him back to 1986, where Helge and Noah have kidnapped Ulrich's brother Mads as a subject for the time travel experiment. Ulrich then moves backward in time to 1953, where he unsuccessfully attempts to stone young Helge to death in order to stop him from abducting his brother Mads 33 years later. Ulrich is arrested and jailed for this brutal crime and denied help even when Hannah travels back in time to save him. (She ultimately decides not to.) Season 2 also develops the storyline of scientist H. G. Tannhaus, author of *A Journey Through Time* and the creator of the machine prototype that he has designed to enable time travel. The season's final episodes find several of Winden's residents retreating to a bunker to ride out the forthcoming apocalypse. In the season's final moments, Adam kills Martha in front of Jonas, yet seconds later *another* version of Martha arrives on the scene to rescue Jonas seconds before the apocalypse destroys the Kahnwald house.

Season 3 begins with the revelation that the Martha who saved Jonas is actually a product of an alternate world. There, Winden remains Winden, and the plot proceeds along lines similar to those in the primary world that we encountered first, but the roles of several characters have been reshuffled: Franziska is now the deaf-mute child instead of her sister Elizabeth; Ulrich attempts (still unsuccessfully) to kill an adult version of Helge in 1954; and Ulrich has left Katarina to be with Hannah while he has an affair with Charlotte Doppler. The most conspicuous difference between these two worlds, however, is the absence of Jonas: since Mikkel never time travels to 1986 in the alternate world, Jonas never travels there to pursue him. Yet shortly after the season begins, the Martha of this alternate world ("alt-Martha") has conceived a child with Jonas.

Season 3 also introduces the character Eva, Adam's counterpart in alt-Winden, who is just as determined to preserve the repeating cycles of time as Adam is to destroy them. Eva is also the elder version of alt-Martha, and in this new world born of destruction, the two figureheads battle it out. Eva becomes convinced that this child, the product of both worlds, will also turn out to be the savior of both worlds; Adam agrees, making him even more intent upon ensuring that the child is never born. The conflict between Adam and Eva ultimately plays out as a staging of alternate and conflicting hypothetical scenarios between their much younger counterparts. No sooner has Adam succeeded in killing the pregnant alt-Martha than the child appears already to have been born.

But neither Adam nor Eva turns out to be correct in this case. It is not the anticipated child who represents the "origin" of the knot that binds the two worlds together; instead, this origin point lies in a world entirely separate from the other two, in an "origin world" that precedes the creation of the primary and alternate worlds that have dominated the narrative. The origin world event that has precipitated the split is a 1971 highway accident that kills H. G. Tannhaus's son, daughter-in-law, and child, occurring just after the son has stormed out of his father's house in a heated argument. After the tragedy, a grief-stricken Tannhaus devotes himself to designing a machine that will let him move backward in time to prevent the accident from ever occurring. Tannhaus is ready to implement this experimental strategy five years later, yet instead of producing the desired result, the time machine splits the origin world into the two worlds to which we have been exposed thus far. In the present-day, Jonas and alt-Martha, descendants of Adam and Eva, intervene to correct the temporal fracture by visiting the origin world and preventing the accident that Tannhaus could not stop. While their intervention succeeds, the strategy results in the annihilation of Jonas/Adam, alt-Martha/Eva, along with the entire existence of the two worlds to which we have born witness. The series ends with a scenario that unfolds in the original, prelapsarian Winden, now inhabited only by Windenites whose existence is not a result of time travel.

Queer Time in Winden

Dark's circuitous temporal manipulations correlate with strategies that queer theorists have used to interrogate the normalcy of ideologically constructed phenomena that uphold the conditions of heteronormativity. Our experience of time is always susceptible to power relations born out of inequities that heteronormativity perpetrates—ideological forces fine-tuned to render it inevitable, for example, that we should strive to establish a legacy, that we should act more maturely as we age, and that, as mature individuals, we should seek legally sanctioned partnerships that support the goal of human propagation. We are expected not to deviate from practices that heteronormative forces have rendered as "given" and that serve us daily doses of temporal content, order, duration, and trajectories of life as it "should" be lived, thereby governing our expectations on what we "should" (and should not) be doing, seeking, or striving for at any given moment.

To disavow or challenge such conditions of temporal hetero-normalcy is to engage in a form of queer resistance that overtly disrespects such conditions and refuses to adhere to them. In *Time Binds: Queer Temporalities, Queer Histories*, Elizabeth Freeman describes the conditions of a heteronormative "chronobiopolitics" that structures time teleologically as the linear progression of "events and strategies of living" that include marriage, reproduction, child rearing, and death (Freeman 2010, 5). Mimicking the logic of an institutional normativity serving as what Freeman describes as "a mode of implantation" that fixes and stabilizes our experience of time, *Dark*'s first several episodes of *Dark* are replete with the orienting indices of time as calendars, work schedules, clocks, maps, and dated letters organize the viewing experience amidst the flashbacks and flashforwards (Freeman 2010, 2).[3] While intertitles initially guide us through the shifting time periods, as the series progresses the temporal groundings feel more unstable. In the post-apocalyptic version of Winden revealed at the end of Season 1, for example, the familiar cadences of structured, heteronormative time have faded away, save for the occasional clicking of Geiger counters tracing radioactive residues scattered across a barren, boundless landscape of the "future." In the Season 2 finale, which reveals the existence of an alternate world populated by familiar characters who have now been assigned unfamiliar identities, attributes, and affiliations, the status of both worlds in relation to the "real" is rendered tenuous. Temporal instability similarly characterizes the series' final episodes, with the revelation of the origin world that positions both of the other worlds as contingent. Designed to move us along a sequential path of disorientation, each revelation necessitates a repositioning of what we have constituted as the "real." Across the series, manifestations of queerness allow us to recognize normative temporality as a set of trappings that insidiously structure our experience of time.

In addition to Freeman's contributions, queer theorists Judith Halberstam, José Esteban Muñoz, and Lee Edelman have explored queerness's potential to resist a heteronormative conception of temporality founded upon progress, linearity, genealogy, and generational thinking. Although their approaches differ, these critics align in their goal of interrogating the presumed integrity of heteronormative temporality, making contributions invaluable to an analysis of *Dark*'s temporal strategies. Seeking challenges to time's assumed status as "given," Halberstam positions "queer time" as a force that recognizes "the potentiality of a life unscripted by the conventions of family, inheritance, and child rearing" (Halberstam 2005, 2), while

Freeman reflects upon the "teleologies of living" that restrict our experience of time to the achievement of the life strategies to which we are expected to adhere in perpetuating a "familial and collective *legacy*" that always depends upon forward movement (Freeman 2010, 5, emphasis in the original). Muñoz invests in the notion of queerness as "horizon," as a "rejection of a here and now and an insistence on the potentiality or concrete possibility of another world (Muñoz 2009, 1)" while Edelman dismisses *any* promise for "another world" that secures our allegiance to the figure of the child, insisting that "*queerness* names the side of those *not* 'fighting for the children,' the side outside the consensus by which all politics confirms the absolute value of reproductive futurism" (Edelman 2004, 4).

Birth and Death

If heteronormative authority over temporality is rooted in a directive for citizens to progress without critique or reflection through the designated stages of a prefabricated life path, *Dark* queers this authority by orchestrating disruptions of "chrononormative" thinking at every stage of a continuum from birth, to adolescence, to marriage, to reproduction, to parenthood, to death. Although heteronormative temporality involves arranging the present in the service of the future, *Dark* strategically positions its viewers within a diegesis that, until the final episodes, *withholds* all images of the future apart from either the impending apocalypse or the endless rehearsal of the past. In the process, the cyclical nature of *Dark*'s primary and alternate worlds disrupts the status of birth as a moment of beginning, or of death as an endpoint. Instead, death prompts recurrence and rebirth with the movement through the 33-year cycles. As central protagonists who at intervals proclaim the intertwining of their destinies by insisting that "we're a perfect match--never believe anything else," Jonas and Martha die more than once in each other's arms, and by each other's hands. As season 2 concludes, for example Adam, the oldest of Jonas's three emanations, fatally shoots Martha, yet moments later a *new* version of Martha (portrayed by the same actress) from the alternate world emerges on the scene to rescue Jonas from the apocalypse. Season 3 approaches the limits of this revival of the dead when it is revealed that *several* versions of Martha are circulating in the alternate world, each of them conjured by Eva (the oldest version of Martha), including one whom Eva summons to kill Jonas.

Reproduction

In the context of Winden's primary and alternate worlds, the narrative "queers" the act of reproduction in the same way that it destabilizes the notion of death as the final or culminating life stage of a prescribed linear progression. In her analysis of the film *Arrival* (Denis Villeneuve, 2016), Heather Latimer draws attention to the "shared contemporaneity" that occurs when characters of different time periods become connected through simultaneous co-presence. In *Arrival*, this phenomenon permits a mother to affectively discern the presence and fate of her future child before it has been conceived, demonstrating the capacity of the film's time travel narrative to "untether reproduction from futurity" (Latimer 2021, 9). The cyclicity in the primary and alternate worlds, combined with Windenites' capacity to move among the designated 33-year cycles without physiognomic changes, produces a host of such paradoxical configurations of family that undermine heteronormative constructions of reproduction and mother–child relations. The narrative sometimes inverts the identities of mother and child, and in the context of "shared contemporaneity," the series' most harrowing instance of reproductive failure arises with the figure of Katarina Nielsen. In the 1986 to which she has time-traveled in search of her son and husband, Katarina meets a nurse named Helene whom Katarina instantly recognizes as her biological mother. Katarina's claim is entirely earnest, since in the 1986 narrative we have seen the teenage version of daughter Katarina suffering abuse at Helene's hands. To Helene, however, this premature encounter with an "older" version of Katarina sparks a misperception of shared contemporaneity with drastic consequences. Since Helene already *has* a teenage daughter named Katarina at home, she misrecognizes the adult Katarina before her as a haunting, spiritual manifestation of an "other" daughter, one whose pregnancy she has already terminated. This misrecognition has tragic consequences, with Helene exclaiming "You're already dead!" as she brutally pounds the adult Katarina's head with a rock until she dies.

The Child

"Queerness names the side of those *not* fighting for the children," Lee Edelman proclaims, and it might initially appear that *Dark* positions itself at both sides of the struggle (Edelman 2004, 3, emphasis in the original). Although the plot begins with the unexplained suicide of a fully grown adult man, it is young Mikkel's disappearance that drives the narrative's search for answers *and* that also ultimately explains the motivation for the suicide. Male children are especially vulnerable in both the primary and alternate worlds. Some are exiled via time travel and condemned to live out their days repeating time cycles of the past, while others are snatched away from familiar environments by Noah and Helge for use as test subjects in time travel experiments using outmoded technologies. Ulrich's invocation of the "grandfather paradox" constitutes one failed, pre-meditated, and conspicuous attempt to "fight for the children": determined to prevent the abduction and murder of his brother Mads in 1986 by murdering the suspected culprit Helge while he is still a young boy in 1953, Ulrich's desperate, ethically suspect act fails when the boy manages to survive Ulrich's presumed fatal blows, and the already dead Mads fails to escape his fate.[4]

After the "origin world" is introduced in the third season, *Dark* appears at first to be hypothesizing mankind's savior in the form of a child (a case of *infans ex machina*?), with Adam and Eva, the eldest versions of Jonas and Martha, identifying the anticipated child to be (or to have been?) produced by their teenage selves as instrumental to the only remaining chance of saving the world—and perhaps *both* worlds. As it turns out, the redemption that Adam seeks involves the *annihilation* of both worlds, including the aforementioned child; Eva, however, protests that alt-Martha's child is now mankind's only hope, although her aim is not to save the world but to perpetuate its infinite cyclical repetition. Accordingly, in versions of the family tree that appear in Season 3, the infinity symbol marks the horizontal connection between Jonas and Martha. True to a narrative invested in the principles of quantum entanglement, *Dark* posits several simultaneously realized outcomes of this hypothetical pregnancy: a prospective child that Adam will have to kill in order to prevent the perpetuation of the cycles; yet one more version of Martha, whom Eva must now arrange to have impregnated after Adam carried out his own murder plot; and no child at all, save for the one who has already been born, matured, and aged, and who appears in tripartite form—the hare-lipped male known only as "The Unknown," whom Eva commissions to enforce the alignment of all historical events required to ensure the cycles' endless perpetuation. None of these hypothetical cases ever produces a savior child, but the ultimate effort to "save the world" from both apocalypse *and* endless cyclical repetition does come to pass, at the expense of the existence of prospective parents Martha and Jonas, who proceed to dissolve in evanescence after their mutual decision to join forces in the origin world, where they intervene to prevent the tragic automobile accident that will later trigger the creation of the first two worlds that we have encountered. In the fractured, cyclical realm of time travel, then, reproduction does not save anyone or anything in Winden; instead, it only reiterates more of the same.[5]

The Directions of Time (Travel)

This generative failure of reproduction connects with a larger set of conditions imposed by temporal cyclicity. "Chronobiopolitics harnesses not only sequence but also cycle, the dialectical companion to sequence," Freeman argues, "for the idea of time as cyclical stabilizes its forward movement, promising renewal rather than rupture" (Freeman 2010, 5). Curiously, however, the more frequently that the cycles of *Dark* play out, the more clearly they are revealed to *impede* progression, constituting renewal only in their guarantee of a steady dose and supply of already recycled iterations. By the time that the series identifies Eva and her devoted followers as the perpetrators of this ceaseless cyclic movement, these impediments have figured too prominently to be disguised. *Dark* confirms the incapacity of its temporal structure to accommodate forward movement, verifying that what appears as progressive momentum involves not only reiteration but *recursion*, a process by which the narrative is revealed to have continuously expanded while temporally folding back upon itself.[6]

In addition to impeding heteronormative "progress," these conditions of repetition and recursion compromise the efficacy of temporal *directionality* in a similar way that tracing a line on a mobius strip paradoxically consolidates two sides of a figure into one. Through such compromise, the concept of opposite directions is rendered meaningless: not only do beginnings become indistinct from endings, but "backward" and "forward" cease to register as discrete vectors of movement that can be differentiated. Yet *Dark* also queers memory and foresight, phenomena that also depend upon directional opposition, since attempts to recall what might appear to be past experiences become indistinguishable from future predictions capable of triggering Windenites to "remember" a *subsequent* cycle. Rather than calling upon its protagonists' capacity to store and retrieve the requisite information on their own that will enable the cycles to perpetuate, *Dark*'s protagonists use other, more reliable strategies to ensure that what happens next is what needs to happen in order to achieve pre-determined outcomes. For instance, when teenage Jonas reflects upon the next course of action in his time-traveling odyssey, the Stranger (the middle-aged version of Jonas) often intervenes to instruct him about permissible and prohibited courses of action according to the terms of cyclical time's "will have happened" so that Jonas does not prevent subsequent, already verified developments from occurring.[7]

Lineage, Heritage, and Generation

"De-linking the process of generation from the force of historical process is a queer kind of project," asserts Halberstam, suggesting that "we may want to forget family and forget lineage and forget tradition in order to start from a new place, not the place where the old engenders the new, where the old makes a place for the new, but where the new begins afresh, unfettered by memory, tradition, and usable pasts" (Halberstam 2011, 70). With reproduction reduced to a non-generative process, and the capacity to differentiate between opposite directions compromised, *Dark* disrupts the tyranny of the future-facing, past-grounded structures of lineage and heritage, along with any efforts to elucidate the connections between generations that require clear distinctions between "before" and "after." Instead of securing stability and order along ancestral lines, lineage in Winden proceeds by seemingly random skips and jumps. Instead of linear movement across generations, Winden yields to instances of simultaneity and overlap, as past and future versions of the same character converge and converse at the same site. This occurs most overtly in the reconfiguration of Martha and Jonas's connection from ex-/future lovers to blood relatives who also become lovers once again in the alternate world, and also in Windenites' searches for lost children (Mikkel, Mads, Helge), fathers (Ulrich, Noah), and mothers such as Charlotte and Elizabeth, after it is revealed that Elizabeth is both Charlotte's mother *and* daughter.

Progress and Heteronormative Futurity

Embedded in an iterable cyclicity that forestalls its protagonists' access to the past *as* past, in both *Dark*'s primary and the alternate worlds any attempts to offer hope for the future (of Winden, of mankind itself) are similarly incapable of evading reiteration and recursion. The troubling circumstances surrounding Winden's decision to

FIGURE 8.1 Progress and forward thinking, the likenesses of the Doppler family grace a billboard at the construction site of Winden's new power plant in 1953. Netflix.

adopt nuclear energy as a sign of "progress" illustrates this failure. In "Everything Is Now" (episode 1.9), a billboard installed at the construction site of Winden's nuclear power plant promotes the image of an idealized, forward-thinking "nuclear" family ready to embrace the future (Figure 8.1), but the 1953 ground-breaking ceremony becomes a sour affair when two dead boys are unearthed at the site. The result of failed time-travel experiments conducted in future time periods, the "surfacing" of the boys' corpses anticipates the forthcoming apocalypse to be precipitated by radioactive isotope caesium-137, itself a by-product of "progress" in the form of waste materials that the nuclear reactors will produce, that the plant's leadership will unsuccessfully attempt to conceal in cylinders that are buried in the caves, and that will also provide the fuel required for Winden's time travelers to effectively *avert* this same apocalypse.[8] Mocking the course of a heteronormative conception of progress, the attempts to forge Winden's future cannot avert the prospect of already being encoded as anticipated endings.

Nostalgia

Dark's queering operations set up the conditions of nostalgia only to highlight and subvert the distinctions among past, present, and future that prevail under the constraints of heteronormativity. If the sync-scheduled apocalypse set to occur across the time periods of the first two worlds renders the future bleak, *Dark*'s turn away from future-facing teleology to past-leaning directives of yearning leads to yet another temporal brick wall. Discussing the paradox implicit in the act of yearning, Svetlana Boym argues that, as "side effects of the teleology of progress" marked by modernity's historical obsession with forward movement, the workings of nostalgia concern an idealized rather than an accurate version of the past," and that "It is this past perfect that one strives to realize in the future" (Boym

2001, 351). Directed toward the past instead of the future, the phenomenon of nostalgia might appear to be well-suited to disrupting the circuit of continuity that plagues existence in the primary and alternate worlds. Just as the logic of "chrononormative," forward thinking in Winden folds in upon itself to reveal evidence of an apocalypse already visible in the quest for the future, however, the crisis of temporal directionality also disrupts time-traveling Windenites' efforts to reverse course in pursuit of any real or idealized past, since nostalgia involves both the attempt to recapture a "lost" time and the rendering visible of that recaptured past to reveal what Boym describes as "an edenic unity of time and space before entry into history" (Boym 2001, 8).

At Home, Homeless

These problems of visualizing the past and future are made manifest by the disjunction between time and space that establishes the requisite conditions for time travel in Winden. Whereas the capacity for intentional movement across time periods (including movement that involves skipping over other time periods along the way) requires only the appropriate technological device and a steady supply of the radioactive isotope required to fuel it, the spatial dimension of time travel remains fixed and constant because *Dark*'s storyscape restricts both the origins and destinations of all time travel to the immediate parameters of Winden. In fact, despite the prevalence of time travel in this narrative, no one ever actually leaves Winden once they arrive or return. This consistency certainly helps audiences to acclimate to the village's spaces and settings across episodes and seasons. For time-traveling Windenites, however, the spatial restriction imposed upon time travel reinforces a sense of displacement and homelessness, a feeling that these once familiar and intimate spaces no longer "belong" to them. If, as Boym suggests, "every return to our actual birthplace or ancestral land gives us the same sensation of returning to where we have never been" (Boym 2001, 352), Winden's time travelers experience this displacement more intensively because of the incongruity between the vast amount of time over which they can travel and the relative instantaneity of the travel "experience" itself. Young Mikkel's journey from 2019 to 1986, for example, involves only a crossing through the caves followed by a short walk to reach places that he immediately recognizes. His house, his school, the police station, and the hospital that he sees were all "there" for him in that 33-year-old yesterday of what now constitutes his future; upon visiting his own house, however, Mikkel is greeted by a teenage boy whom he does not recognize, and Mikkel's odd questions ("Which year is it?") provoke others to mock him. "Homes are effects of the history of arrival," Sara Ahmed asserts, yet especially for the viewer, knowing that the teenager standing before him is also Ulrich, the man who will become Mikkel's own father, exacerbates this sense of the uncanny, marking "home" as a conspicuous absence rather than a physical destination, as something lost even as it remains in view (Ahmed 2006, 9). Travel between the primary world and its mirrored alternate only intensifies the sense of a past (or a future) that does not exist, as Jonas learns when he discovers that in the alternate world the Nielsen's are occupying what was (and is?) his own home, with the staircase now positioned in the "wrong" direction.

The Future as Field of Possibility: Queer Utopia and The Origin World

Boym suggests that the object of nostalgia—its ties to the "real" past notwithstanding—comprises "an affective yearning for a community with a collective memory, a longing for continuity in a fragmented world" (Boym 2001, 10); however, the directive to return to once familiar places only to endure their unfamiliarity accentuates the primary and alternate worlds' inability to accommodate either past or future in a well-rehearsed cyclical replay where "Everything Is Now." Incapable of eliciting nostalgia or of situating home, none of the time periods of the past (1986, 1953, 1920, or 1897) offers conditions of existence that are any more welcoming or embracing than the tenuous present, and in each of these time periods we repeatedly witness similar instances of betrayal, blackmail, deception, manipulation, and coercion. With nothing seeming better (or worse) then than now, the past can provide no anchor or structure of support to justify ceaseless yearning for a once better time. Aligned with his perspective on the impermeable alliance between the future and the figure of the redeeming child, Edelman argues that "The future is mere repetition of and just as lethal as the past" (Edelman 2004, 31). Deviating from Edelman's conception of the future, however, the narrative of *Dark* closes by bringing into view a new world unaffected by cyclical repetition, and replete with bonds and connections that are consonant with a very different conception of the future as utopia. Muñoz rejects the tyranny of the here and now while looking toward the notion of the future as limit, as horizon, and as a realm of possibilities that are not yet realized (Muñoz 2009, 11). In this figuration, queer futurity deviates from "the linearity of straight time," interrogating and undermining straight time's "autonaturalizing tendency" that grounds us in a seemingly inescapable present (Muñoz 2009, 22). This deviation is also a refusal, a search for something else that the "givenness" of the present does not authorize. Ultimately, Muñoz argues, "Queerness's ecstatic and horizonal temporality is a path and a movement to a greater openness in the world" (Muñoz 2009, 25).

The final scenes of *Dark* accommodate this queer openness through the discovery of an "origin" world that existed before Winden's resident horologist Tannhaus inadvertently split it into the two other worlds in 1986, as part of his thwarted attempt to reverse time to save his family. Located outside the parameters of the primary and alternate worlds, the origin world remains insusceptible to the workings of the cycles and to recursive operations that might otherwise contain or reclaim it to neutralize the distinction between past and present. Although they are creatures of time travel who are ineligible for a "place" in this origin world, Jonas and alt-Martha can bring these cycles to a definitive end, even if this resolution will require that they sacrifice the unreal conditions of their time-travel-induced existence for the benefit of a return to the "real." Transitioning from mirror-world machinations comprising the only versions of Winden to which viewers have had access, the introduction of the origin world provides the temporal grounding that ultimately restores directional temporality's distinction between "before" and "after."

We are not exposed to this world for very long, and because of the minimal screen time devoted to exploring it compared to the series' more sustained focus upon the primary and alternate worlds, the final scene of *Dark* both serves as a renewed present and initiates a queer movement toward new future possibilities that resist the pull of straight time. The final scene invites us to a celebration, a sharing of dinner, drinks, and leisure time among six fellow Windenites: Regina Tiedemann, who died of cancer in both of the first two worlds, and who is now being honored; Katarina, whose mother murdered her in the alternate world; Hannah, Jonas's mother in the alternate world; Toben Wöller, a Winden police officer who is now romantically involved with Hannah; Peter Doppler, police chief Charlotte's husband in the primary world and a priest in the alternate world; and Benni Wöller, Toben's transgender brother. The mood of the scene is intimate and convivial, despite a raging thunderstorm.

The origin world does maintain a connection to the two worlds that have just dissipated, through conversations about "a world without Winden" and the loss of electrical power (occurring whenever someone crosses over to another time period through the tunnels) precipitates an immersion in soft candlelight. This loss is paired with the conspicuous presence of a yellow raincoat hanging from the banister where Jonas might have left it in the primary world (or Martha in the alternate), triggering a moment of déjà vu for Hannah as she recalls an intense dream of the night before--a dream of flickering light that only anticipates darkness. Although harrowing, Hannah's dream is also one of cathartic liberation:

> It was just dark, and it never became light again. I had this peculiar feeling that it was a good thing for everything to be over. Like suddenly being free of everything. No wanting. No having to. Infinite darkness. No yesterday. No today. No tomorrow. Nothing.

The connection to the apocalypses of the primary and alternate worlds is undeniable, yet here it has shifted from a menacing premonition of the end of days, to a dream that has already passed, and from which the dreamer herself has awakened after a moment of crisis which, though recent, is now decidedly *past*. Ultimately, Winden's origin world enables an experience of time that abandons ineffectual nostalgia for the prospect of a future distinct from this past, rather than being bound to repeat it.

It is through the prospect of such a future that *Dark* ultimately aligns with a "queerness" that, as José Esteban Muñoz argue, is "essentially about the rejection of a here and now and an insistence on potentiality or concrete possibility for another world" as a utopia, the future-oriented counterpart to nostalgia (Muñoz 2009, 1). As such, Winden's origin world constitutes "The Paradise" of the episode's title, a world that engages with a yet-to-be-realized potentiality "in which multiple forms of belonging in difference adhere to a belonging in collectivity" because it moves forward rather than stagnating in cyclical, atemporal repetition (Muñoz 2009, 20). The players in this "paradise" are all recognizable enough to the viewer who has come this far, yet they resonate as unfamiliar and "new," untainted by the markings of the primary and alternate worlds. What unites the characters in this context is that none of them owes their existence to time travel, and consequently, the interpersonal conflicts that they endured in the other worlds have no place here. That we have entered a recognizable yet unfamiliar Winden is most evident from the absence of Ulrich, Katarina's unfaithful husband who has an affair with Hannah in the primary world and has divorced Katarina to be with Hannah in the alternate world. While Regina dies after suffering from breast cancer in the primary world, the origin world brings her back from a death that was no death at all, and where she is now free of the conflicts that made her the object of Katarina and Ulrich's cruel bullying and Hannah's scapegoating. Another contrast emerges with the revelation that the house where the gathering takes place—Hannah's in the primary world, Katarina's in the alternate—is now Regina's. Spatial territorialities have been curtailed, along with the alienation endured by time-traveling Windenites returning home to domestic spaces that no longer welcome them.

In fact, this respite from the workings of a seemingly endless "now" constitutes a rare instance in the series in which interpersonal connections in Winden are liberated from the intricate schemes, betrayals, and deceptions so prevalent in the primary and alternate worlds. In the realm of queer possibility, however, the most remarkable development in this final scene, is the self-acknowledged, queer relationship between Peter Doppler and transgender Benni Wöller (Bernadette in the alternate world), now welcomed, included, and integrated with the larger community of Winden (Figure 8.2).

Benni's new "place" in the origin world marks a pronounced shift from the primary world, where Peter Doppler was married to police commissioner Charlotte,

FIGURE 8.2 Peter Doppler (Stephan Kampwirth) and Benni Wöller (Anton Rubtsov) in the welcoming community of the origin world in the final scene of *Dark*. Netflix.

their distant, uncommunicative relationship a result of the mutual, unspoken knowledge of Peter's deviation from heteronormativity through his "secret" affair with Benni-Bernadette, there positioned as a sex worker operating from a trailer in the parking lot of a Winden truck stop. With the sources of human discord in the primary and alternate worlds now ontologically dismissed from the table, the proceedings are casual and relaxed. And in place of an isolated forest village harboring the grief-stricken, our first and final night in Winden's origin world is presented in a widescreen aspect ratio that accommodates laterally configured groups of friends, as a fitting testament to a new community undergoing a process of awakening. Following a circuitous journey across more than 25 episodes through a set of time intervals spanning more than 150 years—a journey that navigates the complexities of an elaborate diegesis that we are never prompted to consider as anything else but the "real" world before us, until it is revealed to have inadvertently been set in motion by a local clockmaker's guilt for failing to render "unreal" the car accident that has led to an unimaginable family tragedy, *Dark*'s exhilarating, pilot's-seat journey through queer time ultimately lands its audience in a grounded present and a future receptive to the prospect of queer utopia.

Notes

1 Netflix's official series website provides a yet more elaborate tracing of the time shifts and loops that occur with each episode. See "*Dark*: The Official Guide," https://dark.netflix.io/en.
2 The devastating accident at the Chernobyl nuclear power facility in the Ukraine occurred in April 1986.
3 Freeman identifies "schedules, calendars, time zones, [and] even wristwatches" among these devices of "implantation" (2).
4 Ironically, Episode 3.8 ("Paradise") introduces an instance of trans-interval memory, when Helge accurately recognizes Ulrich as the man who assaulted and disfigured him in the 1953 time interval, acting upon this recognition by murdering him by the same means as Ulrich *failed* to murder Helge.
5 Discussing queer temporality, Alexander Cho includes moments of repetition "as productive places of inquiry, recognizing that queer people, or queerness, has been relegated as adjacent to or incompatible with Western heteronormative historical narratives." See "Queer Reverb: Tumblr, Affect, Time," in *Networked Affect*, eds. Ken Hillis, Susanna Paasonen, and Michael Petit (Cambridge, MA: MIT Press, 2015), 48.
6 The series of episode summaries in "*Dark*: The Official Guide" actualizes this process of recursive temporality by means of progressive, geometric representation, tracing the series' successive forward and backward movements as an elaborate series of loops within loops.
7 Ultimately, this centrality of recursion also informs Adam's crucial miscalculation that the origin world lies within rather than beyond the primary and alternate worlds, with distinctions between inside and outside now rendered ambiguous, or entirely meaningless.
8 With a half-life of roughly 30 years, the pyrophoric caesium-137 is also the isotope that became the primary source of lingering radiation approximately 200 days after the 1986 Chernobyl disaster.

Works Cited

Ahmed, Sara. 2006. *Queer Phenomenology: Orientations, Objects, Others*. Durham, NC: Duke University Press.

Boym, Svetlana. 2001. *The Future of Nostalgia*. New York: Basic Books.

Cho, Alexander. 2015. "Queer Reverb: Tumblr, Affect, Time." In *Networked Affect*, edited by Ken Hills, Susanna Paasonen, and Michael Petit, 43–57. Cambridge, MA: MIT Press.

"*Dark*: The Official Guide." Accessed November 1, 2020. https://dark.netflix.io/en.

Edelman, Lee. 2004. *No Future: Queer Theory and the Death Drive*. Durham, NC: Duke University Press.

Freeman, Elizabeth. 2010. *Time Binds: Queer Temporalities, Queer Histories*. Durham, NC: Duke University Press.

Halberstam, Judith. 2011. *The Queer Art of Failure*. Durham, NC: Duke University Press.

______. 2005. In a Queer Time and Place: Transgender Bodies, Cultural Lives. New York: NYU Press.

Latimer, Heather. 2021. "A Queer Pregnancy: Affective Kinship, Time Travel and Reproductive Choice in Denis Villeneuve's *Arrival*." *Feminist Theory* 22, no. 4: 3–31.

Muñoz, José Esteban. 2009. *Cruising Utopia: The Then and There of Queer Fu*turity. New York: New York University Press.

PART III

Ideological Limitations

The Boundaries of What's Possible

9

THE TELEVISION-INDUSTRIAL CLOSET

Julia Himberg

Between 2020 and 2021, several U.S. television networks and streaming platforms released documentaries on the history of LGBTQ media representation. *Visible: Out on Television* (dir. White), a docuseries on the history of LGBTQ television in the United States was released by Apple. Netflix debuted *Disclosure* (dir. Feder), a documentary that chronicles Hollywood's transgender representation through interviews with writers, actors, producers, and scholars. The cable network FX aired a six-part docuseries titled *Pride*, chronicling the fight for LGBTQ civil rights in the United States as seen through the lens of historical and popular culture events.

Appearing on the heels of the fiftieth anniversary of the 1969 Stonewall Riots, the production and release of these documentaries suggested a triumph of representation wherein a threshold had been met; LGBTQ characters were now an expected and accepted part of the Hollywood landscape, especially on television.[1] No longer a trend, LGBTQ media was officially *out of the closet*.

It is this notion of the being out of the closet that interests me, particularly in *Visible* and *Disclosure*, which are the focus of this analysis. Both are executive-produced by celebrities (*Visible* by Wilson Cruz and Wanda Sykes, and *Disclosure* by Laverne Cox) and are filled with star-studded interviews. They are self-congratulatory pieces of promotion, offering laudatory narratives produced by Hollywood about Hollywood's role in changing (in quality) and increasing (in quantity) representations of LGBTQ people, communities, and stories.

As celebratory stories that signal the fundamental integration of LGBTQ characters and stories into United States media (television in particular), *Visible* and *Disclosure* in different ways and to different degrees offer closure on what has come before and present the incarnation of a new reality, one that includes a deeper and broader range of identities in front of and behind the camera.

This notion that television is out of the closet suggests that television is beyond the closet; *Visible* and *Disclosure* proffer a "post-closet" LGBTQ television landscape

DOI: 10.4324/9781003109044-13

wherein the focus moving forward is on more LGBTQ involvement in making television and on making that involvement more visible (Becker 2007). In making this case, *Visible* and *Disclosure* move forward and backward in time by way of individuals' memories and experiences. Aside from historical footage and clips of television shows (and films), interviews with actors, writers, producers, activists, and newscasters are the center of the documentaries. The privileging of individual voices is a device common to documentary filmmaking, a genre fundamentally invested in "claims to truthfulness" (Aufderheide 2007: 24). The use of voices is one method of validating experiences, providing viewers with a form of witness testimony. As a mode of storytelling, this device gives renewed significance to the past and creates connections among past, present, and futures. In both *Visible* and *Disclosure*, this device allows LGBTQ Hollywood insiders to reflect on their experiences watching television (often as youth) to explain how those experiences informed the strategic performance of their own queerness within the industry, and to describe the ways their television work is the product of those experiences.

These personal stories, in conjunction with the claim that television is beyond the closet, reveal what I call the *television-industrial closet*, a category which shows how the closet has manifested itself in the experiences, beliefs, and practices of industry insiders over time. Defined by dichotomies of agency and autonomy and fear and confinement, the television-industrial closet reflects multiple and conflicting embodiments of queerness and its relationship to discourses of television representation and production. Through this lens, *Visible* and *Disclosure* offer a framework for seeing the interconnections between LGBTQ subject formation and practices of personal conformity and resistance over time, within the specific institutional setting of television.

Setting the Terms: The Television-Industrial Closet

Visible: Out on Television is a five-part docuseries that premiered in February of 2020 on Apple. The series, which chronicles LGBTQ television history since the medium's earliest days, was part of Apple's entry into original content for its streaming TV platform. As part of its initial slate of programming, it was designed to help set the tone for Apple's television brand, run by Tim Cook, who is openly gay. It appeared along with original shows such as *The Morning Show* (2019–) and *Little America* (2020–), offering a brand image that suggests Apple takes a progressive stance on multiple issues. To this end, *Visible* makes explicit attempts to provide a racially diverse range of LGBTQ voices and to cover television's historic lack thereof; its five episodes are narrated by a different actor who each identify with one of the letters in LGBTQ: Lena Waithe as lesbian, Neil Patrick Harris as gay, Margaret Cho as bisexual, Janet Mock as transgender, and Asia Kate Dillon as nonbinary. Notably, white narrators are the minority.

Disclosure was produced as an independent documentary that made its United States debut at the 2020 Sundance International Film Festival. Netflix then acquired the rights to the film and it became available for streaming in June of that same year (a platform that at the time boasted 200 million subscribers) (Spangler 2021). Filled with the voices of famous transgender figures, *Disclosure* is in large part a condemnation of Hollywood's transgender representations, especially on film—television fares better in this history. This indictment is framed as a form of education: we must see and understand the past in order to change representational patterns and tropes in the future. As Yance Ford says early in the documentary, "There are lots of ugly things about our history that feel like an assault…But I think we have to know them. I think we have to learn them." Much of the documentary guides us toward how representational patterns need to change and how this can be accomplished (with more transgender individuals involved at all stages of production).

The opening sequences of the documentaries set a celebratory tone that spotlights the power of television for its role in making LGBTQ lives visible to the greater American public (although the Americanness of this visibility is implicit in the series). In *Visible*, a montage of stars—Ellen DeGeneres, Billy Porter, MJ Rodriquez, Asia Kate Dillon, Adam Lambert, Jill Soloway, Lena Waite, Laverne Cox, and Wilson Cruz—talk about the moment in their careers when they considered walking away from the industry because they weren't, in Rodriguez's words, "being seen." As the montage continues, the tone shifts, sharing moments when their luck changed and their careers took off. Then, as a series of images of contemporary television shows go by, Janet Mock narrates: "Today's television landscape has more diverse LGBTQ visibility than ever before."

Disclosure begins with an equally optimistic tone—the sound of birds chirping plays alongside clips from contemporary transgender films and television series. The first lines of the documentary remark on the moment; Laverne Cox says, "I never thought I'd live in a world where trans people would be celebrated on or off the screen…We are everywhere;" Asia Kate Dillon observes, "We have so much more representation, in government, in media;" and Jen Richards notes, "For the first time, trans people are taking center of their own storytelling."

These opening sequences provide viewers a sense of victory in LGBTQ representation and visibility, suggesting that "we are everywhere" in the twenty-first century. Broadly, this triumph lends itself to the narrative of the multicultural "American Dream," in which incorporation of "Others" in all its forms is linear and infinite, and where all individuals have an equal opportunity to shape their own destinies.[2] For LGBTQ life in the United States, this progress narrative holds that since the mid-twentieth century, there has been a steady rise in LGBTQ social and political equality, including shifts in rights, policy, representation, and public opinion.

Implicit in this narrative—and in the ways *Visible* and *Disclosure* begin—is that television has reached a post-closet moment. Since the 1990s, what have been termed "post-closet," "post-gay," and more recently "post-queer," have gained currency within discourses about television representation. These images have been seen as popular and progressive forms of representation. In them, sexuality and gender identities do not define characters and their motivations on a show. LGBTQ lives on television, as Suzanna Danuta Walters writes, "are largely presented with a world of already-out gays whose coming out is either in the past or fairly inconsequential" (Walters 2014: 63). In a post-closet TV landscape, identity categories have been transcended so that they no longer require self-identification or self-disclosure. Instead, coming out seems to be a relic of the twentieth century.[3]

This televisual mode often has been celebrated because of the ways coming out has long been "the master narrative" of LGBTQ representations in TV history (Walters 2014: 28). Over the previous decades, when LGBTQ (especially L, G, and B) characters appeared in television programs, the storylines focused almost exclusively on their coming out. These storylines also often revolved around the struggles of a character's heterosexual friends and family to come to terms with their sexuality and/or gender identity. In this way, the character's plotline did not move past this "single cataclysmic moment" and privileged the reactions of heterosexual characters over those experiences of LGBTQ characters (Walters 2003: 105).

My focus, though, is not on debating whether U.S. television has reached post-closet status; rather this analysis is invested in examining how *Visible* and *Disclosure's* personal narratives reveal a television-industrial closet. The specificity of this closet comes from how it departs from the stories of representation that both documentaries tell; in other words, walking viewers through the history of LGBTQ representation, insiders complicate that very history. Although *Visible* and *Disclosure* trace LGBTQ history on television as a mix of victory and tragedy, their overall structures move from LGBTQ tele-invisibility to visibility, from the closet to coming out. Both documentaries, but *Visible* in particular, offer largely uncomplicated histories of television's LGBTQ representation, telling straightforward stories of how television representations have changed (read: improved) over time. Yet, the documentaries' personal narratives offer a counterpoint to this overly neat story; the television-industrial closet, instead, is an ambivalent space that moves beyond the cultural studies-based story of representation, offering a deeper, infrastructural, media-industrial transformation that is about how queerness is made within and outside the industry.

The Closet as Career Strategy

The television-industrial closet is fundamentally engaged with the history of twentieth century coming out. The impetus to come out stems from associations with the closet as a place of shame and with coming out as the opposite—as a space of liberation, freedom, and honesty.[4] Stories throughout *Visible* and *Disclosure* engage directly with the persistence of the closet and coming out in television; after all, the titles of these two documentaries themselves betray the centrality of the closet and coming out to their premises. *Visible,* for example, features interviews with Sheila Kuehl talking about her experience realizing her own lesbianism while she starred in *The Many Lives of Dobie Gillis* (CBS, 1959–1963). "Television profoundly affects how people feel about themselves" she says detailing her acute awareness that her sexuality could not be known, within or outside Hollywood. Kuehl's comments underscore that coming out was not a genuine consideration (if she wanted a career in television and later in politics). It was also not, according to her experience, a politically motivated concept; rather, it was a matter of self-preservation and awareness, conscious or not, of the repression that rendered her lesbianism deviant and something to hide.

Visible does not leave this history in the past; in the same episode that features Kuehl, Raven-Symoné describes how her lesbianism came into conflict with the family-friendly genre she had been molded to fit for the Disney Channel's *That's So Raven* (2003–2007). She adds that after the U.S. Supreme Court's 2013 marriage ruling, which struck down the Defense of Marriage Act, she tweeted, "I can finally get married! Yay government! So proud of you." Immediately, she was advised to take down the tweet, as it was the first time she publicly acknowledged her sexuality (she did not remove the post). By presenting both of these personal recountings, especially in the same episode, *Visible* denies the progress narrative that tells us the constraints of the closet were limited to television's early years.

Disclosure also offers stories of working in television from within the closet, ones that reflect the realities of being transgender in Hollywood and the challenging personal choices made to build a career. Candis Cayne, one of the first (if not the first) out transgender actors to play a recurring transgender character on primetime television (in *Dirty Sexy Money*, ABC, 2007–2009), talks about a role she played on the procedural *CSI: Crime Scene Investigation* (CBS, 2000–2015) where her character was dead. In the episode, detectives comment on her "big hands," "big feet," and "breast enhancement." Cayne recalls, "I wanted to sit up off the table and be like, 'you guys, that's bullshit. That is so stupid. Come on.' You know what I mean? But I was just like, 'You know what? Let it go.'" Sandra Caldwell calls Cayne's choice "living stealth." Caldwell describes opting to leave the ballroom world decades earlier in order to work in Hollywood (being part of the ballroom scene would have outed her as transgender). She asks,

> Do you know what it's like to go on a set and be afraid? Your head is trying desperately to stay in the scene. You wake up afraid. You go to sleep afraid. You're trying to figure out if somebody's gonna drop the bomb that day, the next day.

For both Cayne and Caldwell, they explicitly talk about keeping themselves closeted as a means to an end: a career and a livelihood.[5]

These narratives refuse the argument that coming out equals liberation; instead, consciously or not, insiders' active navigation of the closet aligns in part with Judith Butler's widely cited argument that discrete identities themselves are merely ruses of "normalizing power" (Butler 1996). Yet, Cayne and Caldwell's eventual coming out points to the ways that even if a tactic of "normalizing power," LGBTQ insiders' coming out has been a chief organizing principle of television's history.

Indeed, followed to its logical conclusion, it is precisely these careful and intentional negotiations of the closet and coming out that allow *Visible* and *Disclosure* to make their post-closet claim. Caldwell notes this when she talks about coming out later in life and in her career to *The New York Times* in 2016: "It was so frightening. Then I started having meetings with ABC and NBC, and yes, Fox. Who knew?" She explains how stunned she was that as a black transgender actor, she was in demand. After "living stealth" for decades, her identity didn't end her career (as she'd long feared); more than that, television networks were interested in her as an openly transgender woman, not despite it as post-closet rhetoric would have us believe.

In *Visible*, the singer Adam Lambert offers a personal account of his experiences with television that also refuses the liberatory narrative of the closet, although differently from Caldwell. Describing the conditions of appearing as a contestant on *American Idol* (Fox, 2002–2016, ABC, 2018–) he explains that the show, like all reality programming, had "types." In detailing his experience, he says, "there's no place for someone like me" because, he says, he was "too gay." He uses the example of the televised 2009 American Music Awards in which he kissed a male keyboard player and gestured to the audience with his middle finger. This event generated enormous backlash and his appearance the next day on *Good Morning America* (ABC, 1975–) was canceled. As a result, he says the "industry pulled back." Lambert's refusal to stay in the closet, especially not to adhere to its homonormative pressures challenges both the rhetoric of the closet and coming out (in which "clear improvements take place") and demonstrates the industrial disciplining that can come from such a refusal (Barnhurst 2007: 13).

To varying degrees, then, aspects of *Visible* and *Disclosure's* interviews reflect the structures and effects of the closet and coming out, echoing the notion that "'coming out' has its benefits and its disadvantages, but either way, the call to come out presupposes that such an action is in and of itself transformative" (Sullivan 2003: 31). This level of engagement with the closet and coming out is arguably rooted in television's integral relationship to what I would call "Stonewall visibility politics."

Television Insiders as Spectators

Visible and *Disclosure*'s stories of insiders watching television, long before they dreamed of careers in Hollywood, underscore Stonewall visibility politics' mandate that coming out was vital to making change. In the first years after the Stonewall Riots of 1969, gay liberationists "shifted away from arguments for privacy as autonomy, and toward public visibility and publicity" (Duggan 2003: 52). As Michael Bronski writes, "For gay liberationists, coming out was not simply a matter of self-identification. It as a radical, public act that would impact every aspect of a person's life. The publicness of coming out was the decisive break from the past" (Bronski 2011: 209). Seen as a route to social, economic, and political liberation at that time, visibility politics advocates demanded that LGBTQ people come out of the closet in order to form visible communities worthy of anti-discrimination policies, privacy protections, and equal access to American institutions such as marriage.[6]

From the outset, television was seen as vital to this work; as a mass medium uniquely bound up with domesticity and intimacy, television was understood as a crucial site of power and recognition. In the post-Stonewall era, advocates sought influence over mainstream TV content though direct involvement with networks, advertiser boycotts, and use of the mainstream press to generate support from broader society.[7]

On one hand, the emphasis on interviewees as television spectators themselves is leverage for the documentaries' larger argument: we need more LGBTQ representation in front and behind the camera. As Jen Richards says in *Disclosure,* "There is a one-word solution to almost all the problems in trans media. We just need more." On the other hand, LGBTQ insiders' personal stories of watching television in the past are – often emotional – testimonials about the consequences of harmful or damaging representations, thus undercutting claims that coming out equals liberation.

Throughout the series, insiders talk about the influence TV images had on them—how they functioned as affirmation, as lack of representation, and/or as a model of how not to behave. In *Visible*, Lena Waithe describes watching *All in the Family* (CBS, 1971–1979) with her own family; observing their reactions, Waithe notes that her grandmother liked the show and didn't say anything negative about its gay and lesbian characters, confirming the conventional belief that "representations of the [LGBTQ] community move from the marginal to the mainstream" (Barnhurst 2007: 3). She used this experience of watching television to gauge how her family might respond to her own queerness, which she had not yet revealed.

In other stories, television acts as a tool of education and discipline, aligned with critiques about the limits of the closet; Tim Gunn recalls the abuse he received from his father, an FBI agent who lashed out at him as a child after watching TV news coverage about "homosexuals" during the McCarthy era. With tears in his eyes, Gunn talks about his own suicide attempt and hospitalization as a teen, which he says were the result of the images he saw on television, images that taught him "what not to be." In *Disclosure*, Laverne Cox talks similarly about growing up in Mobile, Alabama, where her first exposure to transgender images was on television. "Even when those characters weren't necessarily trans-identified," she says, "they affected how I thought about myself as a trans person and how the general public probably thinks about trans people… These images…just made me hate me." For Gunn and Cox, television reinforced the repressiveness of the closet and its "top-down or macro conception of power" which contain and stigmatize LGBTQ people (Dean 2014: 27).

To a different end, Marquise Vilson recalls watching an episode of the infamous *Jerry Springer Show* (NBC, 1991–2018) that ran with the caption "My boyfriend is a girl." Vilson says,

> Not only was this the first time I was seeing someone transmasculine on television, it was the first time, clearly, that I was seeing somebody Black and

> transmasculine on television…so to see this image…in front of me on TV… it really was empowering.

Vilson's experience speaks to many LGBTQ audiences who have found validation in problematic and even damaging images. Here, their experiences are aligned with theories of "pleasure as jouissance," which Wendy Hilton-Morrow and Kathleen Battles describe as involving "a more purposeful form of engagement that moves beyond taking what is pleasurable, but *making* pleasurable and useful meanings from material that otherwise denies or reviles one's existence" (Hilton-Morrow and Battles 2015: 145).

In *Disclosure,* Jen Richards offers an experience between these two: reflecting on what it might have been like had she never seen herself represented in media, she says,

> On one hand, I might not have ever internalized that sense of—of being monstrous, of having fears around disclosure, of seeing myself as something abhorrent and as a punchline and as a joke…On the flip side, would I even know I'm trans if I had never seen any kind of depiction of gender variance on-screen?

Her account embodies an ambiguity, a both/and framing of the types of LGBTQ representation that have historically populated the medium. Her experience is emblematic of the "paradox of visibility," in which an act like coming out or being out "begin[s] from assertions accepted as true about a positive good…but the value in each case turns out to be at least partly negative, contrary to expectation" (Barnhurst 2007: 2).

These stories are, in part, an educational tool, making the argument that images have real effects on viewers. Cox makes this explicit when she says,

> Seeing trans people loved, uplifted, and well regarded in film and television can endear you to step in when you see a trans person being harassed on the street, and to make sure the trans people in your life are supported in ways that affirm their humanity.

It is true that claims about "media effects" have been complicated and debunked by scholars in the humanities and social sciences. However, as I have written about elsewhere, although the relationship between television and audiences cannot be reduced to cause and effect, the belief in television's power endures and therefore matters.[8]

Indeed, *Visible* and *Disclosure* hinge on the belief that media, especially television, have been drivers of broad-based cultural change. Simply put, both documentaries are premised on the belief that representation matters, a phrase that has become hegemonic: it has become a rehearsed story wherein representation is a form of cultural currency, providing recognition and validation that social minorities are a visible (and valued) part of the national landscape.[9]

Making Television That Is Personal

This belief is particularly evident in the documentaries' stories that express how insiders' queer identities and experiences of those identities determined the ways they made television over the years. Perhaps unsurprisingly, they are often motivated to create a character or to write a storyline based on a desire to offer the queer images they did not see of themselves growing up, images they believe would have positively affected how they viewed their own queerness. These insiders are also equally invested in writing the types of characters and storylines that they feel would have made their experiences of coming out (to family and friends) easier.

In *Visible,* openly gay show creators including Greg Berlanti, Peter Paige, and Max Mutchnick articulate an impulse to provide inspirational and well-rounded LGBTQ characters specifically for youth audiences. Berlanti talks about being asked to take over as showrunner of *Dawson's Creek* in 2000 (The WB, 1998–2003): he said he would agree if the network let two male characters share a kiss. The network did agree but hoped for "some middle ground with regards to its portrayal" (Topel 2020). Instead, Berlanti says he "insisted on a closeup" shot, going against what the network wanted. His insistence, he explains, came from how meaningful it would have been to see that image when he was growing up. Peter Paige co-creator of *The Fosters* (Freeform, 2013–2018) discusses the significance of the character of Jude (Hayden Byerly) in the series. Jude, one of the family's foster children comes out as gay during the series. For Paige, Jude's story resonated with his own and offered youth a vital character to look up to.

Here, insiders identify with the audience in ways that fit with Pierre Bourdieu's "field theory," in which television insiders are "homologous" with their audiences, sharing the sensibilities and tastes of their audiences (Bourdieu 1993). Insiders like Berlanti and Paige assume a set of common outlooks that their audiences have for understanding and assessing television, outlooks usually rooted in experiences of social class. Following Bourdieu's analysis, insiders are innately drawn to producing cultural representations that resonate with their own experiences, in this case of being queer. Notably, as white insiders, Berlanti and Paige's stories align easily with their efforts to bring television further out of the closet because of the whiteness of the closet/coming out paradigm.

This ease is also true for Max Mutchnick who talks about the success of *Will & Grace* (NBC, 1998–2004, 2017–2020). He attributes it to writers' overt attempts to "write for our parents." His comment and others in both documentaries tow a familiar line: the industry's tendency to bring the audience along through normative (assimilationist and often stereotypical) characters and stories. Lynne Joyrich aptly describes this programming as content "that will keep [audiences] 'content,' in the sense of comfortable, via a program of easily digestible content" (Joyrich

2019: 193). In this sense, insiders' anecdotes echo broadcast TV's history of least offensive programming aimed at the so-called middle. Victoria Johnson defines the

> '"middle" [as] both structural and imagined. It is structural as a capital relation expression through strategic market expansion and development and definitions of consumer demography...[The middle] is also symbolic capital, expressed through aesthetic distinctions and presumptions regarding audience disposition or "tastes."
>
> *Johnson 2008: 6*

These creators' stories, though, also imply a degree of agency within the television-industrial closet that is less about institutional policy and more about the personal nature of decision-making among LGBTQ insiders. They reveal that within the television-industrial closet, some insiders in positions of power have the capacity to make decisions based on personal experience even while subject to industrial limitations. Seen this way, even in their normativity, these personal stories make visible a more heterogeneous and less homogeneous landscape of creative labor in television.

Conclusion

The television-industrial closet represents a network of power composed of a community of insiders who deploy their queer identities and experiences in a range of ways. To some degree, they reinforce conventional televisual bounds of the closet and coming out. In other ways, their stories undermine and complicate those hallmarks of LGBTQ television. In tracking the increased numbers and types of LGBTQ people and stories included in TV, *Visible* and *Disclosure's* personal stories offer an antidote to the documentaries' sometimes simplistic narratives that move queerness from invisibility to visibility.

The opening of the television-industrial closet through *Visible* and *Disclosure* then simultaneously marks a definitive historical event and an undoubtedly inflated set of public relations stories. They signal the progress that has been made in representation as television has come out and emphasize future directions focused on more inclusive LGBTQ images and more diverse LGBTQ storytellers in positions of power. This call comes at a time when GLAAD (the nation's largest LGBTQ media watch-dog organization) reported in 2021 that LGBTQ television representation decreased for the first time since the 2013–2014 TV season.[10] The press picked up on the decrease but also focused on another finding in the report: as *The Advocate*'s Daniel Reynolds wrote,

> More troublingly, these [LGBTQ] characters are clustered in shows helmed by only four Hollywood power players: out creators Greg Berlanti, Lena Waithe, and Ryan Murphy and ally Shonda Rhimes. Collectively, their 16

> series accounted for 17 percent of all LGBTQ+ representation (62 of 360 characters).
>
> *Reynolds 2021*

This concentration of power gives credence to *Visible* and *Disclosure*'s insistence that, as *Visible* says in its final episode: "We are not past homophobia, racism, invisibility. We have to add layers of class, language, color, and ability...We [therefore] need more outlets for LGBTQ storylines and creators."

Attention to and interest in queer television insiders behind-the-scenes, although relatively recent, is not unique to these documentaries. However, few commercially made documentaries center queer voices to the extent that *Visible* and *Disclosure* do. Apart from scant others, such as HBO's *The Out List* (2013), they are the only star-studded LGBTQ documentaries I'm aware of that use personal stories as a narrative device to move through historical turning points and to create bridges across time. As such, they underscore the personal influence television has had on Hollywood insiders and their work in television. Indeed, the television-industrial closet makes visible how much character and content development relies on personal experiences with television, rather than on, say, data-driven systems such as audience research (an area that has exploded in the age of algorithms and big data). In other words, the personal stories of queer insiders come to bear on television's past and provide crucial value because they inflect and inform how television is made and how audiences are conceived of. In this way, personal stories are how the television-industrial closet gets unlocked and made visible.

Even curated and produced, *Visible* and *Disclosure* articulate how industry insiders are active agents in the production of images of and knowledge about LGBTQ identities and lives. While these are only one set of personal stories, they offer the notion that, together, there is an institutional structure—a television-industrial closet—for how the closet and coming out have functioned within the industry. The television-industrial closet represents a coming out story of its own. Regardless of whether U.S. television is post-closet, *Visible* and *Disclosure* bring some of Hollywood out of the closet in new ways, ways that offer deeper insights into how LGBTQ television has operated over much of its history.

Notes

1 HBO Max also debuted the four-part series *Equal* in 2020 about the lives and activism of the leaders whose work pre-Stonewall (1940s–1970) set in motion the post-Stonewall LGBTQ rights movement. Although not explicitly about the history of queer media representation, it also emerges to mark a turning point at the fiftieth anniversary of the Stonewall Riots.

2 The progress narrative is problematic because of the ways it leaves some out and doesn't account for the realities of social change, which are not linear and do not affect all people in the same ways and to the same degrees.

3 From the vantage point of cultural critics, post-closet rhetoric is tied up with a host of worrisome implications. As part of a broader neoliberal system, it reflects a shift from a focus on collective consciousness about sexuality and sexual identity to an individualism that emphasizes the free market and consumption as the route to social and political equality. Scholars have also critiqued the assimilationist patterns in these representations where "equality" means characters whose class, race, gender, and ability align with white, gender-conforming, and middle and upper-class heteronormative representations.

4 Scholars have long critiqued, complicated, and contextualized the closet and coming out across multiple registers including the ways the closet/coming out paradigm creates and reinforces a binary between heterosexuality and homosexuality, and by extension normativity and non-normativity as well as how this paradigm does not account for sexuality and gender identity's historically situated nature. In addition, because sexuality and gender identity become organizing principles of one's identity in this framework, they become connected to other aspects unrelated to queer identity, including one's choices in cultural products and leisure activities. One consequence of this understanding of identity is that other aspects of social difference such as race, class, gender, age, nationality, and immigration status become marginalized because of the ways LGBTQ identities are centered above all else.

5 These experiences are not limited to Hollywood but are common across industries and institutions, prompting policy reforms to protect LGBTQ people from employment discrimination.

6 Initially post-Stonewall activists were far more radical in their calls for visibility; visibility was about difference, about liberating oneself from the trappings of heteronormativity.

7 See K. Montgomery, 1990. *Target: Prime Time: Advocacy Groups and the Struggle over Entertainment Television*. New York: Oxford University Press.

8 See J. Himberg, 2018. *The New Gay for Pay: The Sexual Politics of American Television Production*. Austin: University of Texas Press.

9 This investment in representation in both documentaries is unsurprising given that most of those who made them and those who appear in them work in television and thus are committed to beliefs about the medium's power to connect with viewers and to increase rates of LGBTQ acceptance more broadly. Their professions bank on visibility after all—to maintain careers, and recruit and retain audiences (and often advertisers).

10 For full report see: www.glaad.org/wherewereontv20

References

Aufderheide, P. 2007. *Documentary Film: A Very Short History*. Oxford: Oxford University Press.

Barnhurst, K. 2007. Visibility as Paradox: Representation and Simultaneous Contrast. In *Media Q: Media/Queered: Visibility and Its Discontents*, ed. Barnhurst, K. New York: Peter Lang.

Becker, R. 2007. Post-Closet Television. *Flow* 7, no. 3 (November). www.flowjournal.org/2007/11/post-closet-television/. (Accessed November 12, 2020).

Bourdieu, P. 1993. *The Field of Cultural Production*. Cambridge: Polity Press.

Bronski, M. 2011. *A Queer History of the United States*. Boston: Beacon Press.

Butler, J. 1996. *Bodies That Matter*. New York: Routledge.

Dean, J.J. 2014. *Straights: Heterosexuality in Post-Closeted Culture*. New York: NYU Press.

Duggan, L. 2003. *The Twilight of Equality? Neoliberalism, Cultural Politics, and the Attack on Democracy*. Boston: Beacon Press.

Hilton-Morrow, W. and Battles, K. 2015. *Sexual Identities and the Media: An Introduction*. New York: Routledge.

Johnson, V. E. 2008. *Heartland TV Prime Time Television and the Struggle for U.S. Identity*. New York: New York University Press.

Joyrich, L. 2019. Keyword 8: Trigger Warnings. *differences: A Journal of Feminist Cultural Studies*, 30(1), 189–196.

Reynolds, D. 2021. GLAAD TV Report: LGBTQ+ Representation, Driven by Four Creators, Dips. *The Advocate*, January 14. www.advocate.com/television/2021/1/14/glaad-tv-report-lgbtq-representation-driven-four-creators-dips. (Accessed March 2, 2021).

Spangler, T. 2021. Netflix Tops 200 Million Streaming Customers, Handily Beats Q4 Subscriber. Forecast. *Variety* (January 19). https://variety.com/2021/digital/news/netflix-q4-2020-earnings-200-million-subscribers-1234887784/. (Accessed March 3, 2021).

Sullivan, N. 2003. *A Critical Introduction to Queer Theory*. New York: New York University Press.

Topel, P. 2020. 'Dawson's Creek' Producer Greg Berlanti Says He Ignored Network Restrictions to Show Jack's Gay Kiss on TV. Showbiz Cheatsheet (June 24). www.cheatsheet.com/entertainment/dawsons-creek-producer-greg-berlanti-says-he-ignored-network-restrictions-to-show-jacks-gay-kiss-on-tv.html/. (Accessed March 3, 2021).

Walters, S.D. 2003. *All the Rage: The Story of Gay Visibility in America*. Chicago: University of Chicago Press.

Walters, S.D. 2014. *The Tolerance Trap: How God, Genes, and Good Intentions Are Sabotaging Gay Equality*. New York: New York University Press.

10

TV'S INS AND OUTS, OR (BAT) SIGNALS AND (CAPED) CRUSADES

Lynne Joyrich

Televisual Logics in the Age of Trump

It's been common to hear that we now live in a global post-race, post-gender (or at least post-sexist), post-heterosexist (or at least post-closet)—and not at all unrelated to those supposed "posts"—post-television culture. Yet this is certainly belied by the political existence and impact of Donald Trump and by the broader ethos and epistemology of Trumpism (and related –isms around the world). In the wake of those, racism, misogyny, homo- and trans-phobia, and nationalisms have been on the rise, and battles we might have thought were won (for example, in the United States, for fair voting and other civil rights, for affordable health care, for sexual and reproductive freedoms, for equal recognition, legitimation, and the ability to live free of violence for people of color, women, queer folks) are again up for grabs. Indeed, these battles were never simply "won"; they were—and urgently are—areas of critical struggle.

These struggles are not at all unrelated to television, and, just as we are not post-race, post-gender, or post-closet, we are certainly not post-television. Television remains our dominant medium, of critical importance to all, not simply to Donald Trump—who ran not just his campaigns (focused hardly on policy but on media-branded personality), but his presidency like a reality program, treating the country like a game of *Survivor* in which pitting "tribe" against "tribe" was seen as the way to "make it work"—before he himself was declared "the weakest link," told "you're fired" and it's time to "sashay away" (all, of course, catchphrases from popular reality shows, including Trump's own previous program, *The Apprentice*).[1]

While Trumpian politics make clear the significance of television (for Trump, TV ratings are the highest measure of ... well, everything, and, in his use of TV tactics, Trump revealed how powerful televisual formations can be), this significance has blinked in and out of view, potent even, or especially, as it's disavowed. As stated, TV

DOI: 10.4324/9781003109044-14

is still a (if not *the*) central medium, with more people watching more and more television and its convergent media forms (such as online video, also a form of "television" or remote seeing) than ever. Whether broadcast or delivered by cable, satellite, or streaming, across all the devices on which we might watch (including, but hardly limited to, home TV sets, given also, for instance, Jumbotrons in public areas and private screens on hand-held, even wristwatch, devices), television is located on, at, and surrounding our bodies, ourselves, our worlds. Indeed, researchers say, across all those screens, people cumulatively spend more time watching televisual material (broadly defined) than doing anything else aside from working and sleeping.[2]

Yet, oddly, at the same time as this televisual explosion, TV is often pronounced "over": not as revered as cinema and not as cutting edge as digital media forms—even as both cinema and digital platforms are becoming more televisual, given the economics of both industries that have led them to adopt televisual commercial and releasing strategies as well as, relatedly, televisual textual strategies. TV then makes an enormous impact, working to construct the very ways we think (or don't think), even though, or precisely since, we don't often critically think much about TV itself (with people, other than media scholars, typically not bothering to ponder it despite—or paradoxically, exactly because of—its proliferation into all aspects of our lives).[3] The question of how we might ponder not just *about* but, indeed, *through* television has been the focus of my work; I'm fascinated by the complexities of televisual logics and how they yield ways of knowing or not knowing—especially ways of knowing or not knowing about gender, sexuality, and race in the United States. Bringing outer worlds into our interiors, just as we're made privy to the inner lives of its characters (including its fantasy-inducing "real life" characters); sliding across the factual and fictional (and everything in between); generating shock and crisis (the better to keep us watching) while also acting as a shock absorber (again, the better to keep us watching),[4] television both articulates and blurs the boundaries through which we think, feel, and act. In so doing, it produces ambivalent formations, epistemologies, and politics of identity, from the stirring of (some) feminist, queer, and anti-racist affects to, as noted, the stoking of tribal alliances that are not so dissimilar from the "tribes" of reality show competitions.

Television's constructions of nation, race, gender, sexuality, and their intersections are thus crucial to interrogate;[5] indeed, as my particular focus in this piece, the question of sexuality in TV—and sexuality as question for TV—is enormously telling. For sexuality itself spans the interiorized and the relational, the real and the fantasized, the personalized and the publicized, sensation and signification, creation and recreation, making its relation to the media both mutually formative and maddeningly fraught. This is something I've elaborated in my prior work on what, in homage to Eve Kosovsky Sedgwick's "Epistemology of the Closet,"[6] I termed "the epistemology of the console": a reference to the traditional cabinetry housing introduced at the time when TV was becoming a fixture in homes (and thus a major cultural force) both to display and hide television sets, and so already a figure of the closet with its play of concealing and revealing, the screened in and screened out.[7] That doubleness (homey/unhomey, inconspicuous/exhibited, intimate/alienated, able to be tucked away/capable of being anywhere) has been inscribed in television itself: positioned pivotally at the border of ordinary and unusual, domestic and social, familial and extrafamilial, inside and outside, TV is key to our now-fully-mediatized culture's production of sexuality, which is constituted by its position within and across these same borders. Indeed, one might argue that sexuality has been characterized in Western modernity precisely by the terms of "in" and "out," whether as heterosexual cliché or queer struggle.[8]

Television's definition (and redefinition) of these categories, and its construction and confounding of the borders between them, is thus central to the articulation of sexuality today, and its operations of defining sexuality extend beyond the hide-and-seek of the deployment or the disparagement of so-called explicit sexual content. That is, TV's production of sexuality, normative or non-normative, does not only rely on the portrayal of sexualized characters or acts; the mere presence of "out" queer characters on TV thus does not, in itself, erase the dynamics of the "epistemology of the console." That epistemology regulates not only character portrayal but the very structure of commercial TV, encompassing everything from television's temporal organization (which, even with changes in technology and viewing, is still largely ordered around normative patterns of work and leisure, with assumptions about familiar/familial routine determining scheduling and flow, even as there are also specific "fringe" times and "edgy" programming to appease and contain the extrafamilial), through its marketing logic (again defined by familial or "fringe" associations, even as that "fringe" label becomes more and more a fetishized category), to its programs' narrative problematics (which, whether through episodic series or continuing serials, must balance between stasis and change, repetition and alteration, the everyday and the eventful as each program attempts to "reproduce" itself over time).[9]

The latter, for instance, helps to explain why commercial television can still have some difficulty dealing with "regular"—that is, ongoing—queer characters, for whom sexuality is continuous without it having to be of continuous concern.[10] Even in programs that don't seem to founder on that difficulty, there is no simple "post-closet" but a complex configuration—one that may get us to question what we even mean by "regular" and/or "queer," "closet" and/or "reveal," "continuous," and/or "post" and thus one that might help us think about how best to intervene in televisual logics and televisual politics (that is, our politics today) that refuse simple binaries. Let me turn to a reading of a particular text to illustrate.

Bat Signals and Caped Crusading[11]

In October 2019, *Batwoman* premiered on the cable channel The CW, featuring an out queer actor, Ruby Rose, playing out lesbian character, Kate Kane aka Batwoman—"the first lesbian superhero to headline her own series."[12] Per the program's premise, Kate decides to take on the mantle of "caped crusader" after her cousin Bruce Wayne disappeared, abandoning the role of Batman and leaving Gotham City without the protection it desperately needs. As suggested by this narrative device of a cousin swap, *Batwoman* is a superhero program that is also a family melodrama, with the primary plots in its premiere season involving not simply crime-fighting but the miseries, masquerades, and misbehaviors that stem from Kate's family's complicated history and web of relations (which includes a traumatized and now villainous sister; another "good" version of that sister from another dimension; a tough father who treats Kate's ex-lover as almost more of a daughter than his own children; a second wife and her daughter, Kate's stepsister Mary, who longs to be close to Kate; a surrogate brother of the villainous sister; various lovers, exes, friends, associates, and partners-in-crime; and, constantly invoked if never seen, cousin Bruce Wayne/Batman himself). Such a "super-melodrama" is well poised to take on questions of subjectivity and sociality, embodiment and enactment, self-knowledge and awareness (or lack thereof) of others. After all, identity and its performances comprise a central concern not only of melodrama. The superhero genre has long been used, across comics, films, and television programs, to provide allegories for the challenges of identity-in-difference and difference-in-identity, deploying stories of masked heroes with alter-egos and secret identities to comment on political, racial, gender, and/or sexual formations that propel people into double lives—including the double life that can arise from being a closeted queer.

But that is not exactly Kate's problem. Living in a universe that seems oddly both more and less homophobic than ours, Kate is expelled from a military academy given her world's draconian "don't ask, don't tell" policy (whereas that policy was repealed in the United States in 2011) yet seems to face no other problems being out. Rather, her problem is the imbrication of "out" and "in" that she cannot escape, at least if she wants to save her city and the people she loves. In a kind of inversion of the usual "secret identity" trope, in which the superhero mask stands in for other kinds of maskings (such as of sexuality), here sexual identity is invoked as a way to understand the tribulations and trade-offs of being a disguised savior.

The irony of this is made clear early in the series. The fourth episode, aptly titled "Who Are You?," features Kate's voice-over as she reflects on adopting the persona of "the bat," ostensibly musing to her absent cousin Bruce Wayne (so, in effect, voicing these thoughts to herself) about the difficulties of being a superhero:

> I have never hidden who I am. I came out when Brad Morrison told all the kids at school that I was gay. I said "yeah, and?"; then punched him. Ever since then, I've been out and proud, as long as I can remember. So how the hell am I supposed to wake up every morning and hide who I am?

After she vanquishes the villain-of-the-week and gets some clues about her villainess sister for that ongoing narrative arc, Kate returns to her voice-over:

> Dear Bruce... Lies don't make anyone comfortable, especially the one telling them. But no one said anything about this job being comfortable. If I'm going to embrace the bat, then I'm going to have to embrace hiding a part

> of myself from the outside world. Living this double life is a sacrifice—but our city is worth it.

The titular question of "Who Are You?" is not as easily answerable as it seems, and struggling with it—not simply for the self but for others—is apparently inevitable. (It is also not just a question for Kate, as various subplots involve mysteries and misperceptions surrounding the outer appearances and inner character of several others on the show, all of whom have "secret identities" in one way or another.)

Rather than this program, celebrated for its out lead character, being beyond the closet then, it is only possible through it. The maskings and secret identities provide the very basis of the plots and make the characters (both like us yet unlike us, familiar but with more enigmatic and exciting lives) worth televising. Without that closet, yet also without it's being breached, there would be no show—or certainly no queer show. Indeed, it is precisely the mix of "in" and "out" in *Batwoman* that, according to one reviewer of the episode, marks "the critical difference between stories with queer characters & queer stories."[13] That is, the play with and between closeting and uncloseting allows the program to comment on queerness and to produce a narrative that is not a simple story but a multiply inflected one (as is its lead, a multimedia character in a show with its own multi-verse, a superhero with no actual superpowers, a singular person with a double life, saving her city while struggling with her family, figured as "woman" and "bat," situated as "out" and "in").

We are not then, in any simple way, "beyond the closet"—even in a time period that's been called "post-closet," not to mention "post-television"—as those "posts" depend upon the very terms that they, simultaneously, revoke and invoke (that they can only revoke *by* invoking). This is not to say that there are not important historical changes, both in sexuality and in television. It is, though, to argue that the "epistemology of the console" I've discussed is still important to consider—perhaps now more than ever, as television, contrary to dismissals of its continuing impact, is not something that can simply be shut away in those old closet-like consoles but is everywhere (via broadcasting and streaming services, across network programming and digitally convergent offerings, with long form continuing stories and seconds-length video bits, on giant screens on streets and tiny screens we wear). It thus calls out to us like an ever-present bat signal, with pervasive televisual logics truly founding (and confounding) our very senses of subjectivity, sexuality, and sociality.[14]

As elaborated in my prior work on this, TV's mix of founding and confounding paradoxically both impels yet impedes unmaskings, visibilities, and "broadcastings." Indeed, even as it is demanded given television's displays and confessional discourses,[15] any simple sense of "full disclosure" on television of sexual identity and desire is nonetheless rendered impossible because of television's existence, as noted above, precisely at and across the lines between the categories by which we even think "sexuality," "identity," and "disclosure." TV asserts yet blurs the boundaries of private/public, inner/outer, personal/political, solitary/shared, expected/extraordinary, pleasure/boredom, and reality/fantasy. Much like that bat signal (a beam of light and shadow, illuminating yet in the dark—or more precisely, only able to illuminate with and through darkness), television thus produces its own shadows and blind spots along with its exposés and spectacles, which is why a politics simply of visibility, while generative in some ways, is inadequate to combating homophobia (and sexism, racism, ethnocentrism, etc.) in television.

Batwoman itself reflects upon the value yet limitations of a politics of visibility, showing the range of relations that may exist between media visibility/invisibility, knowledge/ignorance, and power/disempowerment. The self-reflexive episode "How Queer Everything Is Today!"[16] finds Batwoman "rescued" while trying to stop a runaway train (a rescue she doesn't need) by a hunky, if publicity-seeking, Gotham City cop—a moment that recreates the old melodramatic cliché of a woman saved off the train tracks, now immortalized for Gotham residents through their cellphones. These images make the Gotham City news—including as the subject of gossip spread by diegetic radio personality Vesper Fairchild, who encourages her audience to "ship" the heterosexual couple (i.e., to root for a relationship between them). Not surprisingly, this does not please Kate Kane, who objects to her assistant Luke Fox that she's "very, very gay." But he reminds her that this gossip could be good, keeping Gotham confused and thus helping to maintain the secret identity necessary for Batwoman.

Here, then, visibility is shown to operate against knowledge and power, with their mismatch giving Batwoman an advantage. Still, Kate struggles with this, not happy about what this kind of visibility implies about both her sexual identity and her supposed need to be rescued by a man. Sophie, Kate's ex-lover, is also struggling, both with her own sexual identity and with what she too has been driven to do in her crime-fighting role as a member of Kate's father's elite (and not always equitable or ethical) security force. While investigating the train incident, Batwoman happens upon her; Sophie, who doesn't recognize her as Kate (and who is forbidden by her boss, Kate's dad, from working with the vigilante Batwoman), asks, "You ever feel like you're hiding from the world?" to which Batwoman quips, "I'm literally standing in a shadow." While Sophie goes on to retort that "You're one to talk" to Batwoman's statement that "We all wear a mask; maybe it's time you took yours off," the dynamics of visibility and knowledge are again more complex than one might expect. Batwoman is suggesting that Sophie come out (Kate has wanted this since they were in the military academy together, when Kate did, and was expelled, and Sophie did not, thereby allowing her to complete the program, get the job with Kate's dad, and become a substitute daughter to him), but it is, indeed, only because she's masked and, in the mise-en-scene, cloaked in darkness (thus protecting both of their identities, jobs, and understandings of their relationship) that Batwoman can make this suggestion.

Yet the time comes for Batwoman herself to remove the mask. She tracks down the culprit behind the out-of-control train, only to find a young hacker named Parker (who was in control of the train all along, in a ploy to extort people for money); she committed the crime, she explains, because she was outed to her parents by an ex-girlfriend of her own (who told her that "being in the closet was prehistoric") and needs money to move out: her parents, Parker claims, see her as a freak and want to disown her. Batwoman tries both to admonish and empathize with her, but Parker will have none of it:

> My parents want me to be someone I'm not. Do you know how that feels? I hate myself, ok? And let's raincheck your "It Gets Better" PSA. We both know I'm going to grow up hiding my girlfriends and aspiring to be represented by an ancillary character on my favorite TV show. Just like you were probably the cool girl in high school, and now you're famous and everyone's shipping you with the hottest guy in Gotham. We have nothing in common.... So could you just leave me alone before I find more reasons to wish I was dead?

Parker almost does wind up dead, but not by her own hand. Kate's traumatized and now evil sister, who goes by the name Alice (and endlessly quotes the only book she was allowed to read when held prisoner as a child, *Alice's Adventures in Wonderland*, which provides the quote for this episode's title, "How Queer Everything is Today!"[17]) captures Parker so as to force her to use her hacking power to out Batwoman as Kate Kane to the whole city. This, Alice thinks, will put an end to Kate's do-gooding ways so that she'll instead join forces with Alice, who, in her own plea for family recognition, begs Kate just to accept her for who she is. Outings, then, cut both ways: causing family tensions for Parker but, Alice hopes, family togetherness for her and Kate. To save Parker, Kate does unmask (sparking contrition from Parker for lashing out against someone who turned out to be "super gay"), but Parker tricks Alice, not sending the photo of an exposed Kate to Gotham residents as Alice believes but instead giving their location, prompting Sophie to arrive to save the day.

Batwoman too is a savior in the melee that ensues—in fact, rescuing the very cop who had "rescued" her from the train tracks earlier. But now when the watching crowd urges them to kiss, she refuses the "ship," telling him it's "not happening." The next thing we know, she's on the cover of the diegetic *Catco Magazine*, with the headline "Batwoman Reveals Herself AS A LESBIAN," earning a quip from Vesper Fairchild about "What ever happened to politics staying out of our superheroes?" (a particularly ironic and "meta" moment in its play with the terms of the real and the fictional, outings and closetings, given that Vesper is voiced by out lesbian and MSNBC host Rachel Maddow, known for her political commentary and queer identity). Kate apologizes to her assistant Luke for the risks now to their secrets, but he assures her they'll "figure it out." Even happier with the situation is Parker, who says, "You know, when you took off your mask, I never in a million years expected it to be you... someone like me. I'm glad it was." In what ways, though, we might ask, is Kate "like" Parker? Kate is rich; Parker is desperate for money; Kate is a hero; Parker is a criminal (though, we presume, on the way to redemption). Identity and difference are not such simple matters, particularly when the confusion and conflation around who someone "really" is (diegetically and extradiegetically, in regard to sexuality and to power, enabling or preventing relationships, announced in media headlines or in intimate talks) is what provides the very basis of the show.

At the end of the episode, we are treated again to Kate's voice-over:

> We all wear a mask of some kind. A cowl, a husband, wife, denial, anger. We all need our shield to protect us from the world. But for people like us, it's not always about stopping a runaway train or disarming a bomb... Sometimes the best way to save someone is to be yourself.

But who is this "self"? Over the voice-over, we see Kate's stepsister Mary, who longs for Kate to care about her as much as she cares about the lost-Beth-now-Alice. And then we see a grown-up Beth—not wearing the "Alice" get-up—who has unexpectedly entered Kate's home and talks as if there never was any trauma, any separation, any Alice persona. Kate forcibly grabs her; "Who are you? Who are you?" she shouts. "Me, Beth; who the hell else would I be?" Who else indeed? As it turns out, she is Kate's sister from another dimension (where the events that damaged Beth didn't happen), with this uncanny doubling opening up what will be a new arc in the narrative and new complications to the questions of sameness and difference, identity and multiplicity, knowledge and recognition, inside and outside. But the question lingers (spilling over too from the title of the prior episode discussed, "Who Are You?"). With one revelation of identity comes another riddle; one outing can yield another closeting, and "being yourself" only happens within and across them. Media visibility—even as the lead, not (as Parker quipped) merely an ancillary character, in a mainstream TV show—may initiate possibilities, but this is only the beginning, not the end, of knowledge production, of relational possibilities, of questions of selfhood, and of complexities of politics—which, to Vesper's question, can never stay just in or just out.

Vesper Fairchild, voiced by Rachel Maddow, is not the only figure for whom these issues resonate both "in" and "out" of the text, given the connections and/or contrasts between the people who play the characters and the characters themselves (many of whom are, within the diegesis, also playing even other characters). Indeed, television scholars have questioned the very limits of "inside" or "outside" of "the text" when it comes to television, in which meaning and knowledge draw as much from extratextual, paratextual, and intertextual material as from intratextual formations.[18] There was extratextual controversy when the production of *Batwoman* was announced, specifically around the season 1 casting of Ruby Rose as Kate Kane/Batwoman. A young, photogenic, white Australian model-turned-actor who had defined herself, to the consternation of some, as both "genderfluid" and "lesbian," Rose was deemed by parts of the LGBTQ+ community to be, at once, both too expected and yet too miscast for the role; too pretty and feminine looking, and so, though heavily tattooed, lacking the "butchness" one might want in a crime-fighter, yet not really a "woman" (because of that genderfluid identification) and so not able truly to qualify as a "lesbian"; hence, too mainstream and yet still too weird, too visible and yet not doing enough for visibility—in sum, too queer in some ways, yet not gay enough in others.[19] (Rose, whose tattoos include a cross with a reference to God, was also critiqued by some as an inappropriate choice because she is not Jewish, which Kate Kane is written as being—an interesting parallel given the closet dynamics that can also operate, if not in quite the same way, with ethno-religious identifications and differences, as Sedgwick details in her reading of the Purim story of Queen Esther as a "coming out" as "one of those"—i.e., in that case, as a Jew.[20])

Tracing the demands and desires here can be dizzying: one must "really be" who they "play," even as that "playing" can valuably destabilize and thus queer "being" and "identity"; one must "represent," even as they should alter conventional representation; one should appear, make oneself visible, and be seen, while not becoming defined by appearance or just framed to be seen; one should be clear, direct, unmistakable (i.e., unmediated) while bringing queerness to TV (i.e., being mediatized). But this dizziness, rather than impeding televisual knowledge, proliferates and multiplies it, revealing the twists and turns of television's continuing (if transforming) "epistemology of the console" and the complications that arise in any simple attempt to crusade (caped or not) against it.

"One Day You're In, the Next Day You're Out"[21]

As indicated by the case of *Batwoman*, television's repetitions, reversals, revelations, and revisions continue to produce that epistemology of the console: even in a world that has "out" characters, actors, and stories, there are always accompanying "ins," as the very terms of knowledge, visibility, and expression circulate through and between those categories. But if this means that television still closets in some ways, it suggests as well that television also queers. Just as Batwoman is positioned between the savior and the outlaw, the dutiful family member and the deceitful outsider, the caped and the crusader, television too (as it both familiarizes the unusual and defamiliarizes what would otherwise be too boring to watch) is positioned between the expected and the odd, the mundane and the fantastic—or, one might say, the mainstream and the queer, both asserting and undermining that very division.

This has important consequences, affecting not only the ability of fantasy figures in textual universes to save their worlds but the ability of people in social reality to save our worlds as well. I began by noting how Donald Trump (and Trumpism in general) deployed a televisual logic, and TV's Trumpverse, while it became terrifyingly mainstream, would seem to be about as far from queer logics as one can go. But this analysis suggests otherwise. Both Trumpian and queer formations emerge from the kinds of conjunctions and conflations, ambiguities and ambivalences that televisuality produces (between fact and fiction, affect and sense, authenticity and performance, personal and political). This is why, for example, Trump fans can, despite all his documented lies, consider Donald Trump to be the most authentic politician ever, in that it is nothing but performance that constructs his identity, and that performance perfectly matches his brand. In other words, it is not despite, but precisely because of how his persona, as a kind of actual superhero (to his fans), is so clearly enacted, performed, and branded that he is read as so "real"—which is not so distinct from how queer theory itself understands identity as formed with and through performativity, reality as formed with and through fantasy, politics formed with and through affect, the natural formed with and through the super- or extra-natural, and vice-versa.

This is certainly not to state an equivalency between Trumpism and queerness, both of which are not only reproduced but produced through mediatizations. Of course, there are critical differences in how these categorical conjunctions and disjunctions are realized and deployed. (For example, Trump uses his performative identity simply to bolster himself while attacking the performances, identities, and legitimacies of others, hardly making this the basis for any kind of alliances as one finds in queer politics.) But it is to suggest that we need carefully to consider the operations of these logics, which can open up new possibilities and dimensions but also create double binds on which we may founder, with life and death consequences (regarding, for example, the fantasies and realities surround race and racism today, the public invasion of women's private reproductive choices, the opening to some forms of queer families along with the closure—or, to use a TV term that's taken on wider resonance these days, the "cancelling" and perhaps even renewed outlawing of other relational possibilities). Given these stakes, Trump himself has been "cancelled" and replaced—though in his wake (given what he was able to do with, for instance, the U.S. Supreme Court), there is the fear, as previously noted, that fights people had thought were won will need to be refought.

Coincidentally, Ruby Rose from *Batwoman* was also cancelled (or willing departed, depending on who you listen to), and she too has been replaced.[22] The program's second season features a different actor, playing another character taking on the mantle of Batwoman—though viewers were assured when the announcement was made that this is still a queer character, indeed now even a queer character of color. This also has a certain resonance with the 2020 U.S. elections, to continue my leaps (like those of television itself) between the fantastic and the real. There were disappointing losses that left the balance of Congress in quite a precarious position, but it was nonetheless a trailblazing year for LGBTQ folks, and particularly queers of color, to be elected.[23]

Such presence and visibility in our representations and for our representatives (both those swooping down from the skies in superhero disguises and those on the floor of Congress in less spectacular but still performed roles) is significant, even if, as I've been arguing, presence and visibility aren't enough. Indeed, breaking-ground and trailblazing are necessarily constrained by the very terms of media recognition (or misrecognition) that we may want our heroes, whether in fantastic television programs or in our "real" politics, to question. One critic exclaimed, "a Black queer Batwoman is the new normal" for our pantheon of luminaries, and one might say the same of the recent changes to the slate of those serving in the U.S. government. But that normality—television's taming of the "untamed" and straightening of the "messy"—operates as a double-edged sword (or Batarang).[24]

Equally double-edged is the position of a Black woman in law-and-ordered crime-fighting (fictionalized or actualized)—a genre that, to say the least, has been extremely problematic in terms of its treatments of race as well as gender and sexuality. While Batwoman is a masked vigilante, not precisely a cop (and, in fact, the program calls out policing in its exposure of the Gotham City police department as ineffective; the private security led by Kate Kane's father as an excessive force-using, for-hire-for the-rich, accountable-to-no-one paramilitary operation; and the diegetic "justice" system as often biased, brutal, and unfair), such a position for a Black woman—even as she takes over the role from a former white savior—is one that raises as many issues for assessing representation as it resolves, given ongoing histories of racist policing and vigilantism both on and off television.[25] Similar perils face those who may not enforce the laws, as Batwoman does, but are dedicated to making them, like those aforementioned newly elected Congresspeople.

In sum, the struggles over enactments, emplotments, and enforcements of gender, race, and sexuality go on. For, as I hope I've shown, unlike the way fights may be staged for TV figures, whether reality stars or fantasy superheroes, there isn't a simple opposition of winning or losing (just like there isn't a simple opposition of inside and outside, the mainstreamed and the marginalized, the affective and the effective). We must instead try to understand and intervene in the terms of struggle themselves. It is thus by thinking carefully *about* (not only unthinkingly operating *through*) the logics (or illogics) of our time—so intertwined with the logics of television—that we can best move ahead, to new seasons in TV, in politics, and in social relations.

Notes

1 These are terms from the reality television programs *Survivor* (CBS, 2000–present), *Project Runway* (Bravo, 2004–2008; Lifetime, 2009–2017; Bravo, 2019–present), *The Weakest Link* (BBC, 2000–2012), *The Apprentice* (NBC, 2004–2017), and *RuPaul's Drag Race* (Logo TV, 2009–2016; VH!1, 2017–present). For a discussion of Donald Trump and televisuality, see Lynne Joyrich, "TV Trumps" in *Unwatchable*, eds. Nicholas Baer, Maggie Hennefeld, Laura Horak, and Gunnar Iversen (New Brunswick, NJ: Rutgers University Press, 2019), 293–298.

2 See, for example, Akrur Barua, "Work, Sleep, TV. How Americans Spend Their Days," *The Wall Street Journal*, January 3, 2019, https://deloitte.wsj.com/cmo/2019/01/03/work-sleep-tv-how-americans-spend-their-days/; Joseph O'Halloran, "Mobile Boom but TV Remains the Most Popular Medium," *Rapid TV News*, June 11, 2019, www.rapidtvnews.com/2019061156318/mobile-boom-but-tv-remains-the-most-popular-medium.html#axzz5yzMNmfvD; Michelle Clancy, "TV Set Viewership Is Still King of the Home," *Rapid TV News*, February 7, 2017, www.rapidtvnews.com/2017020746065/tv-set-viewership-is-still-king-of-the-home.html#axzz6lH1hjLhW; Joseph O'Halloran, "More Time Spent with Traditional TV than Other Media Platforms," *Rapid TV News*, February 28, 2020 www.rapidtvnews.com/2020022858138/more-time-spent-with-traditional-tv-than-other-media-platforms.html#axzz6lH1hjLhW; and Daniel Maina Wambugu, "Which Country Watches the Most TV?," *WorldAtlas*, October 1, 2018, www.worldatlas.com/articles/which-country-watches-the-most-tv.html

3 Of course, many people do like to think and talk about television, discussing the plots, the stars, and the "ships" of their favorite programs; indeed that is part of televisual operations, institutions, and impacts. Yet I would suggest that, while there are important connections to foster between these ways of talking about television and a more critical media theory, there is a difference—one that that TV and media industries literally bank on—between being what we might call a clever viewer (one, say, who enjoys getting TV references) and being a critical viewer thinking about televisuality itself as a cultural form and a social force.
4 This notion of television as both shock and shock absorber comes from Patricia Mellencamp, *High Anxiety: Catastrophe, Scandal, Age and Comedy* (Bloomington: Indiana University Press, 1992).
5 See, for example, my pieces "American Dreams and Demons: Television's 'Hollow' Histories and Fantasies of Race," *The Black Scholar* 48.1 (January 2018): 31–42 and "Tubular Vision: The Ins and Outs of Television Studies" in *New Media, Old Media: A History and Theory Reader*, 2nd edition, eds. Wendy Hui Kyong Chun, Anna Watkins Fisher, and Thomas Keenan. New York: Routledge, 2015, 649–664.
6 Eve Kosofsky Sedgwick, *Epistemology of the Closet* (Berkeley: University of California Press, 1990).
7 Lynne Joyrich, "Epistemology of the Console," in *Queer TV: Theories, Histories, Politics*, eds. Glyn Davis and Gary Needham (New York: Routledge, 2009), 15–47. All of the other essays in this collection are also extremely insightful in thinking about formations of sexuality in and through television.
8 I elaborate this in Joyrich, "Tubular Vision."
9 All of these issues have been discussed in great detail across the history of television studies, but some useful references are listed here. For discussions of television's temporal (and spatial) organization around notions of work/leisure and domestic/social categories, see Jane Feuer, "The Concept of Live Television: Ontology as Ideology," in *Regarding Television: Critical Approaches—An Anthology*, ed. E. Ann Kaplan (Frederick, MD: University Publications of America/American Film Institute, 1983), 12–22; Nick Browne, "The Political Economy of the Television (Super) Text," in *Television: The Critical View*, 4th edition, ed. Horace Newcomb (New York: Oxford, 1987), 585–599; David Morley, *Television, Audiences And Cultural Power* (London: Routledge, 1992), 366; and Gary Needham, "Scheduling Normativity: Television, the Family, and Queer Temporality," in *Queer TV: Theories, Histories, Politics*, eds. Glyn Davis and Gary Needham (New York: Routledge, 2009), 143–158. For a further discussion of television's marketing and commodity logic, see (among many other works): Eileen R. Meehan, "Watching Television: A Political Economic Approach" in *A Companion to Television*, ed. Janet Wasko (Malden, MA: Blackwell Publishing, 2005), 238–255; Amanda D. Lotz, *The* Television *Will Be* Revolutionized (New York: New York University Press, 2007); Sarah Banet-Weiser, Cynthia Chris, and Anthony Freitas, eds. *Cable Visions: Television Beyond Broadcasting* (New York: New York University Press, 2007); and Beretta E. Smith-Shomade, *Pimpin' Ain't Easy: Selling Black Entertainment Television* (New York and London: Routledge, 2007). For founding work on televisual narrative and on the operations of TV series and serial forms, see Jane Feuer's pieces "Narrative Form in American Network Television," in *High Theory/Low Culture: Analysing Popular Television and Film*, ed. Colin MacCabe (New York: St. Martin's Press, 1986), 101–114; "Melodrama, Serial Form and Television Today," *Screen* 25, no.1 (January-February 1984): 4–17, https://doi.org/10.1093/screen/25.1.4; and "Genre Study and Television," in *Channels of Discourse, Reassembled*, ed. Robert C. Allen (Chapel Hill: University of North Carolina Press, 1992), 138–160.
10 An interesting piece that discusses this difficulty of ongoing queer characters is Anna McCarthy, "Must See Queer TV: History and Serial Form in Ellen" in *Quality Popular*

Television, ed. Mark Jancovich and James Lyons (London: BFI Press, 2003), 88–102. For a discussion of the articulations and disarticulations between televisual queerness and "the mainstream," see Lynne Joyrich, "Queer Television Studies: Currents, Flows, and (Main) Streams," *Cinema Journal* 53, no. 2 (Winter 2014): 133–139.

11 A different version of my analysis of Batwoman can be found in Lynne Joyrich, "Bat Signals and Caped Crusading: The Ins and Outs of the CW's *Batwoman*, *Jump Cut* (2021).

12 Jean Bentley, "'Batwoman' Star Ruby Rose Hopes Groundbreaking Lesbian Superhero Appeals to Everyone," *The Hollywood Reporter*, August 4, 2019, www.hollywoodreporter.com/live-feed/ruby-rose-batwoman-1229120

13 Delia Harrington, "Batwoman Episode 4 Review: Who Are You. Kate struggles with her secret identity in an episode showing the critical difference between stories with queer characters & queer stories," *Den of Geek*, October 28, 2019, www.denofgeek.com/tv/batwoman-episode-4-review-who-are-you/

14 Queer Television Studies is a rich field of analysis. For just some useful books, see: Ron Becker, *Gay TV and Straight America* (New Brunswick, NJ: Rutgers University Press, 2006); Rebecca Beirne, ed, *Televising Queer Women: A Reader* (New York: Palgrave Macmillan, 2008); Steven Capsuto, *Alternate Channels: The Uncensored Story of Gay and Lesbian Images on Radio and Television* (New York: Ballantine Books, 2000); Samuel A. Chambers, *The Queer Politics of Television* (London: I.B.Tauris, 2009); Glyn Davis and Gary Needham, eds. *Queer TV: Theories, Histories, Politics* (New York: Routledge, 2009); Alexander Doty, *Making Things Perfectly Queer: Interpreting Mass Culture* (Minneapolis: University of Minnesota Press, 1993); F. Hollis Griffin, *Feeling Normal: Sexuality and Media Criticism in the Digital Age* (Bloomington: Indiana University Press, 2016); Kylo-Patrick R. Hart, *Queer TV in the 21st Century: Essays on Broadcasting from Taboo to Acceptance* (Jefferson: McFarland, 2016); Julia Himberg, *The New Gay for Pay: The Sexual Politics of American Television Production* (Austin: University of Texas Press, 2017); Melanie E.S. Kohnen, *Queer Representation, Visibility, and Race in American Film and Television: Screening the Closet* (New York : Routledge, 2016); Michael Lovelock, *Reality TV and Queer Identities: Sexuality, Authenticity, Celebrity* (London: Palgrave Macmillan, 2019); Quinlan Miller, *Camp TV: Trans Gender Queer Sitcom History* (Durham: Duke University Press, 2019); Tison Pugh, *The Queer Fantasies of the American Family Sitcom* (New Brunswick: Rutgers University Press, 2018); Stephen Tropiano, *The Prime Time Closet: A History of Gays and Lesbians On TV* (New York : Applause Theatre & Cinema Books, 2002); and Amy Villarejo, *Ethereal Queer: Television, Historicity, Desire. Durham* (Durham: Duke University Press, 2014).

15 See for example: Mimi White, *Tele-Advising: Therapeutic Discourse in American Television* (Chapel Hill: University of North Carolina Press, 1992); and Jon Dovey, *Freakshow: First Person Media and Factual Television* (London; Sterling, VA: Pluto Press, 2000). Both pull from Michel Foucault, *The History of Sexuality, Vol. 1: An Introduction*, trans. Robert Hurley (New York: Vintage, 1990).

16 "How Queer Everything Is Today!" *Batwoman*, season 1, episode 10, produced by Caroline Dries, directed by Jeffrey Hunt, written by Caroline Dries, The CW, original airdate January 19, 2020.

17 Lewis Carroll, *Alice's Adventures in Wonderland* (New York: Maynard, Merrill & Co., 1895), 19.

18 For more on paratexts, see Jonathan Gray, *Show Sold Separately: Promos, Spoilers, and Other Media Paratexts* (New York: NYU Press, 2010); relatedly, see Henry Jenkins, "Transmedia Storytelling," *MIT Technology Review*, January 15, 2003, https://www.technologyreview.com/2003/01/15/234540/transmedia-storytelling and *Convergence Culture: Where Old and New Media Collide* (New York: NYU Press, 2008); and Sharon Marie Ross, *Beyond the Box: Television and the Internet* (Malden: Wiley-Blackwell, 2008).

19 See Dino-Ray Ramos, "Ruby Rose Leaves Twitter In Wake Of 'Batwoman' Backlash," *Deadline Hollywood*, August 12, 2018, https://deadline.com/2018/08/ruby-rose-twitter-batwoman-backlash-lgbtq-inclusion-diversity-1202444418/#comments; Michael Cavna, "Ruby Rose Leaves Twitter After Criticism That She Isn't 'Gay Enough' for *Batwoman*," *The Washington Post*, August 13, 2018, www.washingtonpost.com/news/comic-riffs/wp/2018/08/13/ruby-rose-leaves-twitter-after-criticism-of-her-batwoman-casting/?noredirect=on; Emily Price, "Ruby Rose Quits Twitter Over 'Batwoman' Casting Backlash," *Fortune*, August 13, 2018, https://fortune.com/2018/08/13/ruby-rose-quits-twitter-batwoman-casting-backlash/; Matt (user name), "Ruby Rose "Batwoman" Casting Controversy," *Know Your Meme*, 2018, https://knowyourmeme.com/memes/events/ruby-rose-batwoman-casting-controversy; and Patrick Gomez, "Gender-fluid Ruby Rose opens up about the backlash she's received for identifying as a lesbian," *Entertainment Weekly*, June 5, 2019, https://ew.com/celebrity/2019/06/05/batwoman-ruby-rose-lesbian-backlash-interview/

20 Sedgwick, *Epistemology of the Closet*, 78.

21 This, of course, another tagline from a reality program, *Project Runway*.

22 Rick Porter, "'Batwoman' Shocker: Ruby Rose Exits CW Drama Ahead of Season 2", *The Hollywood Reporter*, May 19, 2020, www.hollywoodreporter.com/live-feed/batwoman-shocker-ruby-rose-exits-cw-drama-season-2-1295227

23 See Ally Mutnick and Sarah Ferris, "House Democrats Brace for More Losses," *Politico*, November 6, 2020, www.politico.com/states/new-york/city-hall/story/2020/11/06/house-democrats-brace-for-more-losses-1334909; Lydia Dishman, "2020 Congressional Races See Historic Victories for Women of Color, Indigenous, and LGBTQ Candidates," *Fast Company*, November 4, 2020, www.fastcompany.com/90572193/2020-congressional-races-see-historic-victories-for-women-of-color-indigenous-and-lgbtq-candidates; Hugo Greenhalgh, "LGBT+ Candidates Score Series of Historic Wins in U.S. Elections," *Reuters*, November 4, 2020, www.reuters.com/article/us-united-states-lgbt-elections-trfn/lgbt-candidates-score-series-of-historic-wins-in-u-s-elections-idUSKBN27K1C1; Rachelle Hampton, "The 2020 Election Has Already Resulted in Some Historic Firsts," *Slate*, November 4, 2020, https://slate.com/news-and-politics/2020/11/2020-election-historic-firsts-black-trans-winners-congress.html; Kelly McCarthy, "2020 Election Brought Notable Firsts for LGBTQ Candidates," *ABC News*, November 4, 2020, https://abcnews.go.com/Politics/2020-election-brought-notable-firsts-lgbtq-candidates/story?id=74019639

24 Mel Perez, "With Javicia Leslie's Batwoman, My Favorite Character Is Finally Being Played by Someone Who Looks Like Me," *Autostraddle*, July 29, 2020, www.autostraddle.com/with-javicia-leslies-batwoman-my-favorite-character-is-finally-being-played-by-someone-who-looks-like-me/. For further commentary on the notion of "the new normal" and on the place of queer television in the mainstream, as well as the place of the mainstream in queer television studies (through, indeed, a discussion of the TV program titled *The New Normal*), see Joyrich, "Queer Television Studies: Currents, Flows, and (Main) Streams."

25 For an interesting discussion of this, see Delia Harrington, "How Batwoman Takes on Policing and Social Issues," *Den of Geek*, July 6, 2020, www.denofgeek.com/tv/how-batwoman-takes-on-policing-and-social-issues/. For a discussion of similar issues raised in the program *Watchmen* (also a story of masked identities and superheroes), see Aaron Bady, "Doctor Manhattan Is a Cop: *Watchmen* and Franz Fanon," *The Los Angeles Review of Books*, December 31, 2019, https://lareviewofbooks.org/article/dr-manhattan-cop-watchmen-frantz-fanon/

11

HOW DO TRANS MEN MAKE BABIES?

Transkids and Reproductive Fantasies

Slava Greenberg

Introduction: Documenting Trans Children on Television

A new trans character that appeared on Netflix's animated series *Big Mouth*'s fourth season resurrected the tedious debate over the novelty of trans children and their representation on television.[1] The fundamental assumption of such discussions—that trans children are "new and future-bound"—is meticulously challenged by Jules Gill-Peterson's *Histories of the Transgender Child* in which she compellingly demonstrates that trans children were not only present from at least the 1910s but were also an integral part of the transgender twentieth century and the broader twentieth-century history of sex, gender, and race in medicine.[2] The accelerating public visibility of trans children in the United States in recent years is described by Gill-Peterson as

> sanitized, innocent, and always highly medicalized, they are domesticated figures, either reassuring that the so-called trans tipping point heralds a new generation of liberal progress and acceptance or, to the transphobic agitators involved in political campaigns focusing on bathrooms and schools, acting as proof that trans life deserve to be repressed in its incipient form for the threat to the social order that its future would represent.[3]

This visibility, however, is still dominating nonfiction television. The feature length documentary film *I Am Jazz: A Family in Transition* (Jen Stocks 2011) premiered when Jazz Jennings—now a star of her own reality television series on TLC –was 11.[4] Following, the short documentary film *Trans in America: Texas Strong* (Dresha Kyi 2018) features seven-year-old Kai Shappley.[5] Both Jennings and Shappley have become vocal trans children's rights advocates.[6] In the Israeli media, trans children are medicalized and tokenized like kids in the United States,[7] however, in the

DOI: 10.4324/9781003109044-15

Israeli context, they are also utilized in reproductive fantasies about the nationalist future.

Israeli docu-mini-series *Transkids* (Hilla Medalia 2019) sets out to provide a liberal narrative of acceptance by centering four Jewish transgender teens. Trans feminine Romy (15), and trans masculine Ofri (15), Liron (17), and Noam (16) all feature throughout the show's five episodes. Most topics covered by *Transkids* resemble other docu-reality series in which teens cope with typical adolescent issues such as sexuality, belonging, body image, and independence from their parents. Through a cis and ableist gaze, these issues are heavily medicalized and focus on doctor appointments and surgeries. However, unlike similar shows set in the United States, *Transkids* very casually dedicates an unprecedented amount of screen time to fertility, reproduction, and family planning.

Given the fact that many European countries still require sterilization as a condition for medical gender reassignment,[8] and micha cárdenas's research on trans women's pregnancy findings that existing literature on transgender pregnancy and family planning in the United States, focuses almost exclusively on transgender men with only brief references to the fact that trans women can bank their sperm,[9] this may seem positive. However, in the Israeli context, this focus on procreation is part of both a nationalist ideology and an ableist perspective. The former concerns normalized nationalist ideologies feeding into cultural expectations of Israeli Jews to partake in the "demographic war" against Palestinians. The ableist aspects relate to the medical perspective of "saving" trans youth from the perceived disability of infertility. Both ideologies are inseparable, as the former has led to a flourishing of reproductive technologies (originally intended for cis women).

While some trans men struggle to gain better access and funding, these same procedures are increasingly marketed to trans youth's parents. Israeli endocrinologists recommend such treatments to trans teens as a preparatory step before prescribing hormone replacement therapy, which is presented to them as threat to their future fertility. This practice serves as a double-edged sword simultaneously gatekeeping access to healthcare and nationalizing trans youth.[10] In the context of the "national womb", a tool in the "demographic war" infertility is perceived as a disability. The "national womb" ideology is rooted in the years of pre-statehood and Zionist leaders' concerns about the demographic numerical ratio between the Jewish and Palestinian populations. "[11] Jewish women in Israel were, and to a large extent still are, expected to procreate as part of the national ideology and consequent policies.

In order to increase its emotional appeal, the series does not only use the image of the titular "kid," but also relies on a hybrid style of documentary-medical drama in all the sequences focusing on Liron. Liron is a 17-year-old trans teen, whom *Transkids* follows throughout his encounters with the health care system. These encounters are presented chronologically, making it seem as though fertility preservation procedures are essential to his medical transition. Liron is presumably the youngest trans masculine person in Israel to undergo the in vitro fertility (IVF) procedure.

The series begins its documentation in the midst of the preservation processes, as he enters the fertility clinic with his parents, skipping the stage of decision-making. In all of these scenes, *Transkids* heavily relies on the medical gaze. Its perspective aligns with the doctors' points of view, showcasing rather than problematizing myths and misconceptions about hormone replacement therapy (HRT), testosterone, and the national ethos of reproduction. This complete reliance on the medical gaze is used to amplify the emotional drama, equating and blurring the lines between elective procedures (fertility preservation) and life-saving interventions (HRT and top surgery).

In this chapter, I argue that *Transkids'* hybrid docu-hospital-drama style amplifies the medical gaze, and in so doing, sacrifices the factual and investigative aspects of documentary. This reliance on the medical gaze feeds into nationalist and ableist ideologies; presenting the doctor as a savior, sparing the trans "children" (teens) from disability in the form of potential infertility, and allowing them to join in the nationalist fantasy of a demographic war. Finally, I demonstrate how this style doesn't merely promote these ideologies, but also engages in commercial targeting of trans boys' parents as a profitable market for fertility preservation procedures in Israel.

Docu-Hospital-Drama and the Medical Gaze

Transkids' generic style relies on a conjugation of television documentary and hospital or medical drama. The documentary style is utilized to explore the adolescence processes focusing on the visual changes of the characters while the medical drama style amplifies the emotional intensity by implying life altering and potentially threatening situations. *Transkids* involves multiple scenes showing the teens meeting with medical doctors, endocrinologists, gynecologists, and plastic surgeons. Viewers not only get a glimpse into what goes on during consultation meetings, but also accompany some of the teens throughout their surgical procedures. Many sequences focus on Liron's endeavors with various medical procedures—fertility preservation, HRT, and top surgery. Within these sequences, the series seems to not only sensationalize medical transition but also chronologize and construct these procedures as essential stages followed according to a medical prescription. Presenting the consultation meeting at the IVF clinic as a necessary step before HRT, the series reinforces the medical knowledge presented in this significant scene. It presents fertility preservation as a cure for the irreversible infertility—a presumably disabling process—of HRT. This claim about the irreversible infertility caused by testosterone has been negated both by medical research and the life experiences of thousands of trans men. Nonetheless, the series' alignment with the medical point of view is one of the most apparent ways in which it integrates the direct documentary "fly on the wall" style with the fictional medical drama. Specifically, it does so by aligning with the medical point of view through medical drama cinematography. By so doing the series uses nonfiction's sense of factuality to enhance the medical point of view alongside the urgency and emotional intensity of the hospital drama to amplify nationalist ideologies and practices.

In a comprehensive study of 1990s U.S. hospital dramas, Jason Jacobs (2003) found that within such texts, the body was monitored and policed by medical technology, which has dominated the *mise en scène*. The hospital drama focused on the body in ruins as the subject of the medical gaze, concluding with its healing, and thus resolving the conflict.[12] The medical or hospital dramas glorify the medical gaze in their aesthetics, narrative, and ideology. As mentioned above, *Transkids*' use of this hybrid style of documentary-medical drama increases the show's emotional appeal to viewers by blurring the boundaries between these two components. This documentary-fiction genre mix "use[s] documentary techniques to generate emotional accuracy… Fictional genre techniques from sitcoms, dramas, and soap operas also help make emotional connections to the audience because they garner audience sympathy with characters."[13] This hybridity, in turn, leads "Viewers [...] not [to] experience factual genres in isolation but as part of a chaotic mix of factuality."[14]

This cross between factual direct cinema documentary and fictional medical drama also presents a new conflict of focus: that is, who are the protagonists that spectators are meant to sympathize with? While in documentary conventions, the series aligns its point of view with the trans youth, the medical drama tends to center and idealize doctors. This conflict is not only apparent in most *Transkids* scenes featuring doctors and medical staff but also (and especially) in Liron's narrative. By focusing on this narrative, I explore the trans child's role in the national ethos through the portrayal of a white trans masc teen seeking to preserve fertility.

The series introduces Liron through an action tracking-shot, as if out of a medical drama, following him as he walks out of the elevator alongside his parents into the "IVF and Female Fertility Preservation Unit." This scene is the second one shown in the series, but it becomes the first in the documentary film edited from the same materials. When they are shown in the office, the camera takes the doctor's point of view through an over-the-shoulder shot of her talking to Liron.

The three of them sit across from Dr. Hadar Amir, a senior physician and researcher at the Lis Maternity and Women's Hospital. This office scene opens with Amir verifying the purposes of the meeting, addressing the family in plural: "So I understand we've decided to preserve fertility, before you begin the sex change process. Did I understand correctly?" We see Liron in the corner of the screen, nodding and then smiling in a reaction shot. Amir goes on to explain the necessity of the process:

> When we preserve fertility, it means the individual is about to undergo a process that can *irreversibly* damage their eggs, and we want to preserve the eggs so that we can use them later on, after that *irreversible* process is done. This procedure can only be performed using IVF.
>
> *italics mine*

Liron's father stays silent on camera, while his mother asks the doctor two questions.[15] Neither this scene nor any other throughout the series or the film ask why Liron decided to undergo the procedure, what possible risks are involved, and the procedure's success/failure rate. Nor does it ask for any information supporting the argument about the projected irreversibility of HRT. This is important because as viewers, particularly in medical dramas where they save lives, we are expected to trust doctors and perceive them as having the best interest of their patients.

The emotional intensity reaches its peak in a classic medical drama scene, in which Liron is about to undergo the egg retrieval surgery, while experiencing severe pain. Something is clearly wrong; he is crying as he's examined by Dr. Amir, who decides to go through with the procedure as planned. The concerned parents wait in the corridor until the doctor comes out bearing the good news. Liron is safe, the eggs have been retrieved, and the doctor reassures the parents that Liron's extreme pain was caused by a cyst on one of his ovaries. This nerve-wracking scene achieved the goal of elevated emotional response and gained the series positive media attention.

An Israeli journalist writing about the series opened her article with a mention of this scene:

> Seventeen-year-old Liron is sitting in a waiting room with his mother. This boy, who's always smiling, is now in severe pain. He is held by his concerned mother, as she looks helpless with her inability to help him, crying with him... Liron is a transgender boy, a man's soul born in a woman's body. And as part of his gender affirmation process, he'd come to the clinic to retrieve and freeze eggs –the youngest transgender man in Israel to undergo the procedure.[16]

The series, the film, and their media coverage all undisputedly accept this "helplessness" in light of an elective procedure, which is linked with life-saving, gender-affirming procedures.

This is achieved through the utilization of the fictional aspects of medical drama, alongside the emotional effect of factuality. However, it fails the documentary doubt and critical point view. As demonstrated below, this reliance on the medical gaze achieves emotional appeal at the expense of questioning, doubting authority, and undermining dominant power structures.

The Medical Gaze and the National Womb Myth

Crossing the hospital drama with the documentary style involves a heavy reliance on the medical gaze. In the case of reproductive technologies, this gaze feeds into a larger Israeli national myth. As discussed in the previous section, the series fails to question Liron and his mother's motivations to undergo fertility preservation. In addition, scenes featuring 15-year-olds Romy and Ofri show them being suggested such treatments. Both teens reject the suggestions: Romy dismisses it with the comment "I'll adopt," while Ofri tells his grandmother, "You got an extra twenty thousand?" then later adds, "I want to adopt." However, despite this, no attention is given to their refusal. One of the main reasons for this tendency in the series can be located in the well-rooted Zionist myth of the "national womb." This term describes the ethos of biological production of healthy Jewish children in Israel, which forms an integral part of Zionist ideology, the pursuit and maintenance of a Jewish state in Israel.

Mapping media treatment of reproductive issues in Israel between two wars taking place in 1967 and 1973, Orly Shachar argues that "the Israeli media produce ideology conducive to the preservation of nationalistic objectives, mainly its use of women as national icons—biological reproducers and nurturers of their people".[17] Shachar also investigates "the Myth of the Womb: A Nationalistic Symbol," showing that fertility is a primary priority in Israeli society:

> Writers and politicians placed women in the heart of the national security problem. The "Israeli Womb" was made the source of the problem. Not enough Jewish children were born in Israel. The suggested solution was to produce more children. In the aftermath of the 1967 War, an Israeli morning daily published an article written by David Ben Gurion, the former first PM, attacking the practice of birth control in Israel. He wrote: "A Jewish woman who does not bring into this world at least four children—assuming it is up to her—is defrauding the Jewish mission."[18]

Further, in a study about an Israeli Mothers' protest, Dafna Lemish and Inbal Barzel suggest that "The power conferred by motherhood and the romanticization of its calling, camouflages women's importance as citizens. This is particularly true in a society like Israel which glorifies motherhood as a 'public role' to serve the national goals".[19] Nitza Berkovitch writes that as bearers of children, women are entrusted with the biological and social reproduction of the national collective.[20] Comparing women's magazines from the 1940s and 1950s in the United States and Israel, Eva Illouz and Eitan Wilf (2009) assert that under capitalism, American women were released from motherhood as self-identification, but encouraged to consume beauty products instead. Furthermore, while the American family was increasingly defined as an emotional project between two private individuals, in the Israeli context, the meaning of marriage was formulated as the institutionalization of fertility.[21] Hanna Herzog (1999) argues that in countries that, like Israel, live under a security threat, the exclusion of women from the civil agenda is made possible through the centrality of the family institution. This is particularly salient in Israel, where the assurance of national continuity has become a goal in and of itself. Under this ideology, women are vested with responsibility for achieving this aim, their role being to give birth, pass on the cultural ethos, and educate the next generation.[22]

The Israeli fertility hype, critiqued by feminist activists and scholars, started out with the establishment of the State of Israel, and has been fed by policies aimed to increase Jewish population. The "demographic threat" has set the tone of the political agenda of the Zionist society and has contributed to the massive encouragement of birth and the nationalization of the uterus. In the mid-1990s, Israel has had more fertility clinics per capita than any other country in the world. It is currently the only county where any cis woman may access new reproduction technologies for free.[23]

Israeli feminist NGOs have exposed the aggressive marketing of these technologies to cis women, even while their efficiency was considered low. In addition, the effectiveness of such procedures, as well as their safety, have been contested by feminist activists in Israel. A study on behalf of Isah L'Isha Haifa Feminist Center (ILI), conducted by Tamara Traubmann, investigated the market of egg freezing for fertility preservation in Israel. For example, cryopreservation, a technology intended to preserve fertility in women undergoing chemotherapy, may in fact cause ovary failure. In recent years, this technology has been marketed to healthy women, as a means of preserving and postponing fertility.[24] Through this analysis, the emphasis *Transkids'* Dr. Amir places on the irreversibly of HRT may be explained as a reiteration of the originally accepted threat of chemotherapy.

The American Society for Reproductive Medicine published a document reviewing the scientific knowledge gathered concerning egg freezing. Following its contents, the ASRM commented that the fertilization of frozen eggs from women who experienced problems with fertility should no longer be considered experimental and become routinely used. As for its use with "healthy" fertile women, the document notes the unclear rates of success of the technology, as well as its risks. The document raises concern about the marketing of this technology as a means to postpone the age of fertility, suggesting that it may give rise to false hopes.

Thus, reproductive technologies in Israel operate in a social sphere that glorifies fertility and the traditional family. The marketing of egg freezing technologies to healthy women may impact a decrease in women's freedom not to reproduce, or to do so uncongenially. In the conclusion of its position paper, ILI called for stricter regulation and its enforcement on the marketing of reproductive technologies. By not problematizing or questioning the normalization of trans youth through the vehicle of fertility preservation, *Transkids* does not merely accept the national womb ideology, but actively contributes to it. Furthermore, it reinforces the irreversible infertility myth of testosterone, and assists in the expansion of this market from cis women to young trans men.

The Irreversible Infertility Myth of Testosterone, or Are Doctors Lying to Us?

Following the scene in Dr. Amir's office, Liron injects the follicle-stimulating hormone (FSH)[25] and announces that with that he has finally begun his medical transition. This lengthy scene, showing Liron's struggle with the injection, and the look on his concerned mother's face, are used to intensify the medical drama. However, again, no questions are raised by the text as to why this particular step is perceived by him as the beginning. One possible answer is given as part of his mother's concerns about testosterone: "To be honest, I'm not so nervous about the egg.

I mean, I want it to go well and work the first time by getting enough eggs. I'm stressed about all the male hormones you're going to start taking." This conversation is framed by the previous fertility clinic scene, followed by Liron's conviction that this marks the first step of his medical transition, and ends with convincing his mother about the validity of his identity and need in the medical transition and particularly testosterone. The conjunction of these scenes into one sequence suggests that the fertility preservation procedures may have been pre-conditions set by his parents and or doctors.

The myth of testosterone as a risk for fertility has been disproved by feminist scientist and gender studies scholar Rebecca M. Jordan-Young, and by anthropologist and bioethicist Katrina Karkazis. Their book *Testosterone: An Unauthorized Biography* begins by positioning itself as being in opposition with the "authorized" biography, as presented in the "T episode" of *This American Life* (ep. 220 in 2002).[26] They write: "*This American Life* captured perfectly T's authorized biography, in which T is about libido, aggression, focus, facility with science and math. It's gendered, channeling myriad elements of masculinity."[27] As for the risks involved with T concerning fertility, the authors dismantle the misconceptions regarding "T's detrimental effects, such as inhibiting FSH and causing ovarian cysts that impede fertility." Surprisingly, they provide evidence for its "critical role in ovulation."[28]

The assumption of testosterone as causing infertility has been also contested by various trans men in the United Kingdom and the United States. Particularly, it's been tackled by the experiences of trans men's pregnancies without the use of fertility preservation. This (no longer new) phenomenon is currently being carefully studied by several institutions. For example, the Trans Pregnancy Project is currently conducting a study led by Ruth Pearce, Francis Ray White, and Damien W Riggs, and funded by the United Kingdom's Economic and Social Research Council. According to the project's data, 41 trans fathers participated in a 2013 survey (Light et al., 2014), and 47 trans birth parents have participated in the Trans Pregnancy study so far. In Australia, 205 trans men were recorded giving birth in 2018, from July 1st to June 30th (Medicare, 2019). In addition, an international online support group for trans birth parents, parents, and allies currently boasts 4,300 members. The Trans Pregnancy Project's website goes as far as naming the myth of hormones and infertility "the biggest lie."

One year after *Transkids* first aired, Dr. Hadar Amir led and published a study about trans fertility, concluding that "Transgender men have an excellent response to ovulation stimulation even after long-term exposure to testosterone."[29] The study specifies that "While bilateral oophorectomy results in permanent sterility, *the effect of testosterone on fertility is inconclusive*" (np). This might mean that her introduction to Liron and his parents included this explanation off-screen. If so, it may have included the fact that the irreversible procedure discussed is not HRT, but rather "gender-affirming bottom surgery [which] includes hysterectomy and bilateral oophorectomy with or without reconstruction of male genitalia." However, neither the series nor the film includes any of this information. In fact, as the series unfolds, Liron proceeds to undergo top surgery, while never expressing any intentions to pursue bottom surgery. Thus, instead of deconstructing the myth of HRT as an irreversible cause of infertility, *Transkids* reinforces it.

The threat of infertility has been enshrined in various forms around the world. In the United States, it is classified as a disability under the Americans with Disabilities Act (ADA),[30] and in Israel it serves as an acceptable cause for approval to perform abortions. In her book *A Life (Un)Worthy of Living: Reproductive Genetics in Israel and Germany* (2007), Yeal Hashiloni-Dolev discusses a specific group of genetic anomalies, namely sex chromosome anomalies (SCAs), whose major manifestation is future infertility. Hashiloni-Dolev demonstrates how parenthood and the reproduction of the "national womb" in Israel are understood as the epicenter of human life. Concurrently, Israeli genetic counselors understand infertility to endanger the worthiness of life, thus perceiving it as a higher medical risk. In contrast, their counterparts in Germany do not support abortions on the grounds of SCAs. Thus, had transness been carried by a detectable gene, coupled with the myth of HRT infertility, it may have served as an acceptable cause for abortion in Israel.

Indeed, the same is admitted by Noam's father in *Transkids*. In an honest yet unsettling conversation, Noam, a religious trans masc teen living in a settlement, talks to his father about normalcy. Finally he asks him: "Do you want to fix me?" His father replies without hesitation, while looking straight at him: "I don't want to fix you. But if I could have prevented this thing, I would have. If we had known in that first check-up, that something like this could happen, maybe you would not have been born." Both Noam and his mother are shocked and embarrassed, after which Noam jokingly concludes: "Okay, I'll go stand in the corner and cry about the day I was born." Even while being less common in religious communities, genetic tests are the norm in Israel.

Transkids glorifies the medical gaze by amplifying viewers' emotional response using its medical drama style. This glorification further sidelines *factuality*, through the show's advancement of the myths around reproduction and the effects of testosterone. Coupled with the national womb myth, stressing the pressure to produce able-bodied babies, transness in itself threatens the national fantasies of the future.

Transkids for Profit and National Futurities

In this chapter, I suggested that the hybrid documentary-hospital-drama style of the series sacrifices the interrogative mode of documentary in favor of the emotional intensity of fictional drama. This strategy, which relies on an idealization of the medical point of view, has long prevailed in disability related documentaries, and has recently found its way to trans narratives as well. Examining factual British television, and mainly documentary, Ann Pointon (1997) identifies four themes of "disability" in documentary: the first is "Transformation" as a main theme, in which

> we, the audience, are persuaded that not only will we see a change, but that it will be a change for the (perceived) "better" rather than "worse," and it is transformation of the body that is central to the narrative.

In these narratives, the disabled subject may be the ostensible one, but often the real "hero" and central actor is the "transformer," a role very often given to a doctor. Furthermore, "the scientific elements, or overall utility of the techniques, are rarely held up to hostile analysis."[31]

The documentary *Born to Be* (Tania Cypriano 2019), also titled *Transformation,* centers on the glorification of one particular representative of the medical institution. Dr. Jess Ting, at the Mount Sinai Center for Transgender Medicine in New York City, is presented as the savior within the genuinely heartening stories of several trans people. This bears much resemblance to Liron's narrative in *Transkids*. Through it, the series offers a two-fold type of transformation: the first relating to gender, and the second saving him from an imagined disabled future of infertility.

Following the series' public screening, television premiere, and extensive media coverage, Liron became the center of attention for (presumably) being the youngest trans masculine teen in Israel to undergo fertility preservation procedures. In 2009, the sixth Israeli LGBT Health Conference ("Proud to Talk about Health") took place. The conference was sponsored by the Tel Aviv Municipality and its LGBT community center, the Society for LGBT Medicine—Israeli Medical Association, as well as five pharmaceutical companies. It consisted of six panels, each featuring one community member sharing a personal experience, and a medical practitioner.

Of the six practitioners presented in the panels, four were affiliated with the Tel Aviv Sourasky Medical Center (Ichilov Hospital), home to the IVF unit represented in *Transkids* (which itself comprised two of the six panels). The panel that inspired the title of this chapter—"How do Trans People Make Babies?"—consisted of three panelists: Dr. Hadar Amir, Liron Matzas, and his mother, Ofrit Matzas.[32] Liron has become the poster child for trans fertility preservation. The homogeneity of the panel's answer to the question in its title overlooks several issues. Firstly, it neglects to engage with trans feminine experiences; secondly, it makes no note of the more common practice of trans men taking a break from testosterone and getting pregnant either through intercourse, or through other assisted reproductive technology; and finally, and significantly, it fails to provide a successful case study of long-term use of frozen eggs. In fact, the panel utilized Liron and his mother in order to enhance the IVF market and expand it to the new consumer sector of trans boys.

ILI's study (discussed in the previous section) investigated the commercial market around these medical technologies and found that egg freezing has a high profitability potential to its operators. The procedure is currently marketed by private clinics and hospitals. Its cost for customers is about 15,666 ILS in Israel (approx. $5,000), and even more abroad (€7,666). A study conducted by ILI indicated that most information accessible to women on the issue of egg freezing is distributed by private parties for the purposes of financial gain. Such advertisements report high success rates and downplay the risks.

However, the use of trans teens to promote reproductive technologies is not only invoked by capitalist ideology but also nationalist and eugenic ideologies: Whose reproductive futures are protected? Whose lives are desirable? Jake Pyne analyzes the case of Ashley X, a seven-year-old girl from Seattle who was subjected to forced sterilization in 2004. Pyne compares her sterilization to the anticipated infertility of trans youth: Ashley's perceived lack of a reproductive future was the basis for her sterilization. However, in contrast, "For trans youth [...] when they are perceived to have reproductive futures, this can slow down their access to transition care, while clinicians or parents deliberate about the loss of fertility that may occur with these procedures".[33] Furthermore, the comparison leads to an ethical question: "While supporting trans youth in their employment and fertility options is positive, this support also signals the future value of their bodies, a value not accorded to all."[34]

Furthermore, the series, the film, and the panel, used Liron as the promise of an imagined future white able-bodied, reproductive Jewish child in Israel. The protection of imagined, often unborn, future children was the main strategy of the eugenicist ideology. Social fantasies about the future often exclude anyone and anything undermining familial and national structures, thus exposing present concepts (and policies). Disability Studies scholar Alison Kafer (2013) has demonstrated how entire populations have been determined as unworthy of a future due to their race, class, gender, and disability. The imagined child is a stand in for a desirable future: "The Child through whom legacies are passed down is, without doubt, able-bodied/able-minded." The same child is also cis. Gill-Peterson articulates the role of the dominant figure of the trans child in the U.S. public sphere today as

> a potent "racial innocence" that empties trans childhood of its content, including race, rendering it conceptually white while simultaneously liberating the existence of black trans and trans of color childhood. There is tremendous damage in the figurative separation of racialized trans negativity and white trans childhood futurity.[35]

The trans poster child in the Israeli context was "played" by *Transkids'* representation of Liron as an advocate for the IVF clinic: He is a white, green-eyed, able-bodied, sweet young trans teen. While he was offered to preserve fertility, Black Jewish women of Ethiopian origin in Israel were offered long-lasting birth control.[36]

Notes

1 Allen, Samantha. "I Didn't Expect Much from Big Mouth's New Trans Character—But She's Amazing," *Them*, December 4, 2020, www.them.us/story/big-mouth-season-four-josie-totah-patti-harrison-transgender-character, Accessed May 26, 2021.

2 Gill-Peterson, Jules. *Histories of the Transgender Child*. Minneapolis and London: University of Minnesota Press, 2018, 3.

3 Gill-Peterson, *Histories of the Transgender Child*. 2018, 2.

4 *I Am Jazz* (Colin K Miller and Aegnus James 2015) is a current popular reality television series on TLC about a 19-year-old trans rights advocate named Jazz Jennings. "*I Am Jazz* documents Jennings' life as a transgender teen and activist, including her gender-confirming surgeries, dating life, mental health, family, and college dreams" (Dorwart 2020). 'I Am Jazz': Jazz Jennings 'Unravels' Under Pressure on the New Season Laura Dorwart, January 17, 2020 www.cheatsheet.com/entertainment/i-am-jazz-jazz-jennings-unravels-under-pressure-on-the-new-season.html/

5 Strangio, Chase. "ACLU Short Film Series Highlights the Resilience of the Trans Community." *them.*, October 10, 2018. www.them.us/story/aclu-film-series-transgender/ Accessed May 26, 2021.

6 Yvonne S. Marquez, "10-Year-Old Activist Kai Sahappley on Fighting for Trans Kids in the Texas Lege," *Texas Monthly.* April 16, 2021, www.texasmonthly.com/news-politics/10-year-old-trans-actor-activist-kai-shappley-texas-lege/ Accessed May 26, 2021.

7 Lee, Vered. "'Inside I Was a Girl, but No One Knew It': The Incredible Story of Rina, a Transgender Fourth-grader" *Haaretz*, May 15, 2020 www.haaretz.com/israel-news/.premium.MAGAZINE-i-was-a-girl-but-no-one-knew-the-incredible-story-of-rina-a-trans-fourth-grader-1.8845974. Accessed May 26, 2021.

8 "24 Countries in Europe Require Sterilization of Trans People." *TGEU.* May 17, 2013. https://tgeu.org/24-countries-in-europe-still-require-sterilization-from-trans-people/

9 See micha cárdenas's *Pregnancy* Project, Digital HD video, 13:15, https://michacardenas.sites.ucsc.edu/pregnancy/ Accessed May 26, 2021.

10 For more about the gatekeeping of HRT and trans youth's care models see: Florence Ashley's Thinking an Ethics of Gender Exploration: Against Delaying Transition for Transgender and Gender Creative Youth," *Clinical Child Psychology and Psychiatry* 24, no. 2 (2019): 223–236 and "Homophobia, Conversion Therapy, and Care Models for Trans Youth: Defending the Gender-affirmative Approach," *Journal of LGBT Youth* 17, no. 4 (2020): 361–383.

11 Leibler, Anat. "Disciplining Ethnicity: Social Sorting Intersects with Political Demography in Israel's Pre-State Period," *Social Studies of Science* 2014, 44(2): 271–292 (282).

12 Jacobs, Jason. *Body Trauma TV: The New Hospital Dramas* (London: British Film Institute Publishing, 2003), 69–70.

13 Edwards, Leigh H. "Mashup: Hybrid Genres and Emotional Appeals." *The Triumph of Reality TV: The Revolution in American Television* (New York: Praeger, 2013), 48.

14 Hill, Annette, *Restyling Factual TV: Audiences and News, Documentary and Reality Genres* (London: Routledge, 2007), 2.

15 "Have you ever performed this procedure on such a young person?" (For which the answer is yes, and even younger people, for various reasons), and: "Is he the first transgender person to undergo fertility preservation?" (No, but the only one under 18).

16 Nahum Shahal, Maya. "Tnu Chance Latrans: Sidrat Docu Merageshet Al Naarim Transgenderim Israelim" [Give a Chance to the Trans: A Moving Docu-Series about Israeli Transgender Teens]. *Calcalist* (2019): www.calcalist.co.il/consumer/articles/0,7340,L-3758132,00.html

17 Shachar, Orly. "The Israeli Womb: Images of Gendered Nationalism in the Israeli Press." In *Women and the Media: Diverse Perspectives*, edited by Theresa Carilli and Jane Campbell (Lanham and Oxford: University Press of America, 2005), 20.

18 Ben Gurion, Ha'aretz, Dec. 8, 1967, p. 13, qt in Shachar "The Israeli Womb," 25.

19 Lemish, Dafna and Inbal Barzel. "'Four Mothers' The Womb in the Public Sphere." *European Journal of Communication* 15, no. 2 (2000): 147–169.

20 Berkovitch, Nitza. "Motherhood as a National Mission: The Construction of Womanhood in the Legal Discourse in Israel." *Women's Studies International Forum* 20, no. 5–6 (1997): 605–619.

21 Illouz, Eva, Wilf, Eitan. "Hearts of Wombs? A Cultural Critique of Radical Feminist Critique of Love," Debra Hopkins, Jochen Kleres, Helena Flam, and Helmut Kuzmics (eds.) *Theorizing Emotions: Sociological Explorations and Applications* (Frankfurt/New York: Campis Verlag, 2009), 121–142.

22 Lachover, Einat. "Women in the Six Day War through the eyes of the Media." *The Journal of Israeli History* 28, no. 2 (2009): 117–135.

23 Shkedi-Rafid, Shiri, Hashiloni-Dolev, Yael. "Egg Freezing for Age-related Fertility Decline: Preventive Medicine or a Further Medicalization of Reproduction? Analyzing New Israeli Policy," 9, no. 2 (2011): 291–294.

24 Traubmann, Tamara. *Egg Freezing for Fertility Preservation in Israel: Mapping the Market.* Position Paper by Isha L'Isha: Haifa Feminist Center, November 2012.

25 Behind the doctor hangs a [EMD Serono's Gonal-f] poster with an ad for a brand of Follitropin alfa, an injection that contains follicle-stimulating hormone (FSH) to help stimulate healthy ovaries to produce eggs. The same brand is seen in the following scene in which Liron opens the package with the brand name visible and injects it.

26 "Testosterone." *This American Life*, August 30, 2002, www.thisamericanlife.org/220/testosterone

27 Jordan-Young, Rebecca M., Karkazis, Katrina. *Testosterone: An Unauthorized Biography.* President and Fellows of Harvard College 2019, 5.

28 Jordan-Young and Karkazis, *Testesterone,* 38.

29 Amir, Hadar, Iris Yaish, Nivin Samara, Joseph Hasson, Asnat Groutz, and Foad Azem. "Ovarian stimulation outcomes among transgender men compared with fertile cisgender women." *Journal of Assisted Reproduction and Genetics* (2020). Accessed October 4, 2020. https://link.springer.com/article/10.1007/s10815-020-01902-7

30 www.cga.ct.gov/2005/rpt/2005-R-0145.htm

31 Pointon, Ann. "Disability and Documentary." In *Framed: Interrogating Disability in the Media*, edited by Anna Pointon and Chris Davies (London: British Film Institute/The Arts Council of England), 1997, 84–92 (87).

32 Soon after the premiere of the series Ofrit Matzas has published her book about her son's transition titled "I Always Wanted a Daughter" and went on tour to promote it.

33 Pyne, Jake. "Arresting Ashley X: Trans Youth, Puberty Blockers and the Question of Whether Time is on Your Side," *Somatechnics* 1, no. 7 (2017): 95–123 (109).

34 Pyne, "Arresting Ashley X," 110.

35 Gill-Peterson, *Histories of the Transgender Child*, 2.

36 Eyal, Hedva, Yali Hashash, and Adva Shai. "Depo Provera: A Contraceptive Method Given Via Injection, a Report on Its Prescription Policy Among Women of the Ethiopian Community in Israel." Haifa: Isha LeIsha Center, 2013. http://isha.org.il/wp-content/uploads/2014/08/%D7%93%D7%A4%D7%95-%D7%90%D7%A0%D7%92%D7%9C%D7%99%D7%AA.pdf

12

QUEER AESTHETICS IN THE STREAMING AGE

Jake Pitre

Introduction

Is there something queer about algorithms? Or rather, is there anything queer about algorithms? Algorithms are developed and used to gather data, analyze it, and provide strict definitions and categorizations. Is it even possible to queer such a normalizing system?

Queer aesthetics are being harnessed for internet television, and both content and form are being led by algorithmic decision-making. In this chapter, I argue that despite some meaningful exceptions, major streaming platforms like Netflix and Amazon Prime are generally averse to creating and distributing work that employs queer aesthetics of radical transgression and transformation. Despite lip service to queer communities, streaming platforms in the post-network era utilize and weaponize algorithmic knowledge while undermining queer aesthetics—and this is not a coincidence. In fact, I argue that the very structures that organize these platforms are fundamentally incompatible with queerness and will continue to be until these structures have been thoroughly adjusted, or wholly destroyed and rebuilt.

We can begin by asking: what is an algorithm, and how does it operate within television? In the simplest terms, an algorithm takes an *input*—information in the form of data—and transforms it into an *output*, a new piece of data that may or may not be presented to a user. These processes can be compounded together into complex systems of computational power, and machine learning allows this to occur automatically as computers learn from previous decisions, inputs, and outputs. As Ed Finn argues in *What Algorithms Want: Imagination in the Age of Computing*, algorithms are also *culture machines*:

DOI: 10.4324/9781003109044-16

> While the cultural effects and affects of computation are complex, these systems function in the world through instruments designed and implemented by human beings. In order to establish a critical frame for reading cultural computation, we have to begin with those instruments, jammed together in the humble vessel of the algorithm.
>
> *Finn 2017: 16*

With that framing, we can start to see how this can be seen within the television industry. What often gets missed in discussions about algorithms is that they aren't unknowable, or completely abstract, as is often suggested. The symbolic language of algorithms has real consequences, both computationally and materially. Finn continues: "Unlike the proverbial black box, the culture machine is actually porous, ingesting and extruding cultural and computational structures at every connection point with other sociotechnical systems" (48). This means that there is a give and take, with algorithms acting as an interface between us and data, to the point that algorithms "reshape the spaces within which we see ourselves" (50)—including in the television shows that we watch.

Think of it this way: if a platform like Netflix can gather endless amounts of data about what you watch, when you watch, how you watch, and where you watch, that means it can input all of this data into algorithms which will then deliver an output in the form of recommendations for what you should watch next. This data, though, can be used for many more things by a company like Netflix, including which brands it chooses to partner with for product placement or advertising, or how much of a monthly increase in subscription cost is considered palatable to your financial demographic (yes, they can infer how much money you make), or how many seconds after an episode ends before the next one autoplays (it's seven). It should not be surprising, then, to consider how this data, processed through algorithms over years, has impacted the television shows that Netflix and other companies choose to produce, at every possible level. Indeed, it has become a common criticism against middling Netflix Originals to declare them to have been made or written by an algorithm, precisely because there is some truth to it. Netflix is obsessed with *watch time*, the metric that measures how long you spend on the platform. Naturally, if they have all this data on what shows keep us watching longer, this will help guide investment decisions and content creation. Interestingly, the way that Netflix, and its chief content officer (CCO) Ted Sarandos in particular, have talked about this process has changed over the years. At the beginning, with *House of Cards* and *Orange is the New Black*, the company's reliance on data was front and center. In 2015, Sarandos described these decisions as 70% data-based and 30% human judgment, and in 2019 he adjusted to 70–80% "art," based on human intuition, and 20–30% "science," based on data (Hayes 2019). This transformation may reflect an actual shift in company practice, or it may merely be a way to narrativize their growth, but data and algorithms undeniably inform Netflix's content. As we'll see, this includes not only which shows are greenlit, but also what form they ultimately take.

It is troubling to consider how mechanisms like algorithms, with the cooperation of human judgment, handle nuanced human identities and characteristics. For instance, in this chapter I aim to firstly acknowledge previous attempts to analyze and theorize queer technologies (such as the Gay Bombs manual and theories of QueerOS) while pointing out their limited scope and adjacent aims. As Zach Blas and micha cárdenas put it, "today's technologies are products of globalizing neoliberalism and, therefore, are powerfully centered in the interests of multinational corporations" (Blas & Cárdenas 2013: 565). Of course, queer media makers are always looking for and developing alternative futures within such systems, and there may be some potential within conceptions of queer technologies, possibilities for theorizing and enacting practices that harness the vision of queer futurities. However, under the domination of *algorithmic* production, little space is provided for the unconventional or the unpredictable. Algorithms, as programmed by corporate engineers and developers, are intended to provide us with what we want, yet these parameters are inevitably shaped by what has come before (which tends to be what is mainstream, particularly with data built on a platform like Netflix, which hosts a limited library), and they also function to *mitigate risk*. Put simply, they exist to provide what is likely to be successful (and generate capital).

I am focusing on Netflix because they are leaders in the streaming industry but also because of these routine publicizations of their algorithmic approach to entertainment production. Other streamers, such as Hulu and HBO Max, utilize algorithms of their own, but Netflix has been at the forefront of data gathering and algorithmic strategization, in all aspects of their business. For Netflix, we can think of examples like *Queer Eye*, *Grace and Frankie*, *Orange is the New Black*, *Special*, *The Politician*, *Sense8*, *She-Ra and the Princesses of Power*, *Elite*, *Halston*, *I Am Not Okay With This*, *Tales of the City*, *Heartbreak High*, and *Sex Education* for insight into how this production process operates. These Originals are indicative of the approach these platforms consistently take to production, with little to no incorporation of aesthetics to begin with. Moreover, even if catering to a queer audience *was* part of the decision to greenlight these shows, it was due to the influence of a piece of data, not any authentic interest in appealing to niche demographics.

It would be helpful at this point to briefly explain what I mean by queer, to better situate our understanding of queer aesthetics and how this model of television production is largely antithetical to its aims. As Cathy Cohen has defined it, queerness is about embodying the experience of alterity, a "shared marginal relationship to dominant power" (Cohen 2005: 43). Alexander Cho builds on this approach by adding a relational element of the image, arguing for an understanding of "queer feeling as a function of image moving along the vector of time, a trajectory that is warped, coiled, broken, and multiple, or at the very least, *not straight*" (Cho 2015: 47). This helps orient my positioning on queer aesthetics, which I would define as being informed and structured by this fluid and aberrant affect. In other words, as images are constructed and distributed, they are experienced not only chronologically but coherently and without rupture, but a queer aesthetic to image-making would challenge and distort these expectations. In this chapter,

I will argue that the approach taken by streaming platforms and their algorithms is not sustainable if these companies hope to maintain the approval of marginalized audiences, and moreover that if the term "queer algorithms" is an oxymoron, we must envision (as queer scholars always do) a way out of "aesthetic gentrification" (Keegan 2016) and into the queerness of post-network television.

Queer Technologies, Queer Aesthetics

For decades, scholars and queers and queer scholars have looked to technology for answers, community, and theories of identity. Particularly with the mainstream use of the internet, queer theorists have mapped existing frameworks onto technological bases and, more often, attempted to imagine queerer futures that either incorporate or are entirely reliant on internet technology. Zach Blas has been a key figure in these formulations, working throughout his career as a scholar and as a filmmaker and artist to articulate how to use technology queerly and how queer users can and should use technology. In *Gay Bombs: User's Manual* (2008), published via Blas' activist group and art collective Queer Technologies, Inc., Blas instructed readers to "use this manual as a weapon," a guide for queer political action through the use and understanding of queer technologies (14). He argued that the standards set by technology tend to place us within the grasp of capitalism. In such an environment, then, what does *queer use* mean? To start with, it involves employing a strategy of disidentification, as theorized by José Esteban Muñoz. Muñoz argued that disidentification is the only move to make, that it describes "the survival strategies the minority subject practices in order to negotiate a phobic majoritarian public sphere that continuously elides or punishes the existence of subjects who do not conform to the phantasm of normative citizenship" (Muñoz 1999: 4). In other words, queer users must rethink encoded meanings, turning what was considered unthinkable into something real. Queer users must resist and reconfigure.

We can begin to think about the aesthetic dimension of these systems by focusing on the relationship between code (understood as obscure, beneath the surface, unseen) and its representation on a screen. In Lev Manovich's *The Language of New Media* (2001), he presented a dialectical understanding of a computer layer and a cultural layer, and how they interact: "we can say that they are being composited together. [...] Cultural categories and concepts are substituted, on the level of meaning and/or language, by new ones that derive from the computer's ontology, epistemology, and pragmatics" (64). Something like queer programming, then, would offer a way to interrupt the circulation of technical and visual interfaces, creating a possible route to technological agency for queer users by hijacking existing networked flows, as Blas and micha cárdenas argue: "Queer technologies identifies its larger discursive practices as a viral aesthetics, in that it encrypts itself within flows of capital to replicate/permeate itself in relation and tension to capital's own modulating, viral structure" (2013: 562). This positioning puts queer technology precisely within the realm of an aesthetic environment that is typically unable to permit its transgressions, and this tension is where possibility may reside.

What does this have to do with streaming platforms and queer television? For starters, consider the realm of politics. If you want to make a difference in the world, or in your community, should you become a politician and make change from inside the system, or should you become an activist and push for change from outside? A crude analogy, but we can think of queerness and technology in the same way. Netflix, Amazon, and other streamers are chief operators of the capitalist system, and queer creators or those hoping to create queer-themed content may or may not see an opportunity there to find a massive audience, taking advantage of the oppressive structure's techniques to spread counterhegemonic messages. After all, through their mythological recommendation engines, Netflix in particular is capable of turning something into a phenomenon overnight, like when *Schitt's Creek* (a CBC Television/Pop TV production created by Daniel Levy, who is gay; his character in the show is pansexual) was added to the platform and proceeded to blow up (shows like The CW's *Riverdale* and the Lifetime Network's *You* experienced similar boons) (Adalian 2019). The Wachowski sisters and J. Michael Straczynski, for instance, took their concept for *Sense8* and some spec scripts to Netflix, emphasizing the themes of identity, gender, sexuality, and privacy, along with an intention to depict the ways "technology simultaneously unites and divides us," as the Wachowskis put it in the Netflix press release about the series' announcement (PR Newswire 2013). As Netflix CCO Ted Sarandos said about the Wachowskis and Straczynski, "Their incredible creations are favorites of Netflix members globally and we can't wait to bring *Sense8* to life," referring to the data Netflix had about how many people had been watching *The Matrix* films and Straczynski's series *Babylon 5*, presumably. The creative team behind the series and Netflix executives found a data-driven synergy, then, with an opportunity to bring a decidedly queer story to a massive audience *and* an opportunity to release something with a built-in audience to serve your customers, respectively. Of course, the show's subsequent premature cancellation is part of this story, which we will soon return to. At any rate, this example illustrates how queer aesthetics and technology intersect within a system as standardizing as Hollywood using a mechanism of classification like algorithmic decision-making. Is *Sense8* a fluke, wherein this tension is only temporarily relieved for the expression of these queer aesthetics which rethink, reconfigure, and reimagine, or is there lingering potential?

Others are, perhaps unsurprisingly, less convinced about such synergistic approaches to queer technologies and aesthetics. To get there, we should make sure we fully understand what we mean when we say that technology, data, algorithms, and computational programming can be, or are, queer. Kara Keeling, who describes *queer* as "an orientation toward various and shifting aspects of existing reality and the social norms they govern," (2014: 153) articulates what a "Queer OS" could look like within the confines of a hegemonic technological system. She suggests it would acknowledge "its own imbrication with and reliance on those logics while still striving to forge new relationships and connections" (154). Perhaps this is inevitable. As Jacob Gaboury has found in charting his "Queer History of Computing" (2013), "queerness is itself inherent within computational logic," a self-shattering that engenders a queer digital method. In this formulation, we must embrace queer *as* a technology.

Blas, Cárdenas, Gaboury, and others followed Keeling with a collaborative project called "QueerOS: A User's Manual," which sought to provide a largely speculative vision of a queer operating system in practice, wherein difference and social formation would be fused with technology that is defined by both resistance and potentiality, a "relational network of queer kinship with and between people and systems" (2015: 51). The idea is to make a case for *queerness as systemic*, embracing a technology that is uncertain, precarious, illegible, unreliable, unstable, yet liberated—a reflection of queer subjectivity. Yet here they regularly note the project's utopian futurity, its speculative form and use. As Muñoz has convincingly argued, queerness is

> not yet here...We may never touch queerness, but we can feel it as the warm illumination of a horizon imbued with potentiality. We have never been queer, yet queerness exists for us as an ideality that can be distilled from the past and used to imagine a future. The future is queerness's domain.
>
> *Muñoz 2009: 1*

This is undeniably inspiring and invigorating as a theoretical project, yet perhaps unavoidably these speculative proposals are further reminders of what we have now—put differently, while it is useful to envision an ideal, we should at the same time reckon with what we're given, because it may be that it's *too late* to fuse queerness with actually existing technology.

Cáel M. Keegan has argued that in mainstream representations of queerness, there is a pattern of "*disruptive innovation* in the portrayal of past LGBTQ lives and the resulting *aesthetic gentrification* of queer and trans cinematic worlds" (2016: 50). Charting the recent history of queer cinema, Keegan notes that the radical filmmakers of the New Queer Cinema in the 1990s have been largely displaced by executives and producers more interested in appealing to a broader audience, particularly in an age of marriage equality in the United States that coalesces with the rise of data-driven demographics. Building from Sarah Schulman's work on urban space and aesthetics and on Harvard Business School professor Clay Christensen's work on disruption and innovation, Keegan contends that aesthetics, much like gadgets or computers, follow the logic that

> consumers are often willing to tolerate a downgrade in product quality (e.g. streaming video or music over high-resolution hard media) in exchange for a more flexible delivery system, and that such downgrades are often effective in penetrating previously disinterested markets.
>
> *51*

This is the logic of immediacy and convenience that dominates Silicon Valley solutionism, but applied to aesthetics and to cultural products, it can also explain the downgrades consumers (i.e. audiences) accept in exchange for the ease of use Netflix and other streamers provide. It is incredibly easy to log into Netflix, peruse their "LGBTQ" section, and pick something to watch. Moreover, LGBTQ+ audiences have been primed by advertisers and the media over decades to accept and celebrate the morsels given to us by these companies, a *good enough* gratefulness for being represented at all in an ecosystem that typically evades us (think of the mid-credits reveal that the protagonist teen girl of *The Mitchells vs. The Machines*, an animated 2021 Netflix film, is seemingly queer). Using examples such as *Dallas Buyers Club* (2013), *Stonewall* (2015), and *The Danish Girl* (2015), Keegan diagnoses mainstream queer cinema as being "saturated with fear" as it "struggles to reflect anything but our obsession with safety, familiarity, and sameness" (56). This gentrification is endemic to modern cinema and television, he argues, which "appropriate aesthetic capital from communities that already have little to no cultural representation" (55). The logics of safety, familiarity, and sameness are further operationalized by algorithms, a standardizing technology being utilized to help create and market marginalized stories. What better way to understand Netflix's approach to content than as aesthetic capital?

The relationship between aesthetic gentrification and algorithmic production is key to understanding the state of queer aesthetics in the streaming age of television. The more we learn about the value of data to companies like Netflix, the clearer it becomes that the symbolic nature of algorithmic functions is perpetuating existing systems of watered-down aesthetics and representational service. Consider, for instance, Netflix's partnership with Ryan Murphy, one of the company's first high-profile development deals. The deal, worth $300 million over five years, has thus far resulted in *The Politician*, *Hollywood*, *Ratched*, *Halston*, and the film *The Prom*, with projects based on Jeffrey Dahmer and *A Chorus Line* in the works at the time of writing. Regardless of what one thinks about any of these projects, it is worth considering the cost/benefit to Netflix's pricey deal with Murphy. Put simply, as Netflix relies less on expensive licensing (letting *Friends* and *The Office* lapse, for example) and more on building a hefty Originals library to compete with other streamers, it depends on risk management and algorithmic determinations thereof. Netflix surely had data on how many subscribers watched *Glee*, *American Horror Story*, *Nip/Tuck*, and *Scream Queens* on their platform, all Murphy productions. We can infer, then, that $300 million was resolved to be an amount worth paying to ensure that this engagement would replicate itself through new Murphy series, and that this could draw a number of new subscribers. This process was undoubtedly assisted by algorithms, processing endless amounts of viewer data to reveal the value of Murphy himself to the company. Importantly, Netflix would not spend hundreds of millions of dollars on a creative talent that would risk their reputation or provoke outrage among their subscribers or shareholders. Like any publicly traded corporation, Netflix is beholden to the whims and interests of its shareholders, which includes giant asset management companies like BlackRock and Vanguard, who themselves specialize in risk management for investment, which is what we're talking about here anyway, creative investment. Like any subscription-based platform, Netflix wants to maintain existing subscribers and draw new ones with the content it has to offer and the promise of more. If we take a step back and remember that queer aesthetics are about *interrupting the flow* of what has come before, it follows that a company like Netflix has no real incentive to take that kind of risk within a streaming ecosystem full of fierce competitors. Murphy, then, provides palatable content that is easy to binge, populated with queer characters and romances, but rarely daring to interrupt the flow. These shows are, by and large, aesthetically indistinguishable from most network television, defined by overblown or harsh lighting, sanitized production design and sets, an abundance of white performers, and coherent storytelling and editing that holds the viewer's attention through a visual logic that is familiar and safe, purposefully bereft of formal transgression. This is by design.

Platformed Desires

Netflix, as Matthew Ball, an analyst, writer, and venture capitalist, suggests, is "as much a technology and product company as Google, Apple or Amazon" (2018). This has become common knowledge in recent years, as its status as a media company is inextricable from its tech and product operations. As Ball explains, Netflix's primary KPI (key performance indicator) is *hours per subscriber per month*, and so every decision they make is geared toward customer retention and consumption, from the intuitiveness of their interface (which is far easier and more pleasurable to navigate than Amazon Prime Video, for example) to what content is emphasized for each user. For example, cover art, Ball says, is algorithmically determined to personalize a product to a user to make them more likely to take a chance on it (which has led to some issues, as some users reported being targeted by their race, which is not information that Netflix users provide [Zarum 2018]). Ball points to Netflix's own materials about how it evaluates new content deals. The company says:

> We utilize detailed statistical models to determine expected hours of viewing for each piece of content over its license period. We compare cost per hour viewed against other "like" content deals (i.e. exclusive versus non-exclusive, TV versus movies, etc.) We look for high engagement and cost efficiency. For renewals, we look to renew content that performs well (based on hours generated relative to the cost) and do not renew content where the price doesn't make sense relative to the value generated. We feel we have [a] good breadth of content so that no specific title or set of titles is must-renew.
>
> *"Top Investor Questions"*

It's worth quoting Netflix at length here, as it highlights our reliance on the company's own reports to make sense of its operations, as it notoriously fiercely protects its proprietary information. We can extrapolate from this that they employ a number of algorithms and models to generate how they should act through content-as-engagement principles. In effect, we can assume that the cost-per-hour of a series like *The Crown* must be relatively low (meaning that it has quite a high rate of engagement) for such a lavishly expensive production, considering its renewal for six full seasons (most Netflix Originals do not last that long). Taken together, this tells us that Netflix is able to weaponize the well-documented database of user behaviors that it collects (from how many episodes in a row users watch to how often they pause) to inform every decision the company makes. Tech, product, media—it's all one. Again, queerness is founded in risk, and risk is the antithesis of KPIs and hours per subscriber per month and proprietary data. Murphy's $300 million deal, then, was struck based on what their "detailed statistical models"—algorithms—told them about his engagement and cost. The projected "value generated" was presumably deemed to be sufficient for the price. What is queer about a risk-free decision that seeks to provide subscribers with more of what they (or their data says that they) already like?

Ed Finn (2017) points out that this data gathering, especially in terms of aesthetic content, is an "ambitious leap forward in expanding the calculabe terrain, declaring that complex cultural concepts like the lightness or darkness of a film's humor can be quantified" (93), and moreover that these quantifications can have direct consequences on Netflix production, distribution, and consumption. Finn rightly emphasizes that this is enormously significant to Netflix's brand, which is tightly controlled: "For Netflix, the brand is algorithmic, the magic computational, and the humans are kept carefully out of the spotlight" (94). Of course, human taggers and designers are a part of the process at every step, but their role is likewise deliberately black boxed from view and obscured through the brand's techno-solutionism. The implications of this system on production are many. As the story goes, Netflix's algorithms kept showing *Perry Mason*, the original CBS series that ran from 1957 to 1966, at the top of countless algorithmic lists: the top directors based on Netflix data included *Mason* director Christian I. Nyby II, and besting all others for favorite actor was Mason himself, Raymond Burr. Netflix had no explanation for this, according to Finn, but trusted in it all the same. The data doesn't lie.

In a context where the stakes are not only recommendations but productions, this takes on added weight. As Finn articulates, the result of this system is that in most cases, the actual content of what is created barely matters, as long as it will fill a series of quadrants as identified by the company's algorithms. With *House of Cards* as an example, "the most important pieces were in place as soon as the ink dried on the contract: Fincher was there; Spacey was there. Let the artists make two seasons and Netflix would make sure we watched them" (Finn: 99), with algorithmically targeted trailers (arty shots for Fincher fans, a focus on Robin Wright for those who watch a lot of strong female leads) and in-platform interface placement. In effect, the show itself only matters insofar as it performs as well as Netflix anticipates, so creators are generally given a wide latitude. This could be a possible opportunity for queer content and aesthetics, then, as a way to take your creation in any direction once you've been fingered as fulfilling the basic algorithmic purpose that Netflix desires. Much of the discourse around Netflix and its algorithms has been about how it directly impacts the narratives of their shows, but the larger impact is felt in marketing, interfacing, and aesthetics, the enveloping forces of a platform with specific requirements that have less to do with character arcs and more to do with camera and lens selection or casting—or which productions are algorithmically deemed valuable to begin with. Finn argues that this is a "new form of authorship," and so "the aesthetic of abstraction" permeates each series "from inception to delivery, demanding a new literacy from viewers in order to participate in the work of the Netflix culture machine" (109). To even be in a position to enjoy the latitude given to Netflix creators, a "queer series," so to speak, would need to be proved demographically appealing enough through the platform's data to warrant being greenlit.

Sense8, for example, offered Netflix the chance to help make its claim as a globalized entertainment leader, as the show was filmed in countries all around the world and its global setting was repeatedly highlighted in marketing material. Any queer content, aesthetic or otherwise, would essentially be consequential. Combined with the Wachowskis and Straczynski being involved and being able to serve a variety of demographics not often catered to, including the transgender community, the series was put into production with a cost of $4.5 million per episode in the first season, and $9 million in the second. It was praised for its queer storylines, its global appeal, and for its visual effects and intersecting storytelling. Notably, though, the show experimented with narration and legibility, using Netflix's insistence on the use of 4K resolution cameras to play with its capabilities and weave characters together across space and time in inventive or even confounding ways that relied more on emotional logic than editing. The series gained a cult following, especially among LGBTQ+ audiences, and though Netflix does not release viewership data, it never became a mainstream cultural phenomenon. In some ways, we can see the decision to cancel the series as a traditional one for the television industry: the series was too expensive to justify the smallness of its impact. Putting aside the purposeful unknowability of the show's actual viewership numbers (which would allow us to more holistically evaluate its demise), its ultimate cancellation tells us that Netflix's models ran the numbers and simply found that hours per subscriber per month was not being improved enough by *Sense8* to justify its cost. Netflix repeatedly praised the show for its success, especially in markets such as Brazil and France, and used it to help promote their brand's global growth and dominance. Sarandos said that despite the show's passionate fandom, the numbers didn't support a renewal: "We couldn't support those economics. If you put all your money into something that a very few people are watching, eventually you'll have nothing for people to watch" (Ge 2017). Even more interestingly, Sarandos went on to specifically highlight how the series broke new ground, "being a show rooted in concepts of gender and identity," suggesting that he personally felt the show had been "beautiful" and "incredibly ambitious," but that the company was powerless against the numbers. Sarandos is, however indirectly, acknowledging the show's tendency to interrupt the flow of traditional television, not only through its themes and characters but also in its very form and in its (admittedly exorbitant) production needs. This comingling of queer content and materiality suggests that the series was simply too outside of the norm, too disruptive, too aesthetically flamboyant. Given the rare opportunity to take advantage of streaming-era creative latitude, *Sense8* essentially bit off more than the company was willing to give based on what their data told them about risk, cost, and value. In the end, the episodes that already existed had fulfilled their demographic purpose. Letting it finish on its own creative terms was not important. The second season ended with a cliffhanger, in the hope of managing to land a deal for a third season, so after fan reaction, Netflix did put a series finale into production. Nevertheless, even this example is a rarity within the streaming ecosystem and its deference to data, which tends to delimit the boundaries of sure-things and safe bets.

Algorithmic Abstractions

For years, financial analysts have argued that Netflix's spending cannot maintain its momentum as debt piles up into billions. The company's debt, around $15 billion at the time of writing, has yet to bring them to heel. This is because financialization has altered the operations of capitalist firms to such a degree that credit and debt are not only expected but necessary as networked flows of capital travel between firms through intermediaries and banks to offset any risk while sustaining at least the appearance of solvency. In other, simpler words, Netflix's debt drive is not a bug but a feature by which they are able to leverage its debts to generate more value. As a result, the company is able to spend billions annually on original content and it is almost always low risk thanks to the algorithmic decision-making that facilitates a practice of mass customization. And yet, as Finn noted, these customizations are, more often than not, attributable to an aesthetic of abstraction. An acquisition's actual performance is almost beside the point in an environment where it simply fills in a gap, as yet another piece of content to slot into predetermined genre categories in the app interface. To put it crudely: quantity over quality. Finn points out that Netflix has tens of thousands of hyper-specific genres to offer users in their interface, including many that have yet to be populated with a single piece of content—why not fill those gaps with new content, to give your algorithms more data to help you make better decisions about new content, and so on. Feeding the algorithm feeds the beast of capital, and the cycle continues. *Sense8*, then, was a casualty of this aesthetic—once it had served its purpose of filling that gap (let's say something like Global Sci-Fi LGBTQ Action/Adventure?), its costs were seen as an unnecessary suck on Netflix's resources that could be better spent on greenlighting something that would fill a new gap.

In his book *Never Alone, Except For Now: Art, Networks, Populations*, Kris Cohen argues that there are two social models best suited for understanding the particular spaces of networked life: the population form and the group form. Group form combines data production with self-conscious group production to create a networked collectivity. Populations, for Cohen, are aggregations of data. "Populations are not individuals amassed so much as the effect and source of variance," and populations "are collectives of protocol and algorithm rather than of autopoesis or recursivity or conscious action" (Cohen 2017: 32, 38). The tricky thing about populations is that they have a veneer of benevolence and representational acuity. Populations create collectives, which can have the appearance of being formed around something tangible, an identity or an allegiance. This is an illusion, Cohen argues. "There is no equality in a population; just more data, more and more personalized forms of address, more deployments of that data" (70). In other words, we are grouped into populations as abstractions, all the better to target with personalized subgenres of TV shows that "people like you," within a population, also watched. This is largely how the online advertising industry is run, as companies like Facebook and Google likewise have less interest in you specifically and more in what your data can do to help form larger but distinct populations of users to better target with ads. Finn reaches a similar conclusion, finding that in our everyday online experience, "the ever-lengthening trail of judgments, indulgences, and other cultural decision points we leave behind on digital platforms can lead to the algorithmic assemblage of digital selves that are both *highly specific and highly abstract*" (109–110). It's not that the logic of the algorithm replaces all, but that aesthetic and representational concerns are forced to cooperate with the algorithm, and to forfeit any instincts (of resistance, of disruption, of transgression) that would contradict the algorithm. If a Netflix user, then, is being shown *The Politician* and *Sense8*, that's not because they have been identified as a *queer user*, but as a *population* that is to be served via highly specific but highly abstract categorizations.

This aesthetic of abstraction, as I've suggested, is incompatible with any proper notion of queer aesthetics. A queer aesthetic would be defined by its fluidity, its anti-normative understanding of formalism and narrative, its refusal to kowtow to accepted standardizations. If users, queer or otherwise, are fundamentally abstracted by algorithms, then they cannot be represented by them—moreover, perhaps they don't want to be. Noah A. Tsika writes in his book *Pink 2.0: Encoding Queer Cinema on the Internet* (2016) that if

> the internet makes it hard to parse a profoundly disruptive queerness, then perhaps that's a good thing—it means that queerness, imagined as a limitless process, hasn't yet been monetized, that its promises and particularities remain too powerful and too plentiful for extant interfaces and algorithms to assimilate them.
>
> *56*

Perhaps, then, we are looking in the wrong place to begin with and must take heed of the utopian visions of Blas and others to inform how we can build other spaces for queer aesthetics in the streaming age. Until then, of course, there's probably a new Ryan Murphy series up on Netflix.

Bibliography

Adalian, Josef. "The Unlikely Rise of Schitt's Creek," *Vulture* [*New York Magazine*], April 7 2020 [originally published January 2019], www.vulture.com/2020/04/schitts-creek-netflix-pop-success-story.html

Ball, Matthew. "Netflix Is a Product & Technology Company," *Blog*, May 12, 2018, www.matthewball.vc/all/netflixproduct

Barnett, Fiona, Zach Blas, micha cárdenas, Jacob Gaboury, Jessica Marie Johnson, and Margaret Rhee. "QueerOS: A User's Manual," in *Debates in the Digital Humanities 2016*, Matthew Gold and Lauren Klein, eds. Minneapolis: University of Minnesota Press, 2015.

Blas, Zach. *Gay Bombs: User's Manual*. Queer Technologies, Inc., 2008.

Blas, Zach and micha cárdenas. "Imaginary Computational Systems: Queer Technologies and Transreal Aesthetics," *AI & Society* 28.4 (December 2013): 559–566.

Cho, Alexander. "Queer Reverb: Tumblr, Affect, Time," in *Networked Affect*, Susanna Paasonen, Ken Hillis, Michael Petit, eds. Cambridge: MIT Press, 2015.

Cohen, Cathy J. "Punks, Bulldaggers, and Welfare Queens: The Radical Potential of Queer Politics?" in *Black Queer Studies. A Critical Anthology*, Patrick E. Johnson and Mae G. Henderson, eds. Durham/London: Duke University Press, 2005.

Cohen, Kris. *Never Alone, Except For Now: Art, Networks, Populations*. Durham: Duke University Press, 2017.

Duffy, Nick. "Ben Platt on Ryan Murphy and How Everyone is 'a Little Bit Queer' in Netflix's The Politician," *Pink News*, September 20 2019, www.pinknews.co.uk/2019/09/20/ben-platt-the-politician-ryan-murphy-queer-interview/

Finn, Ed. *What Algorithms Want: Imagination in the Age of Computing*. Cambridge: MIT Press, 2017.

Gaboury, Jacob. "A Queer History of Computing," *Rhizome,* February 19, 2013, https://rhizome.org/editorial/2013/feb/19/queer-computing-1/

Ge, Linda. "Netflix Boss on 'The Get Down,' 'Sense8' Cancellations: 'We Couldn't Support Those Economics'," *The Wrap*, June 10, 2017, www.thewrap.com/netflix-ted-sarandos-defends-get-down-sense8-cancellation/

Hayes, Dade. "Netflix's Ted Sarandos Weighs In On Streaming Wars, Agency Production, Big Tech Breakups, M&A Outlook—Update," *Deadline*, June 22, 2019, https://deadline.com/2019/06/netflix-ted-sarandos-weighs-in-on-streaming-wars-agency-production-big-tech-breakups-ma-outlook-1202636595/

Keegan, Cáel M. "History, Disrupted: The Aesthetic Gentrification of Queer and Trans Cinema," *Social Alternatives* 35.3 (2016): 50–56.

Keeling, Kara. "Queer OS," *Cinema Journal* 53.2 (Winter 2014): 152–157.

Manovich, Lev. *The Language of New Media*. Cambridge: MIT Press, 2001.

Muñoz, José Esteban. *Disidentifications: Queers of Color and the Performance of Politics*. Minneapolis: University of Minnesota Press, 1999.

Muñoz, José Esteban. *Cruising Utopia: The Then and There of Queer Futurity*. New York: NYU Press, 2009.

Netflix, "Research Areas: Machine Learning," https://research.netflix.com/research-area/machine-learning, last accessed December 15, 2022.

Netflix, "Top Investor Questions," https://ir.netflix.net/ir-overview/top-investor-questions/default.aspx, last accessed December 15, 2022.

PR Newswire, "Only on Netflix: Sci-Fi Giants The Wachowskis And J. Michael Straczynski Team-Up To Create 'Sense8'", May 27, 2013, www.prnewswire.com/news-releases/only-on-netflix-sci-fi-giants-the-wachowskis-and-j-michael-straczynski-team-up-to-create-sense8-200215501.html

Tsika, Noah A. *Pink 2.0: Encoding Queer Cinema on the Internet*. Bloomington: Indiana University Press, 2016.
Wu, Tim. "Netflix's Secret Special Algorithm is a Human," *The New Yorker*, January 27, 2015, www.newyorker.com/business/currency/hollywoods-big-data-big-deal
Zarum, Lara. "Some Viewers Think Netflix Is Targeting Them By Race. Here's What To Know." *New York Times*, October 23, 2018, www.nytimes.com/2018/10/23/arts/television/netflix-race-targeting-personalization.html

PART IV

Industrial Contextualization

Studying Production Processes

13

TELEVISING LESBIAN FEMINIST LOVE-POLITICS ON *DYKE TV*

Lauren Herold

In 1993, *New York Magazine*'s May issue declared the arrival of "lesbian chic." Featuring interviews with lesbian celebrities Martina Navratilova and k. d. lang, the article claimed that lesbians in the 1990s could finally be "stylish" and "corporate" as well as "political" and "proud" (Kasindorf 1993). This article was quickly followed by *Newsweek*'s June issue, which claimed lesbians were "coming out strong" at the same time as it questioned, "what are the limits of tolerance?", as well as *Vanity Fair*'s now-famous August issue, in which lang posed with supermodel Cindy Crawford in a butch-femme barbershop fantasy photoshoot for the magazine's cover.

The lesbian chic phenomenon seemed to indicate an increase in the visibility and cultural capital of lesbians. For perhaps the first time, lesbian celebrities and executives could have successful careers while being open about their sexualities. Yet the phenomenon was marked with much skepticism from lesbian activists and academics, who were uncertain about the impact of this new media attention. Journalist and activist Ann Northrop argued that these articles did not do justice to myriad political concerns of lesbian activists and in fact exploited lesbians for commercial gain ("Episode 1" 1993). Similarly, Ann M. Ciasullo concluded that the 1990s lesbian chic representations made queer women into objects of desire for a heterosexual majority: "the lesbian body is marked and made 'tasteful' for the viewing public—made, in essence, palatable for mainstream consumers to consume" (Ciasullo 2001, 579). Lesbian chic stories typically portrayed lesbians as white, wealthy, and normatively feminine, a characterization that many felt misrepresented the diversity of their communities.

Dyke TV (1993–2006), a half-hour public access cable television program focused on feminist and lesbian public cultures and community issues, premiered during the same summer of "lesbian chic." Created by three lesbian artist-activists—Cuban

DOI: 10.4324/9781003109044-18

playwright Ana Maria Simo, theater director and producer Linda Chapman, and independent filmmaker Mary Patierno—*Dyke TV* intervened in the "lesbian chic" phenomenon by creating television by and for lesbians. Designed as a magazine-format program, *Dyke TV* covered a wide range of topics, including community news and events, health issues, activism, art and film, and sports, with a focus on stories affecting lesbian, bisexual, and queer women. *Dyke TV* aired on one of the two Manhattan Neighborhood Network access channels from 1993 to 2006, as well as on Free Speech TV, a national, independent news network that amplifies underrepresented voices, from 2000 onward. In 1994, *Dyke TV* expanded its distribution outside of Manhattan to 14 other cities; at its widest distribution, the show aired on public access channels in 78 cities around the country ("Dyke TV ·Herstories: Audio/Visual Collections of the LHA" n.d.). Critically acclaimed by both LGBTQ and mainstream news publications—*The New York Times* called the show "its own best advertisement"—*Dyke TV* brought the diversity of lesbian communities into living rooms across the United States for perhaps the first time (Witchel 1994, 14).

This chapter explores *Dyke TV*'s significance as the first nationally cablecast show dedicated to discussing lesbian feminist community and culture. I define the term "lesbian community" loosely here, referring to individuals with a wide variety of gender and sexual identities. *Dyke TV* profiled a range of issues, including segments that discussed women living with AIDS, lesbians in prison, domestic violence, Black lesbian literature, butch and transgender masculinity, trans femininity, as well as spirituality, nightlife, and hate crimes. The show's purview included LGBTQ people marginalized by heteropatriarchal systems, rather than just women who identified as dykes. Indeed, *Dyke TV* included trans people as guests and producers on the show and covered issues affecting trans people. The capacious understanding of "dyke" in *Dyke TV* is worth exploring.

An analysis of *Dyke TV* demonstrates the significance of noncommercial and local television and older media as historical sites of possibility for LGBTQ television producers. I examine the show's development and content, arguing that *Dyke TV* embraces what I call lesbian feminist love-politics: a willful sensibility and political orientation committed to celebrating queer women's community culture. Drawing upon Jennifer Nash's conception of love-politics, I establish love—the love for one's self, love for one's partners, and love for one's community—as the political and affective orientation of *Dyke TV*. I explore how *Dyke TV* responded to the lack of "love" for lesbian communities on the broader social and political level, opposing the homophobic and sexist ideologies that rendered lesbian sexuality deviant, abnormal, and/or fetishized, by mobilizing lesbian feminist love-politics toward cultural and political commentary and activism. While declining resources eventually caused the show to stop production entirely, the legacy of the show remains its investment in lesbian feminism: an embrace of love-politics enabled *Dyke TV* to imagine forms of "dyke" relationality marked by an orientation to an expansive queer community rather than exclusive and precise definitions of identity.

Lesbian Feminist Love-Politics on *Dyke TV*

The development and on-screen content of *Dyke TV* are marked by what I call lesbian feminist love-politics. In "Practicing Love: Black Feminism, Love-Politics, and Post-Intersectionality," Jennifer Nash argues that Black feminist theory generates a theory of justice based in the care of self and community. While Black feminist thought has been "reduced" to intersectionality theory in ways that limit its political potential, Nash asserts that this writing evokes "a broad activist conception of love" that reimagines one's relationship to the self and to broader political formation (Nash 2013, 4–5). Nash (2013, 19) claims that love is

> a call for a labor of the self, an appeal for transcending the self, a strategy for remaking the public sphere, a plea to unleash the radical imagination, and a critique of the state's blindness to the violence it inflicts and enables.

Black feminist love-politics calls for a utopian future free from the oppressive conditions of the present and built upon connection and collectivity. Rather than imagining community based on shared identity, love-politics, Nash argues, imagines connection based on communal sentiment. As a nonidentitarian project, Black feminist love-politics "offers a powerful reconception of the public sphere" oriented around collectivity rather than identity and difference (Nash 2013, 13).

Lesbian feminist theory has similarly been marginalized in academic texts; it is frequently relegated to the past, considered a necessary but outdated precursor to queer theory. As Sarah Ahmed (2017, 222) writes, "the lesbian appears as an abject figure we were all surely happy to have left behind" in much of queer theoretical writing. Lesbian feminism is often rewritten as an essentialist project limited to simplified understandings of identity, womanhood, gender, and power, where queer theory emerges as a project invested in deconstructing and rethinking the terms of these debates. This chapter intervenes in this scholarly conversation by rereading lesbian feminism as a liberatory ideology for all those marginalized by heteropatriarchal systems.

What I call a lesbian feminist conception of love-politics emerges from the canon of lesbian feminist theory. Lesbian feminist love-politics adds to Nash's conception of the term by exploring the radical potential of erotic connection between women. From these theories, a version of love-politics emerges that imagines the utopian possibilities of lesbian relationality. For example, in their 1970 essay manifesto, the collective the Radicalesbians asserts the need for women to realize the "primacy of women relating to women" (The Radicalesbians 1997, 157). According to the Radicalesbians (1997, 156), women must free themselves from patriarchal definitions of womanhood and embrace a new sense of self, or a new "consciousness," based on solidarity with other women. The Radicalesbians suggest that this new consciousness sparked by relationships between women will ignite a revolutionary movement toward women's autonomy. In another foundational essay, "Compulsory Heterosexuality and Lesbian Existence," Adrienne Rich critiques the way in which heterosexuality is produced as a social expectation for women, rendering lesbian sexuality a deviant aberration. Rich (1980, 648) theorizes the possibilities of what she calls "the lesbian continuum" as an alternate social form to compulsory heterosexuality. Rich describes the lesbian continuum as a variety of experiences "of primary intensity shared between and among women," ranging from breastfeeding and childrearing to friendship, community, political alliance, and sexual intimacy. In Rich's formation, the existence of the lesbian continuum destabilizes compulsory heterosexuality; it can "undo the power men everywhere wield over women" by placing a primacy on relationships among women rather than relationships between women and men (1980, 660). Cheryl Clarke's "Lesbianism: An Act of Resistance," originally published in the feminist anthology *This Bridge Called My Back: Writings by Radical Women of Color*, similarly explores the personal and political power of lesbian relationships. Clarke (1983, 130) sharply critiques heterosexuality as an oppressive norm that contributes to the marginalization of women. Clarke passionately believes in the power of lesbianism to oppose these systems of oppression: lesbianism is "an ideological, political, and philosophical means of liberation of all women" (1983, 129).

These theories envision relationship as a key site through which women can reimagine the public sphere as a space free from patriarchal oppression. For the Radicalesbians, Rich, and Clarke, love and intimacy between women hold transformative possibilities. Interestingly, each of these writers embraces a non-identitarian love-politics in their respective pieces. As Nash (2013, 19) writes, love-politics crafts a "future-oriented community held together by affiliation and 'public feeling' rather than an imagined—or enforced—sameness." While Rich, the Radicalesbians, and Clarke discuss the significance of lesbianism and lesbian relationships, each defines the term "lesbian" in expansive ways. The Radicalesbians imagine lesbianism as the psychological state of women under patriarchal oppression; Rich argues that lesbianism is not an aberration but a continuum of behaviors which many experience; and Clarke considers lesbianism as an anti-oppressive ideology as much as a sexual preference. By including but not limiting lesbianism to erotic connection, these definitions expand the meaning of the term so that it applies to a greater number of women.

Dyke TV televises lesbian feminist love-politics through its commitment to covering queer women's community in New York and around the country. The show emerged as a part of the resurgence of radical queer activism in New York in the 1980s and early 1990s. Following years of government inaction on the AIDS crisis, many in LGBTQ communities joined grassroots activist groups, such as the AIDS Coalition To Unleash Power (ACT UP) and Queer Nation, to work together to end the AIDS crisis. While women participated in these groups as allies, activists, as well as people living with AIDS, lesbian activists like writer and public intellectual Sarah Schulman criticized the fact that ACT UP never made central lesbian issues. "The time has come for a new lesbian activism—in or out of ACT UP," Shulman wrote in 1991, "We have to fully participate in activism to create a country that *we* want to live in" (Schulman 2018, 216). In 1992, Shulman, along with five other lesbian activists in New York, created the feminist visual collective the Lesbian Avengers, a group that Schulman called "a post-ACT UP lesbian movement" (Schulman 2018, 282). A group "focused on issues vital to lesbian survival and visibility," the Lesbian Avengers coordinated both local and national protests and demonstrations, including the first Dyke March in 1993, using public intervention as a tactic to bring media attention to the intersections of homophobia and sexism (Cogswell 2014, 9). As Schulman wrote at the time, "The Avengers represent a turning point in lesbian politics, a belief in grass-roots, a commitment to direct action and creative organizing" (Schulman 2018, 286).

Dyke TV both chronicled and helped shape this historical moment. It is not a coincidence that one of its executive producers, Ana Maria Simo, was also a prominent Lesbian Avenger—the two projects were deeply related. I interviewed ten people involved in the production of *Dyke TV* to learn more about the history and development of the show. Over a series of emails, Simo shared that she pitched the idea of a lesbian cable access show to Linda Chapman and Mary Patierno in the autumn of 1992. Simo hoped the show would become a "stealthy agitprop instrument" on television editorially independent from, but politically aligned with, the Lesbian Avengers (Ana Maria Simo, email interview with the author, August 2019). "The Avengers urgently needed to set up our own alternative media" in order to "report on our work and, crucially, to expand our reach beyond the initial dyke activist community," Simo believed (Simo, interview). This activist impulse is palpable on the show: as each episode opens, the host of the show announces, "You're watching *Dyke TV*: television to incite, subvert, provoke, and organize."

After joining the team, Patierno and Chapman quickly added to Simo's vision: whereas Simo was primarily interested in reporting on the news and covering political demonstrations around the city, Chapman and Patierno used their connections in the professional arts world to expand the purview of the show. They both suggested using a magazine format on the show, which would allow it to cover a wide variety of issues, vary the content from episode to episode, and incorporate video made by and with volunteers from across the city and the country (Linda Chapman, interview with the author, September 2019). Working with a large network of volunteers was crucial to *Dyke TV*'s success, Simo, Patierno, and Chapman largely volunteered their own time and energy to produce weekly half-hour episodes, an overwhelming amount of work for three people. Consequently, they relied on volunteer producers to help create the show's content. In 1994, Manhattan Neighborhood Network offered the team a crucial grant: it provided funding for *Dyke TV* to hold free and low-cost workshops to teach women with little to no filmmaking experience how to produce video.

The *Dyke TV* founders continually affirmed that including a diverse array of lesbian voices in production was central to the mission of the show. Patierno explained:

> It was a real activist time, so there was these other lesbian groups in town… we would've been completely remiss if we didn't reach out…it just felt like a no brainer, to be honest. We lived in New York. It's a very diverse city…It

> would have been just a big void and a big problem if we didn't try to make the show reflect at least what our city was looked like and what the women in our city were doing.
>
> *Mary Patierno, interview, interview with the author, September 2019*

For Patierno, racial and ethnic diversity on *Dyke TV* was a "no brainer," in large part because the lesbian art and activist community in New York was itself diverse: including women of color as producers, hosts, and guests of the show was a natural byproduct of working and living in New York. The producers conducted ongoing outreach campaigns to other lesbian and LGBTQ groups to recruit a diverse group of volunteers. Women were quick to participate, Associate Producer Harriet Hirshorn suggested, because it gave them the opportunity to tell their own stories: "that notion of, you know, picking up a camera and telling your own story and telling the story of your community and telling the story of your community's ancestors…all of that was just really kind of riveting for people" (Harriet Hirshorn, Skype interview with the author, October 2019). Over the years, *Dyke TV* worked with the Asian Lesbians of the East Coast, the African Ancestral Lesbians United for Social Change, the Bronx Lesbians United in Sisterhood, and Las Buenas Amigas, among others, whose members each produced segments for the show on a wide range of topics.

The name of the show, decided at an early planning meeting in 1993, was purposefully provocative. "We felt like it really encapsulated the times, which was a little bit in your face," Patierno said (Patierno, interview). The word "dyke" is an historically pejorative term leveled against women whose gender expression and/or sexuality falls outside of heterosexual norms. Chapman shared that the *Dyke TV* founders wanted to "take back that title" and turn it into something "affirmative"—reclaiming the word "dyke" as something positive was part of the mission of the show because it helped the team "confront lesbian invisibility" (Chapman, interview). The *Dyke TV* founders' interest in "confronting lesbian invisibility" exemplified what Ann Cvetkovich calls a "countercultural politics of visibility" in lesbian media, a form of representation invested in making lesbians, and alternative lesbian cultures, visible to each other (Cvetkovich 2001, 289). If the term "politics of visibility" usually refers to analysis of how underrepresented groups are portrayed in commercial media, a "countercultural politics of visibility" examines how marginalized groups create images themselves for one another in the service of non-hegemonic representation. Using the word "dyke" in the title simultaneously got viewers' attention and demonstrated lesbian activists' desire for their own forum to create cultural and activist work. In an interview with *The Independent Film & Video Monthly*, Chapman expressed frustration that other LGBTQ television programs lacked coverage of lesbian topics: "Gay Cable Network just didn't satisfy us. *In the Life* wasn't really addressing the needs of the lesbian community. Nothing we were aware of was talking about our issue" (Saafied 1993).

Dyke TV's provocative tone is reflected in early logos for the show, in which the phrase "Dyke TV" is styled to resemble the logo of a superhero (see Figure 13.1).

FIGURE 13.1 Jocelyn Taylor hosts an episode of *Dyke TV*. The *Dyke TV* logo, pictured here inside the television screen on set, was styled to resemble the logo of a superhero.

Black and white capital letters spell out the word "dyke" and the letter "T" is placed vertically one on top of the letter "V," forming the shape of a triangle. Perhaps inspired by the irreverent demonstrations of the Lesbian Avengers, a group whose name calls to mind an image of vigilante caped crusaders fighting for justice, the style of the *Dyke TV* logo references popular culture understandings of heroism. The logo embraces the provocative sensibility of the show, as well as its irreverent spirit, playfully imagining the show as an intervention in the status quo.

Dyke TV most notably embraces love-politics in its recurring segments, which explored a wide variety of topics related to queer women's community issues. These segments provide an instructive example of what Cait McKinney calls information activism. Looking at lesbian community and advocacy projects from the 1970s to 1990s, McKinney argues that lesbian activists "generated information infrastructures" including newsletters, databases, switchboards, indexes, and archives to address "their frustrated desire for information about lesbian history and lesbian life" (McKinney 2020, 2). Lesbian information activism draws upon "a longer history of how lesbian feminists appropriate commonplace media technologies toward the goal of better, more accessible information that might sustain feminism, and the everyday lives of lesbians" (McKinney 2020, 6). A televisual form of information activism, *Dyke TV* circulates information about lesbian life, history, and advocacy in the service of sustaining lesbian community culture. The televisual information activism of the show aspired to a radically inclusive lesbian feminist love-politics throughout its segments.

Dyke TV's recurring "Lesbian Health" segments, for example, urged viewers to educate themselves about their physical and mental health. Topics included AIDS and HIV transmission, menstruation, menopause, breast cancer, family planning, and vaginal and cervical health. These segments recall the ethos of women's health movement of the 1970s, reminding viewers that, as argued by publications like *Our Bodies, Ourselves*, it is important to empower themselves in a world in which women's health care is marginalized. Sexual health was a particularly salient issue for LGBTQ people in the early 1990s, who desperately needed education and services around HIV/AIDS, and for queer women in particular, who were typically left out of mainstream news and medical research about the epidemic. The fact that cable access television in New York was relatively uncensored at the time was an asset to queer health activists, who could openly discuss sexual health on their own shows, thus allowing them to convey important information to their communities.

Other *Dyke TV* segments uplift the diversity of queer communities. Episodes typically open with a five-minute "News" segment reporting on LGBTQ current events around the country, focusing on but not exclusive to lesbian issues, followed by an "Eyewitness" segment offering an in-depth (5–15 minutes) investigative account of a particular subject. Many episodes include an "Arts" segment, profiling lesbian cultural producers; over the years this included Barbara Hammer, Cheryl Dunye, Carmelita Tropicana, Su Friedrich, Toshi Reagan, Nicole Eisenman, Barbara Smith, and Dorothy Allison. These recurring segments foreground a wide range of lesbian culture and issues, providing news coverage of arts and activism that would likely have otherwise gone unmentioned on television.

As *Dyke TV* expanded its reach via national distribution, it began incorporating national and international stories into its purview as well. In 1995, *Dyke TV* secured grant funding to attend the World Conference on Women in Beijing, China; producers combined their footage into an Eyewitness segment on lesbian organizing worldwide. In the early 2000s, *Dyke TV* fundraised to send producers on a road trip to different cities in the United States; the result was "*Dyke TV* On the Road," a recurring segment that shined a spotlight on lesbian organizations in cities like Seattle, Denver, and Portland. During this time period, *Dyke TV* similarly expanded its purview to include more stories about transgender people. In 2000, *Dyke TV* covered the political funeral and memorial service for Amanda Milan, a trans woman murdered in New York. In the same episode, a segment titled "Genderfuck" explores the fluidity of gender roles, identity, and presentation via interviews with a variety of people about how they understand their genders. Often aided by documentary aesthetics like the interview format, these segments provided trans people with the opportunity to speak about their own experiences on camera. By expanding its mission, *Dyke TV* implicitly and at times explicitly called for lesbian and queer communities to support trans issues and LGBTQ people around the world.

Finally, many segments on *Dyke TV* are infused with an erotic energy that celebrates love, sex, and healthy relationships between women. These included "Dyke Dish," a segment that shared lesbian celebrity and entertainment news and gossip, "Lexa's Lesbian Love Signs," which provided insight into dating via astrology, "Blind Date," a reality TV-esque segment that filmed lesbian couples on their first dates, "Clubland" and "Oh What a Night!," nightlife-themed segments that interviewed guests and staff at lesbian bars and parties throughout the city, and "What's Your Problem?", a call-in show within the show whose hosts gave viewers advice about their relationships. In these numerous segments, *Dyke TV* explored the many facets of lesbian dating: "U-hauling" (the common stereotype that lesbian relationships tend to progress quickly in emotional intensity), butch and femme gender presentation, the "lesbian bed death" stereotype, cruising, queer fashion aesthetics, monogamy, and infidelity. *Dyke TV* promoted erotic lesbian representation on screen in the service of making lesbians visible and accessible to each other, rather than making lesbian sexuality legible for a mainstream audience. It's notable that women of color consistently appear on screen in *Dyke TV* segments about sex and dating: racial and ethnic diversity are crucial to the project. By including women of color on screen in every episode, the show embraces an expansive and anti-racist imagination of lesbian community.

Promotional content for the show often imagines *Dyke TV* in the context of dating and relationships. One recurring commercial for the show, aired between its other segments, shares the story of two women who leave behind their heterosexual lifestyles in order to date each other. At the end of the commercial, voiceover narration declares, "Lesbianism, what a beautiful choice! Keep it that way. Support *Dyke TV*!" As the narrator speaks, the words "Lesbianism what a beautiful choice" appear superimposed over the image of the women in bright pink lettering (see Figure 13.2). Depicting a happy-go-lucky lesbian couple who leave behind heterosexuality, this commercial imagines the freedom-making potential of lesbian sexuality. While tongue-in-cheek, the rhetoric of the commercial suggests that women have the agency to choose loving relationships with one another. These *Dyke TV* commercials celebrate lesbian sexuality as a rejection of compulsory heterosexuality and a commitment to a better life.

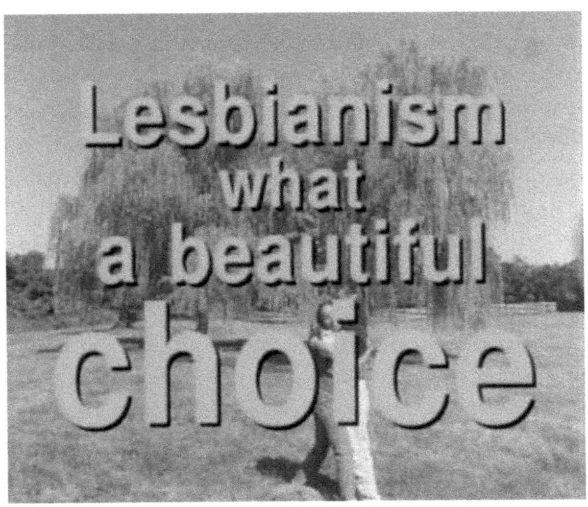

FIGURE 13.2 A still from an in-show commercial for *Dyke TV*.

Taking a closer look at examples of recurring segments on the show illuminates how its content televises different aspects of lesbian feminist community culture. Whether focused on the health and wellness, in-depth reporting on news and current events, erotic connection between women, and/or an expansive sense of community, lesbian feminist love-politics on *Dyke TV* embrace queer women's culture and community in the service of sustaining and celebrating it. Significantly, lesbian feminist love-politics on *Dyke TV* retains the nonidentitarian focus of Black and lesbian feminist theory. *Dyke TV*'s expansive understanding of "dyke" community culture imagines a lesbian community united by anti-sexist, anti-homophobic, and anti-racist politics rather than by sameness and identity. The content of the show generates lesbian feminist love-politics, implicitly and explicitly exploring and honoring lesbian community in all its diverse forms in order to advocate for a more just world in which queer life is celebrated rather than stigmatized. Analyzing *Dyke TV* highlights the expansiveness of lesbian feminist love-politics as a sensibility, a mode of thought, and a political project. Moving LGBTQ television studies toward a deeper engagement with feminist theory, studying *Dyke TV* suggests that the study of queer media may be enriched by a deeper dialogue with Black and lesbian feminist scholarship.

Dyke TV Evolves into the 2000s

Dyke TV faced a number of financial, technological, and social challenges into the mid-1990s and 2000s. A bequest from Mary Patierno's brother, David Miller, who passed away from complications due to AIDS in early 1993, provided the bulk of the early funding for *Dyke TV* (Patierno, interview). After funding from Miller's bequest ran out, the team began to have trouble raising funds to match all of its expenses, which included rent, office supplies, video equipment, and small salaries for its few staff members. As a result of the financial difficulties, *Dyke TV* episodes began airing biweekly and later monthly. Decreasing the production output lowered costs and reduced the constant pressure on staff and volunteers to create and edit content for the show. *Dyke TV* also began to offer workshops focused on digital media rather than just video production, including introductory courses to using the Internet, designing a website, and digital video editing, creating a new source of revenue for the show. Finally, *Dyke TV* moved offices to cheaper locations as rents rose across Manhattan and eventually moved to a storefront in Brooklyn. Lowering expenses and finding creative new sources of income allowed the show to continue production despite financial insecurity.

Dyke TV's move to Brooklyn, where it operated until the last episode aired in 2006, signaled a number of bigger shifts that may have led to the show's end. By the early 2000s, the founding producers of the show were largely not involved in its operations. Patierno, Chapman, Simo, and Hirshorn were more focused on their own projects and careers. By 2003, the most senior staff member was Jules Rosskam, a 23-year-old transgender filmmaker who served as the Executive Producer until 2005. While Rosskam, along with a number of volunteers, organized to produce

Dyke TV segments and episodes, the lack of mentorship from more experienced filmmaking professionals impacted the consistency and format of the show, as well as staff morale (Jules Rosskam, Skype interview with the author, November 2019). Constant financial insecurity plagued the small team, making it difficult to envision a sustainable future for the show (Rosskam, interview).

Technological and representational changes impacted the show as well. Cheaper video technologies and digital video editing software became widely available. By 2005, new digital streaming websites, YouTube in particular, provided a free (if corporate-funded) platform for video distribution. A burgeoning LGBTQ and feminist blogosphere shifted interest away from cable access toward new opportunities and platforms for writers online. These technological changes meant that many marginalized filmmakers could use new media technologies to tell their stories and share their perspectives without relying on *Dyke TV*'s resources. Similarly, as commercial media outlets grew interested in representing lesbian culture, *Dyke TV*'s efforts to claim a space for lesbian visibility on television became less urgent. In the years between 1993 and 2006, broadcast and cable channels began incorporating lesbian storylines into their programming. It is perhaps not a coincidence that *Dyke TV* closed its doors two years after the premiere of *The L Word* (Showtime, 2004–2009), the first commercial cable show to focus on the lives of queer women. While the "lesbian chic" phenomenon was short-lived, it created a model for commercially viable lesbian content adopted by marketers, advertisers, and television executives throughout the 1990s and 2000s that appealed to heterosexual viewers and consumers (Sender 2005). The increase in lesbian representation sparked hope that commercial television might finally provide opportunities for LGBTQ representation, seemingly lessening the need for independent LGBTQ television.

In 2005, lawyer Cynthia Kern was hired to serve as the Executive Director of *Dyke TV*; while hoping to revive the organization, she closed it by the end of 2006. "In the end, the money wasn't there anymore," Kern told me (Cynthia Kern, telephone interview with the author, November 2019). Fewer volunteers, increasing rent prices in Brooklyn, and a lower demand for services meant that *Dyke TV* was quickly running out of money as well as video content. Without the money to fund operations, Kern had no choice but to close *Dyke TV* for good. With the help of a volunteer, Kern packed up the *Dyke TV* storefront and drove the records up to Patierno's house in Western Massachusetts. Some years later, Patierno donated the archives to the Smith College Library, where the video content and paper records are accessible for researchers. Examining the struggles of independent television producers to succeed in a competitive marketplace, Aymar Jean Christian writes, "risk and failure are inextricable from innovation" (Christian 2018, 163). Persistent financial struggle, changes in television representation, and the development of digital technologies eventually made it difficult to continue producing *Dyke TV*. Without the financial backing of mainstream 2000s-era LGBTQ television shows like *The L Word*, there was no way for *Dyke TV* to compete in the marketplace.

While *Dyke TV* went off the air in 2006, contemporary screenings of the show have generated a new audience. Video journalist Ainara Tiefenthäler organized a series of *Dyke TV* screenings in Brooklyn between 2018 and 2020. "Every lesbian I know is hungry for content," Tiefenthäler told me over the phone (Ainara Tiefenthäler, telephone interview with the author, October 2019). Despite the increase in media representations of lesbian and queer life over the last two decades, Tiefenthäler expressed frustration that these stories do not usually resonate with her experiences of lesbian community. *Dyke TV*, on the other hand, felt familiar: "It doesn't seem very dated to me…overall the way topics are treated, the kind of humor, what kind of issues are covered or discussed, still seems awfully relevant" (Tiefenthäler, interview). *Dyke TV*'s scrappy, homegrown feel contrasts with commercial media made about lesbian lives. The show's community-oriented mission still feels novel in a media landscape where LGBTQ representations are typically designed to appeal to a mainstream (straight, cisgender) audience.

As Tiefenthäler suggests, what seems to draw contemporary viewers to *Dyke TV* is its utopian vision of queer and feminist community and activism. "Black feminist love-politics is staunchly utopian," Jennifer Nash (2013, 17) reminds us; it is a politics bound not by shared identities but by a shared dream for a new society. As an archive of lesbian feminist love-politics, *Dyke TV* offers a glimpse of one such dream: the collected and repeated efforts at creating a television show in the service of an expansive lesbian community. When I asked the producers what they liked most about working on *Dyke TV*, many described the feeling of community generated by participating in the production of the show: working among a group of queer women inspired and emboldened the *Dyke TV* volunteers and staff and often shaped their future careers. The determination of the staff and volunteers to continue to produce episodes, and to adapt, evolve, and change their tactics and politics as new challenges, conflicts, and community norms arose, reveals how experiments in television production can reflect queer and feminist principles. As a reporter for *The Washington Blade* wrote, "The mere survival of *Dyke TV* may prove to be more political than anything they air" (Tasse 1994). The hundreds of people who worked with *Dyke TV*, who helped produce over 300 episodes spanning *Dyke TV*'s 13-year run, provide contemporary viewers with an example of how dedication to love-politics can generate new forms of cultural production and new understandings of the legacy of lesbian feminism.

Dyke TV presents an alternative vision of late twentieth-century feminism: one not curtailed by transphobia or racism, but enriched by an expansive, unbounded, and freedom-seeking politics. The show's circulation of love-politics reveals the underlying potential of the show, and of lesbian feminist theory itself: it demonstrates the imagination of a community oriented toward a sense of justice in the service of LGBTQ liberation, rather than an organization around narrow definitions of identity.

References

Ahmed, Sara. 2017. *Living a Feminist Life*. Durham: Duke University Press.

Christian, Aymar Jean. 2018. *Open TV: Innovation beyond Hollywood and the Rise of Web Television*. New York: NYU Press.

Ciasullo, Ann M. 2001. "Making Her (In)Visible: Cultural Representations of Lesbianism and the Lesbian Body in the 1990s." *Feminist Studies* 27 (3): 577. https://doi.org/10.2307/3178806

Clarke, Cheryl. 1983. "Lesbianism: An Act of Resistance." In *This Bridge Called My Back: Writings by Radical Women of Color*, edited by Cherríe Moraga and Gloria Anzaldúa, 2nd ed, 128–137. New York: Kitchen Table/Women of Color Press.

Cogswell, Kelly J. 2014. *Eating Fire: My Life as a Lesbian Avenger*. Minneapolis: University of Minnesota Press.

Cvetkovich, Ann. 2001. "Fierce Pussies and Lesbian Avengers: Dyke Activism Meets Celebrity Culture." In *Feminist Consequences: Theory for the New Century*, edited by Elisabeth Bronfen and Misha Kavka, 283–318. Gender and Culture Series. New York: Columbia University Press.

"Dyke TV · Herstories: Audio/Visual Collections of the LHA." n.d. Accessed September 6, 2019. http://herstories.prattinfoschool.nyc/omeka/exhibits/show/dyke-tv

Dyke TV, season 1, episode 1, "Episode 1," 1993, executive producers Mary Patierno, Linda Chapman, and Ana Maria Simo, aired June 8, 1993 on Manhattan public access TV, https://media.smith.edu/departments/ssc/dyketv/dyketv1993_playlist.html.

Kasindorf, Jeanie Russell. 1993. "Lesbian Chic." *New York Magazine*, May 10.

McKinney, Cait. 2020. *Information Activism: A Queer History of Lesbian Media Technologies*. Sign, Storage, Transmission. Durham: Duke University Press.

Nash, Jennifer C. 2013. "Practicing Love: Black Feminism, Love-Politics, and Post-Intersectionality." *Meridians: Feminism, Race, Transnationalism* 11 (2): 1–24.

Rich, Adrienne. 1980. "Compulsory Heterosexuality and Lesbian Existence." *Signs* 5 (4): 631–60.

Saafied, Catherine. 1993. "Lesbians Want Their Dyke TV." *The Independent Film & Video Monthly*, October.

Schulman, Sarah. 2018. *My American History: Lesbian and Gay Life during the Reagan/Bush Years*. 2nd ed. New York: Routledge.

Sender, Katherine. 2005. *Business, Not Politics: The Making of the Gay Market*. New York: Columbia University Press.

Tasse, Tania. 1994. "Dyke TV: Television to Incite, Subvert, Provoke." *The Washington Blade*, February 11.

The Radicalesbians. 1997. "The Woman Identified Woman." In *The Second Wave: A Reader in Feminist Theory*, edited by Linda J. Nicholson, 153–157. New York: Routledge.

Witchel, Alex. 1994. "Vox Pop Video: A Public Access TV Guide." *The New York Times*, October 30.

14

PRODUCING INCLUSION AND INTERSECTIONALITY

Queer Showrunners of Color in Contemporary Television

Sarah E. S. Sinwell

Introduction

In an attempt to acknowledge the historical absence, invisibility, and erasure of people of color within the television industry at the 2020 Emmy Awards, Lena Waithe (Emmy Winner for *Master of None* (Netflix, 2015–2021), and creator of *The Chi* (Showtime, 2018–present), *Boomerang* (BET, 2019–2020) and *Twenties* (BET, 2020–present)) was interviewed as part of a slate of appearances by people of color such as Issa Rae (*Insecure*, HBO, 2016–2021) and Zendaya (*Euphoria*, HBO, 2019–present). Introduced as the creator of *The Chi* and discussing "the right to tell our own stories," Waithe recalled her own memories of the television series *A Different World* (NBC, 1987–1993) and how she felt seen through the character of Lena played by Jada Pinkett. Then, she remarked, "I still think there is a lot more territory to be covered in terms of intersectionality, with blackness and queerness."

This essay looks at how queer showrunners of color in contemporary television such as Waithe, Janet Mock (*Pose*, FX, 2018–2021), and Tanya Saracho (*Vida*, Starz, 2018–2020) use "showrunning as advocacy" to create LGBTQIA-positive series that are inclusive not only of the queer community, but also women and people of color. To this end, this essay also focuses on how the embodiment, presence, and visibility of queer people and queer people of color in media representation *and* media production can be seen as advocacy. For instance, the hiring and signing of Janet Mock for Netflix will likely continue this showrunning advocacy and enable more queer women of color to be hired both above and below the line for its future series and film slots. Additionally, a new digital content series from GLAAD called NEON focuses on black LGBTQ experiences and aims to increase the visibility of black LGBTQ people by sharing their voices and histories. Using feminist theory, queer theory, critical cultural studies, and media industry and production studies approaches to these showrunners, their casts, and their content, this essay

DOI: 10.4324/9781003109044-19

will show how these showrunners have worked to create a politics of inclusion and intersectionality that refuses to deny the embodied realities of these marginalized identities. To this end, I will be analyzing how casting queer people and queer people of color enables new possibilities for understanding the intersections between media production and media representation.

The presence of women, queer people, and people of color on the stage, in the writing room, and in the board room also points to the ways in which marginalized bodies and identities challenge cultural understandings of the media industry itself. Showrunners like Mock, Waithe, Saracho, and others are making and (re)making media history not only by casting queer people, women, and people of color in their series, but also by including them in other positions both below and above the line. To this end, these showrunners are also attempting to create a safe and empowering space for women, people of color, and the queer community.

To this end, this essay first focuses on intersectionality, labor, and casting within the television industry. I then study the hiring and casting practices of Mock, Waithe, and Saracho as a means of analyzing how queer showrunners of color are creating a space for marginalized voices within the television industry and enabling more inclusivity on television, both on the screen and on the set.

Intersectionality, Labor, and Casting in the Television Industry

In 2017, 28 years after her 1989 seminal essay "Demarginalizing the Intersection of Race and Sex: A Black Feminist Critique of Antidiscrimination Doctrine, Feminist Theory and Antiracist Politics" was published, when Kimberlé Williams Crenshaw was asked to revisit the meaning of intersectionality, she stated,

> Intersectionality is a lens through which you can see where power comes and collides, where it interlocks and intersects. It's not simply that there's a race problem here, a gender problem here, and a class or LBGTQ problem there. Many times that framework erases what happens to people who are subject to all of these things.
>
> *2017*

As Patrick Grzanka notes in his "Introduction" to *Intersectionality: A Foundations and Frontiers Reader*,

> Intersectionality is a structural analysis and critique in so much as it is primarily concerned with how social inequalities are found and maintained: accordingly, identities and the politics therefore are the products of historically entrenched, institutional systems of domination and violence.
>
> *2014, xv*

Studying the "multiple dimensions of inequality" that Grzanka and other authors such as Julia Himberg (2018), Ralina Joseph (2018), Alfred L. Martin (2014, 2018,

2019), Isabel Molina-Guzman (2018), and Kristen Warner (2015, 2017) critique in their work on race, gender, and sexuality in the media, this essay examines the ways in which these structures of production, labor, and industry frame contemporary television, both above and below the line. This focus on intersectionality via the power of storytelling and mediamaking serves not only as a means of empowering these marginalized identities, but also as a means of investigating how embodiment and representation are tied to the material conditions of labor in these media productions.

In their 2013 essay, "Toward a Field of Intersectionality Studies: Theory, Applications, and Praxis," Sumi Cho, Kimberlé Williams Crenshaw, and Leslie McCall, explicitly refer to intersectionality as a means of "analyzing the multiple ways that race and gender interact with class in the labor market" (785). This essay seeks to examine showrunning activism, television hiring, and queer casting in order to map out the way in which queer showrunners of color are not only acknowledging the inequities of the labor market, but, pushing the limits of those boundaries by insisting on the inclusion of queer people and people of color both below and above the line.

In this context, casting is a significant means of examining the presence, visibility, and embodiment of queer identities and people of color. As Alfred L. Martin (2018) points out in "The Queer Business of Casting Gay Characters on U.S. Television," casting for gay roles in U.S. television occupies an important space within media production studies because it exposes the patterns involved with who is allowed to work within the culture industries. And, as Aymar Christian argues, in smaller scale work, "cultural production value asserts more importance, as producers create with and for their community" (2019, 255). In her book *Below the Line: Producers and Production Studies in the New Television Economy* (2011), Vicki Mayer discusses the historical divisions between above the line (showrunners, producers, directors, actors, and writers) and below the line (editors, grips, line producers, art directors, etc.) television professionals. Analyzing how the publicity around television production often does not account for the invisible labor of those working below the line, Mayer draws attention to the need to account for other laborers such as editors, line producers, and grips, that are "structuring absences" within discourses around television production (2011, 4).

Queer television itself is highly contested, intertwining narratives of not only representation, but also production, reception, form, and the industry. Like many queer media scholars have noted, including Becker (2006), Brennan (2019), Chambers (2009), Davis and Needham (2008), Doty (1993, 2000), Griffin (2016), Himberg (2018), Kohnen (2015), Martin (2020), Miller (2019), Parsemain (2019), Pugh (2018), Raun (2016), Steinbock (2019), and Villarejo (2014), representations of queer characters are still largely white and male, although shows with more inclusive queer casts and queer casts of color such as *Pose*, *The Chi*, *Twenties*, *The Bisexual*, and *Vida* have also become popular over the last few years. Both Julia Himberg (2018) and Alfred L. Martin (2019, 2020) have referred to the contemporary desire for "realistic" representations in terms of casting and writing

LGBTQIA+ characters on television. For instance, audiences and critics have searched for LGBTQIA+ characters that are as multidimensional and complex "as their heterosexual counterparts" (Himberg 2018, 58).

As F. Hollis Griffin notes in *Feeling Normal*, "I see in gay and lesbian media a process of circulation that hinges on the shared investments of gay and lesbian producers and gay and lesbian audiences in particular practices, ideologies, and institutions" (2016, 11). As noted in the histories of gay and lesbian cinema in *The Celluloid Closet* (Rob Epstein and Jeffrey Friedman, 1995) and *Fabulous: The Story of Queer Cinema* (Lisa Ades and Lesli Klainberg, 2006), as well as in the recently released documentary about trans representation *Disclosure* (Sam Feder, 2020), the concern within queer film and television history has been not only the focus on representation, but who is making that representation and for whom. Are there queer characters present on screen at all? Are those characters represented positively? Are they represented in as complex and diverse ways as their straight counterparts? Whose stories are being told? Who is telling them? How do audiences gain access to these stories?

Queer Showrunners of Color and Showrunning Advocacy

Queer showrunners of color like Mock, Waithe, and Saracho are advocating for changing both above the line and below the line hiring practices as a means of involving and advocating for the LGBTQIA+ community. In June 2019, Janet Mock became the first transgender person to land full creative control with a major content company at Netflix. Mock will continue to write, produce, and direct for Ryan Murphy and *Pose* (FX, 2018–present), but also become a TV showrunner for future Netflix series and feature film projects. In 2019, *Pose* received Golden Globe nominations for Best Television Series—Drama and Best Actor in a Television Series—Drama, a Primetime Emmy nomination for Outstanding Drama Series and a Primetime Emmy Award for Outstanding Lead Actor in a Drama Series for Billy Porter, as well as a GLAAD Media Award for Outstanding Drama Series.

Janet Mock said of *Pose*, "We made history in many senses, not just the cast. I'm the first trans woman of color not only to be in a writers' room of a Hollywood series or movie, but to also direct" (Dry 2019). At the Television Critics' Association, Mock spoke about trans representation and stated that the characters in *Pose* were being written as "beyond the struggle with their bodies, with people calling them by their right name. These are people who are creating new ways of having family—chosen family through the ballroom networks." Mock's comments center upon "a post-transness that suggests that the trans characters within the series are "beyond" the concerns of gender dysmorphia gesturing toward the notion that the "transition story" is one of the most frequent tropes within mainstream media when engaging with trans people's stories" (Martin 2019).

At the same time, Janet Mock is not the only queer of color writer and showrunner on *Pose*, writer and director Steven Canals is also an openly queer Puerto Rican and African American, writer Lady J is a transgender nonbinary woman, and director Tina Mabry is a Black lesbian. Following the controversy over the casting and subsequent firing of Jeffrey Tambor on *Transparent* (Amazon, 2014–2019), it is also significant that the show features *multiple* transgender actors in trans roles, including Mj Rodriguez (the first trans actor to be nominated for an Emmy in a lead acting category), Indya Moore, Dominique Jackson, Hailie Sahar, and Angelica Ross. Including the largest transgender cast ever for a scripted series, it must also be noted that over the course of the series, more than fifty LGBTQIA+ actors and characters appear on the show (Andreeva 2017).

The inclusion of queer and trans people of color both onscreen, as well as in the writer's room and behind the camera, also impacts the kinds of stories that are told within the series. For instance, in season one, episode six (the first episode of the series that Janet Mock both wrote and directed), not only are trans characters Bianca (played by Mj Rodriguez) and Angel (played by Indya Moore) at the center of the storytelling, but the show also acknowledges the complexities of how trans people are seen both within their own communities and outside of them. In the opening scene of the episode, Angel is speaking with a married straight white woman (played by Kate Mara) about her own identity. When asked why she would be at a drag ball, Angel not only responds by coming out as trans, but also refers to the drag ball community as "my home, my community, my familia." Refusing to believe that such a femme-presenting person could be trans, when the woman asks to "see her dick," Angel responds by saying she's got boundaries, "If you want to see who I am, that's the last place you should look." Angel's insistence upon defining her own identity outside of its association with her genitalia and anatomy and her emphasis upon valuing the queer kinship of her chosen family rather than her biological family also highlights the complexities of both the queer experience and queer histories. At the same time, as multiple characters get tested for HIV and as Pray Tell (played by Billy Porter) copes with the fact that his partner is dying of AIDS and that he himself has tested positive, the episode also addresses the embodied and emotional realities of the AIDS epidemic and its impact on multiple generations. Additionally, this episode features multiple representations of gay and straight masculinity as multiple queer men of color compete for the title of "realness" at the drag ball. Both upholding and questioning the idea that the ideal male body is muscular and masculine-presenting, the show also enables multiple understandings of what masculinity, femininity, and trans identities look like, both through its casting, as well as through its portrayal of the stories and experiences of queer people of color.

Likewise, writers and showrunners such as Lena Waithe (the first Black woman to win an Emmy for comedy writing for *Master of None* and the creator of the Showtime series *The Chi* and BET's *Twenties*), and Tanya Saracho (showrunner of the Starz series *Vida*) have also advocated for queer women and people of color on their shows. For instance, *Twenties* is the first show on BET to be helmed by a queer person and the first time a show on BET has featured an LGBTQIA+ character as the lead. *Twenties* is loosely based on Lena Waithe's own start in the entertainment industry and features a Black masculine-presenting lesbian (Hattie, played by Jonica T. Gibbs) who is trying to make it as a TV writer in Los Angeles. In the pilot episode, we are introduced to Hattie, as one of "two people enjoying each other's bodies and company all morning." As the camera shows the image of a nude black back, it plays with audience expectations as that back is revealed to be that of a Black woman in bed with another Black woman. The show also points out that while Hattie is a lesbian, the other woman is not a lesbian. In fact, "their orientations aren't important." In this way, the show also questions our expectations of not only black femininity, but also, lesbians, queerness, and how those identities intersect and intertwine. The show not only includes a masculine-presenting Black woman as the central character, but it also includes straight Black female characters as her best friends, thus imagining alternative means of representing the intersections between queer and Black communities beyond more typical series such as *The L Word* (Showtime, 2004–2009) or *Noah's Arc* (Logo, 2005–2006).

For Lena Waithe, mentorship is part of her advocacy and showrunning. She says,

> I have a ton of mentees…They're all people of color. Some of them are poor. And I'm just trying to help them learn how to be great writers; and for those that have become really good writers, I help them get representation; and those that have representation, I want to help get them jobs. That to me is a form of activism. I was doing this before Time's Up was created. I am doing it now. Activism is me paying for a writer to go to a television-writing class.
> *Woodson 2018*

At the same time, Waithe also points out the need for queer people and people of color to tell their own stories, saying, "I am tired of white folks telling my stories. We gotta tell our shit. Can't no one tell a black story, particularly a queer story, the way I can, because I see the God in us" (Woodson 2018).

Tanya Saracho created an all Latin-x writer's room of mostly queer women and hired all women-of-color directors for *Vida,* a show that tells the story of two Mexican-American sisters who are facing the challenges of racial prejudice and gentrification in their Los Angeles community. In addition, the casting director, composer, and editor of the series were also all female and Latina. Thus, *Vida* breaks expectations not only by including multi-generational stories of Latin-x queer women, but also by intertwining Spanish, Spanglish, and English languages throughout the show (and without subtitles). Even from the very first episode, the show questions what it means to "pass" for straight and white. Both sisters are called "gringas" and "whitinas" by another Latin-x woman within their community. The characters on the show are also constantly code switching as they interact with various member of their community. At the same time, Emma Hernandez (played by Mishel Prada) struggles with how to define herself, not only in relation to her race, ethnicity, class, and sexual identity, but also in relation to her own familial history as she learns that her deceased mother's "roommate" is actually her wife. Though we do not learn of Emma's sexuality in the first episode, it is significant that the show includes a variety of Latin-x queer characters throughout the series, including femme-presenting, butch, nonbinary, and gender-queer women. The show also overtly addresses the plight of the undocumented within the community, as well as the increasing gentrification and white development of the neighborhood. Thus, the show's inclusion of Latin-x and queer women, both below and above the line, also enables more complicated and nuanced narratives of these identities to be shown onscreen.

In an interview with *Variety*, Saracho noted the systemic changes that are necessary in order to change the television industry, stating, "It's about the gatekeepers believing that our worlds are worthwhile—and that is what we have to change, because that's systemic," Saracho said. "I'm talking about the people in the towers" who have the power to greenlight diverse projects" (Herman 2019). In an interview with *bitchmedia*, Saracho stated, "I do have a little agenda. I want to complicate Latina women and put them front and center. It's super simple, but you need a big platform for that so you can affect perception" (Mora 2018). By including these voices on networks such as FX, Showtime, BET, and Starz, these queer showrunners of color are also creating a space not only for queer people of color's stories, but also for their presence onscreen as well as on set, both above and below the line.

Conclusion

In 2018, one of the writers of the animated television series *Central Park* (AppleTV+ , 2020) launched the #ShowUsYourRoom Social Media Initiative in an attempt to draw attention to the social inequities and lack of diversity and inclusion of writers' rooms within the television industry, but, also to encourage agencies, studios, and other media organizations to interrogate their hiring practices and workplaces (Turchiano 2018). Six months later, creator of the hashtag Amanda Idoko told the *Chicago Tribune*,

> Only 52 rooms participated in the Show Us Your Room Challenge. There are over 500 scripted shows on TV, so only one-tenth of TV writers rooms were proud to share a photo of their staff in support of diversity and inclusion. That's shameful. I also want to point out that 75 percent of the rooms that participated in the challenge are run or co-run by women or people of color. If this industry actually wants to improve its terrible diversity numbers, studios should hire more women and POC showrunners, because women and POC are clearly the ones hiring diverse staffs.
>
> *Metz 2019*

Thus, the positioning of queer women and people of color both below and above the line is becoming a more and more necessary element of the television industry's productions. As more marginalized voices demand to be heard and are enabled to be heard by companies such as Showtime, Starz, and Netflix, these showrunners are creating a safe and empowering space for women, people of color, and the queer community to tell their own stories. Though *Vida* was canceled after three seasons (and received a shortened final season) and Desiree Akhavan's *The Bisexual* (2016) lasted only one season, *The Chi* was renewed for a fourth season in 2020 and *Twenties* was also renewed for a second season. In February 2020, Janet Mock announced that she would be partnering with producer Ryan Murphy on her feature film debut *Janet* for Netflix, a film which chronicles the true and complicated story of *Washington Post* journalist Janet Cooke (Andreeva 2020). Additionally, as part of the annual AT&T Film Mentorship Program, ten aspiring writers and directors have been working diligently under the close mentorship of Lena Waithe to create their own short films.

In October 2020, as founder of the Untitled Latinx Project (an all-Latina advocacy group) Tanya Saracho along with 270 other Latinx writers including Lin-Manuel Miranda, John Leguizamo, and Gloria Calderon Kellett (creator of *One Day at a Time* (Pop/Netflix, 2017–2020)) created her own initiative. Among the five demands laid out in the letter, "the writers note the importance of hiring more Latinx talent, including in decision-making roles like creator/showrunner: 'No stories about us without us'" (Braxton 2020). In 2020, Saracho also signed a deal with Universal Content Productions that also enabled her to "establish a lab and incubator program aimed to nurture, amplify, guide, and empower intersectional Latinx voices" (Otterson 2020). Thus, these queer showrunners of color continue to mentor, participate in activism and showrunning activism, and fight for the representation of people of color and queer people on television despite the systemic racism and homophobia of the industry itself.

Bibliography

Andreeva, Nellie. 2017. FX's Pose: Ryan Murphy Sets Largest Transgender Cast Ever for Scripted Series. *Deadline Hollywood*. October 25. https://deadline.com/2017/10/pose-ryan-murphy-transgender-cast-fx-series-1202194718/

Andreeva, Nellie. 2020. Janet Mock & Ryan Murphy Team On Netflix Film About Former Washington Post Journalist Janet Cooke. *Deadline*. February 27. https://deadline.com/2020/02/janet-mock-ryan-murphy-team-on-netflix-film-about-former-washington-post-journalist-janet-cooke-1202870078/

Becker, Ron. 2006. *Gay TV and Straight America*. New Brunswick: Rutgers University Press.

The Bisexual. 2018. Hulu. Produced by Desiree Akhavan.

Boomerang. 2019-2020. BET. Produced by Lena Waithe.

Braxton, Greg. 2020. "We Are Tired": Read the Open Letter 270 Fed-up Latinx Writers Just Sent Hollywood. *LA Times*. October 15. www.latimes.com/entertainment-arts/tv/story/2020-10-15/latinx-writers-open-letter-to-hollywood-united-latinx-project

Brennan, Joseph. 2019. *Queerbaiting and Fandom: Teasing Fans through Homoerotic Possibilities*. Iowa City: University of Iowa Press.

The Celluloid Closet. 1995. Directed by Rob Epstein and Jeffrey Friedman.

Central Park. 2020-present. AppleTV+.

Chambers, Samuel. 2009. *The Queer Politics of Television*. London and New York: I.B. Tauris.

The Chi. 2018–present. Showtime. Produced by Lena Waithe.

Chiba, Kirsten. 2018. Ryan Murphy on "Showrunning as Advocacy" and the Post-Me Too "Age of Enlightenment." *Variety*. July 18. https://variety.com/2018/scene/news/ryan-murphy-ronan-farrow-showrunning-as-advocacy-1202877298/

Cho, Sumi, Crenshaw, Kimberlé Williams and McCall, Leslie. 2013. Toward a Field of Intersectionality Studies: Theory, Applications, and Praxis. *Signs,* Summer 38.4: 785–810.

Christian, Aymar. 2018. *Open TV: Innovation Beyond Hollywood and the Rise of Web Television.* New York: New York University Press.

Christian, Aymar. 2019. Expanding Production Value: The Culture and Scale of Television and New Media. *Critical Studies in Television* 14(2): 255–267.

Crenshaw, Kimberlé Williams. 1989. Demarginalizing the Intersection of Race and Sex: A Black Feminist Critique of Antidiscrimination Doctrine, Feminist Theory and Antiracist Politics. *University of Chicago Legal Forum,* 1989(1), Article 8.

Crenshaw, Kimberlé Williams. 2017. Kimberlé Crenshaw on Intersectionality, More than Two Decades Later. *Columbia Law School.* June 8. www.law.columbia.edu/news/archive/kimberle-crenshaw-intersectionality-more-two-decades-later

Davis, Glyn, and Gary Needham, eds. 2008. *Queer TV: Theories, Histories, Politics.* London: Routledge.

Davis, Glyn, and Gary Needham, eds. 2008. Introduction: The Pleasures of the Tube. In *Queer TV: Theories, Histories, Politics.* London: Routledge.

A Different World. 1987-1993. NBC. Created by Bill Cosby.

Disclosure. 2020. Directed by Sam Feder.

Donnelly, Matt. 2019. Jane Mock Signs Landmark Overall Netflix Deal. *Variety.* June 19. https://variety.com/2019/tv/features/janet-mock-netflix-deal-pose-1203246917/

Doty, Alexander. 1993. *Making Things Perfectly Queer.* Minneapolis: University of Minnesota Press.

Doty, Alexander. 2000. *Flaming Classics.* New York and London: Routledge.

Dry, Jude. 2019. How Ryan Murphy's "Showrunning As Advocacy" Led to Janet Mock's Historic Netflix Deal. *IndieWire.* June 19. https://www.indiewire.com/2019/06/ryan-murphy-pose-interview-janet-mock-lgbt-1202151338/

Euphoria. 2019-present. HBO. Created by Sam Levinson.

Fabulous: The Story of Queer Cinema. 2006. Directed by Lisa Ades and Lesli Klainberg.

Goddard, Michael N. and Hogg, Christopher. 2019. Streaming Intersectionality: Queer and Trans Television Aesthetics in Post-Medium Transformation. *Critical Studies in Television* 14: 4: 439–444.

Griffin, F. Hollis. 2016. *Feeling Normal: Sexuality and Media Criticism in the Digital Age.* Bloomington: Indiana University Press.

Griffin, F. Hollis. 2018. Queer Media Studies. *Feminist Media Histories* 4(2): 167–172.

Grzanka, Patrick R., Ed. 2014. *Intersectionality: A Foundations and Frontiers Reader.* Boulder: Westview Press.

Grzanka, Patrick R., Ed. 2014. "Introduction: Intersectional Objectivity." In *Intersectionality: A Foundations and Frontiers Reader.* Boulder: Westview Press.

Herman, James. 2019. How 'Vida' Showrunner Tanya Saracho Became a Leading Voice for Latinx Creators. *Variety,* July 29, https://variety.com/2019/scene/news/tanya-saracho-vida-latinx-1203283204/

Himberg, Julia. 2018. *The New Gay for Pay: The Sexual Politics of American Television Production.* Austin: University of Texas Press.

Insecure. 2016–2021. HBO. Created by Issa Rae.

Joseph, Ralina L. 2018. *Postracial Resistance: Black Women, Media, and the Uses of Strategic Ambiguity.* New York: New York University Press.

Joyrich, Lynne. 2001. Epistemology of the Console. *Critical Inquiry* 27: 3.

Jude, Dry. 2019. How Ryan Murphy's 'Showrunning As Advocacy' Led to Janet Mock's Historic Netflix Deal. *IndieWire.* June 19. https://www.indiewire.com/2019/06/ryan-murphy-pose-interview-janet-mock-lgbt-1202151338/

Kohnen, Melanie. 2015. *Queer Representation, Visibility, and Race in American Film and Television: Screening the Closet*. London and New York: Routledge.
Lotz, Amanda. 2007. If It's Not TV, What is it? The Case of US Subscription Television. In *Cable Visions: Television Beyond Broadcasting*. Edited by Sarah Banet-Weiser, Cynthia Chris, and Anthony Frietas, 85–102. New York: New York University Press.
The L Word. 2004–2009. Showtime. Created by Ilene Chaiken.
Martin, Alfred L. 2014. Scripting Black Gayness: Television Authorship in Black-Cast Sitcoms. *Television and New Media* 16(7): 648–663.
Martin, Alfred L. 2018. The Queer Business of Casting Gay Characters on U.S. Television. *Communication, Culture, and Critique* 11(2): 282–297.
Martin, Alfred L. 2019. Pose(r): Ryan Murphy, Trans and Queer of Color Labor, and the Politics of Representation. *LA Review of Books*. August 2. https://lareviewofbooks.org/article/poser-ryan-murphy-trans-queer-color-labor-politics-representation/
Martin, Alfred L. 2020. For Scholars…When Studying the Queer of Color Image Alone Is Not Enough. *Communication and Critical/Cultural Studies* 17(1): 69–74.
Master of None. 2015–2021. Netflix. Produced by Aziz Ansari.
Mayer, Vicki. 2011. *Below the Line: Producers and Production Studies in the New Television Economy*. Durham and London: Duke University Press.
McCarthy, A. 2001. *Ellen*: Making Queer Television History. *GLQ: Journal of Lesbian and Gay Studies* 7(4): 593–620.
Metz, Nina. 2019. Hollywood May Say It's All for Diversity, But TV Writers Tell a Different Story. *Chicago Tribune*. March 20. www.chicagotribune.com/entertainment/tv/ct-mov-equality-and-inclusion-in-tv-writing-still-a-problem-0322-story.html
Miller, Quinlan. 2019. *Camp TV: Trans Gender Queer Sitcom History*. Durham: Duke University Press.
Molina-Guzman, Isabel. 2018. *Latinas/Latinos on Television: Colorblind Humor on Post-racial TV*. Tucson: University of Arizona Press.
Mora, Ruby. 2018. Be About It: Tanya Saracho Wants To Wake Up Hollywood With "Vida." *Bitchmedia*. May 4. www.bitchmedia.org/article/bitch-interview/tanya-saracho-is-changing-television?utm_source=newsletter&utm_medium=email&utm_content=we%20have%20not%20historically%20gotten%20a%20chance%20to%20handle%20our%20own%20stories&utm_campaign=Weekly%20Reader%2005.05.2018
Noah's Arc. 2005–2006. Logo. Created by Patrik-Ian Polk.
Normal. 2003. Directed by Jane Anderson.
O'Falt, Chris. 2018. "The Chi" Creator Lena Waithe: Inclusive Casting Changed My Writing and My Life—Toolkit Podcast. *IndieWire*. January 25. www.indiewire.com/2018/06/lena-waithe-the-chi-master-of-none-casting-advice-filmmaker-toolkit-podcast-episode-59-1201978298/
One Day at a Time. 2017–2020. Pop/Netflix. Created by Gloria Calderon Kellett.
Orange Is the New Black. 2013-2019. Netflix. Produced by Jenji Kohan.
Otterson, Joe. 2020. "Vida" Creator Tanya Saracho Signs Overall Deal with UCP. *Variety*. August 19. https://variety.com/2020/tv/news/vida-tanya-saracho-overall-deal-ucp-1234740022/
Paris is Burning. 1991. Directed by Jennie Livingston.
Parsemain, Ava Laure. 2019. *The Pedagogy of Queer TV*. Cham: Palgrave Macmillan.
Pose. 2018–2021. FX Network. Produced by Ryan Murphy.
Pugh, Tison. 2018. *The Queer Fantasies of the American Family Sitcom*. New Brunswick: Rutgers University Press.
Raun, Tobias. 2016. *Out Online: Trans Self-representation and Community Building on YouTube*. New York: Routledge.

Real, Evan. 2018. Ryan Murphy Says 'Pose' Could Have Never Happened without Trans Talent. *The Hollywood Reporter*. June 1. www.hollywoodreporter.com/live-feed/ryan-murphy-pose-hiring-transgender-talent-1116572

Steinbock, Eliza. 2019. *Shimmering Images: Trans Cinema, Embodiment, and the Aesthetics of Change*. Durham: Duke University Press.

Transparent. 2014–2019. Amazon. Produced by Joey Soloway.

Turchiano, Danielle. 2018. 'Central Park' Writer Launches 'Show Us Your Room' Social Media Initiative. *Variety*. September 18. https://variety.com/2018/tv/features/show-us-your-room-social-media-initiative-1202939127/

Twenties. 2020–present. Showtime. Produced by Lena Waithe.

Vida. 2018–2020. Starz. Produced by Tanya Saracho.

Villarejo, Amy. 2014. *Ethereal Queer: Television, Historicity, Desire*. Durham and London: Duke University Press.

Warner, Kristen. 2015. *The Cultural Politics of Colorblind TV Casting*. New York and London: Routledge.

Warner, Kristen. 2017. In the Time of Plastic Representation. *Film Quarterly*, 71(2): 32–37.

Woodson, Jacqueline. 2018. Lena Waithe is Changing the Game. *Vanity Fair*. April. www.vanityfair.com/hollywood/2018/03/lena-waithe-cover-story

15

LIVING IN THE GRAY AREA

Bisexual Resignifications in Desiree Akhavan's *The Bisexual*

Maria San Filippo

#StillBisexual After All These Years: from Stigma into the Spotlight

"The entire conceit of a TV series debating what bisexuality even means in 2018 feels 20 years too late." So judged *The Hollywood Reporter* in reviewing Desiree Akhavan's Channel 4/Hulu series *The Bisexual*.[1] Dismissed here as "too late," perennially in need of defending as not "just a phase," bisexuality has long been subject to erasure and negation. Meanwhile, a *Vox* thinkpiece noted the proliferation of bisexual representation proffered by Peak TV, observing that bisexuality had "evolved" into "a vital storyline" in series ranging from network comedies to premium cable dramas to children's programming.[2] This just three years after Akhavan, on the heels of releasing her acclaimed debut feature *Appropriate Behavior* (2014), had shopped *The Bisexual* script to "all the networks in LA and was rejected everywhere," on the grounds that "they already had a gay series, or a series starring a brown woman, or [so said Amazon] *Transparent*."[3] It would seem bisexuality's shift from representational tokenism to reputed heyday was not rapid enough for Akhavan, who made her second feature *The Miseducation of Cameron Post* (2018)—a YA adaptation awarded the Sundance Grand Jury Prize—in the intervening time. After Akhavan impulsively relocated in 2015 to London to live alongside writer/producing partner Cecilia Frugiuele, they, along with co-creator Rowan Riley, landed the Channel 4 production deal, with co-distribution by Hulu to follow.

Despite its reported promotion to "vital storyline", and contrary to the relaxed expectations of positivity and palatability placed on lesbian and gay media imagery, bisexuality's burden of representation is ongoing and self-effacing; or as Elijah (Andrew Rannells) on *Girls* memorably put it, "Bisexuals are like the last group you can make fun of. Bisexuals and Germans. And I happen to be both." Enter Akhavan, who consistently if ambivalently identifies as bi even while ruing being repeatedly

DOI: 10.4324/9781003109044-20

dubbed "the bisexual Lena Dunham" in the wake of *Appropriate Behavior*'s release—an experience that inspired *The Bisexual*, in which she plays Leila, an Iranian-American in London who starts dating men after ending a decade-long relationship with girlfriend/business partner Sadie (Maxine Peake). In branding herself and her series with "the last taboo" (as its tagline proclaims), Akhavan asserts that "the b word" retains personal and political valence within a purportedly post-queer era still sufficiently bi-averse to have birthed the #StillBisexual social media campaign.[4]

As defined by fansite TV Tropes, "But Not Too Bi" refers to the representational predominance of femme cisgender women open to same-sex flirtation who nevertheless partner only with cismen. Even in the expanding field of bisexual visibility, *The Bisexual* stands out by virtue of its titular and representational forthrightness, and in its willingness to risk alienating straight *and* gay viewerships. For the former, Leila overturns female bisexuality's representational appeal to straight men with her unruly body humor involving queefing, farting, and (to the horror of flat mate Gabe [Brian Gleeson]), flaunting unshaven armpits. Akhavan dares alienating another key demographic by configuring bisexuality as ex-lesbianism; as she reports "It was lesbians in my life who said that's inherently offensive—the narrative of a woman leaving a woman and dating men is just wrong. I want to know why is it wrong?...Why is it inherently negative to see that narrative?" (Figure 15.1)[5]

Recalling *Sex and the City*'s maligning of bisexuality as "greedy double-dipping," Akhavan boldly owns, then dismisses, the accusation: "It is greedy, but who cares?"[6] Assuming the role of her ego-unbridled screen-self Leila further liberates Akhavan to voice (as she puts it), "the stuff that we're uncomfortable to say out loud."[7] After embarking on her first sexual experience with a man, Leila marvels over its

FIGURE 15.1 Not "not too bi": Female bisexuality not for straight men's visual pleasure.

ultimate sameness: "I thought sex with a man would be so different, and it's not. Sex is sex." Such pronouncements dissent from the "born this way" belief system that mythologizes sexual identity out of proportion to its utility as a tool for political advocacy. Doubling down on stereotypes of bisexuals as opportunistic, defaulting to relationships with men, and disinclined to come out, Leila continues her post-coital reflection in classic Akhavanese, musing "Sometimes I think that if a guy had swept me off my feet the way that girl did in my support group for cutters when I was nineteen that maybe I'd have been straight." Questioned that surely having been with Sadie so long rules that out, Leila responds, "I'm definitely attracted to women, but maybe I'd have gone the path of least resistance? Coming out to my parents was hands down the worst thing I've ever had to do. They're from Iran. It was awful. I don't think I would have put my family through that if I felt I had another option." Even as it admits to the personal and political cowering for which bisexuals are chastised, this confession indicates both the complex intersectionality of identity and desire's contingency upon time and circumstance.

Leveraging its six half-hour episodes to explore these dynamics of attraction, *The Bisexual* aims for more inclusive representation and broader queer resignification than its title suggests. It does so first within its central storyline, following Leila *and* Sadie's reckonings with the inconvenient truths masked by their decade of monogamy. Second, *The Bisexual* examines generational identifications with queerness among characters whose age range spans three decades, presenting an important reminder of queer history's not-so-distant past and an affective rendering of the trauma and shame embedded within it. Third, by gradually displacing romantic coupling from the narrative's center, *The Bisexual* probes what Akhavan sees as "a real parallel between being bisexual and being the child of immigrants...you live in the gray area."[8] Shifting to center stage its other narrative uncoupling between same-sex (albeit platonic) partners—Leila and best pal Deniz (Saskia Chana), a first-generation Londoner and partly closeted lesbian who manages her Turkish parents' off-license—the series gives more weight still to the complications of reconciling one's sexuality with one's familial-cultural heritage, and aspires even further in its attention to socioeconomic and systemic barriers (for queer women of color especially) to experiencing sexuality as a choice.

Still Unsayable: Making Use of 'the B Word'

Building on her also autobiographically informed earlier works—self-proclaimed "superficial, homophobic" web series *The Slope* (2010–11), co-created with then-partner Ingrid Jungermann, and (the ironically named) *Appropriate Behavior*, a self-described "gay *Annie Hall*" about an Iranian-American bisexual's breakup with her lesbian girlfriend—*The Bisexual* amplifies Akhavan's now-distinctive defiance of GLAAD-friendly rhetoric and identity policing in favor of the provocative and individuated.[9] Given that bisexual representation has conventionally been conflated with/configured as white privilege, Akhavan's voice as a first-generation woman of color speaks volumes about shared *and* divergent aspects of bisexual alterity.

Particularly urgent for Akhavan is the persistent experience of external *and* internal biphobia; of her response to being termed "the bisexual Lena Dunham," Akhavan recalls "I didn't mind that they were calling out my sexuality but there was something about being called a bisexual publicly—even though it's one hundred percent true!—that felt totally humiliating and in bad taste, and I wanted to understand why."[10] Or as Leila replies after Gabe suggests that her hitting it off with hairstylist Jon-Criss (John Dagleish) could mean she is bisexual:

> When I hear bisexual I think lame slut. It's tacky, it's gauche, it makes you seem disingenuous. Like your genitals have no allegiance, you know? Like you have no criteria for people, just an open door policy. It's not a nice thing to be, it's not a cool thing to be, and it makes my fucking skin crawl.

Akhavan's chutzpah in choosing this loaded identity term as the series' title indicates her urge to explore her own cringe-inducing ambivalence while provoking (she hopes) that of her audience: "I think it will turn off a lot of viewers. I want to know why that is, and to stand by it: I know that I'm playing the long game and I want you to watch this thing and be like 'Oh, it's not what I thought it would be.'"[11] Ironically, given that Akhavan's inability to shake "the b word" inspired *The Bisexual*, the term often disappeared from descriptions of the series in its promotional rollout, as in its introduction on a queer pop culture podcast as "a show about a lesbian in her early 30s," or in a public radio announcer's describing Leila as "a woman who is not entirely queer."[12] Yet that erasure is unsurprising given the still-kneejerk impulse to dismiss and de-queer bisexuality and its representations. Bisexuality remains, as well, the bastard child of queer media studies, which endorses the enduring necessity of gay-, lesbian- and now (finally) trans-specific scholarship while casting bisexuality as redundant (at best) or retrograde (at worst) within queer critical-theoretical frameworks.[13]

Rather than tally such slights to bisexual specificity, this chapter aspires to Akhavan's model of creatively mining those enunciations, whether crassly reductive ("the bisexual Lena Dunham") or (self-)effacing ("lame slut," "not entirely queer"), to resignify bisexuality. Such resignification is important not only, Akhavan reminds, "because the more you use a word the more you can destigmatize it,"[14] but also to provoke reassessment of bisexuality's potential for unthinking monosexist logics of erotic-emotional subjectivity, as well as of screen representation, reception, and interpretation. Thus reconceived, bisexuality becomes a pluralistic rather than prescriptive (much less binary-reinforcing) construct, with a historical lineage and idiom that, in emphasizing determinants of desire beyond gender-of-object choice, offer routes to explore and question sexuality's contours, and to reconceptualize identity formations. Lacking the space here to delineate this critical bisexual theory taken up in *The B Word*, this chapter's focus on time-based implications of resignifying bisexuality as representational trope, authorial praxis, and coalitional site finds ample illustration in *The Bisexual*'s single-season (para)text and Akhavan's on/offscreen self-inscription.

Time to Be Bi: Using Televisual Temporality to Resignify Bisexual Stereotypes

Akhavan's forthright titling immediately settles a question that typically demands considerable labor of justification on the part of bisexual representation—and scholars thereof—: the legitimacy of claiming a character as bisexual. That bisexuality must be explicitly and consistently named for it to be recognized stems from monosexist modes of reading characters, like actual people, as straight until proven gay—with anything between regarded as a waystop to an ostensibly "real" (read: mature and sustainable) monosexual identity. Or as Akhavan (2019a) puts it, "It's really hard to stand by a bisexual narrative".[15] In explaining her titling as playing "the long game", Akhavan alludes to the importance of TV seriality. Alongside the onus on bisexuality to name itself, a temporal component weighs on its representational legibility and hence legitimacy; at any given moment a bisexual character (or person) might appear monosexual depending on their present object choice. As Akhavan observes, "You're defined by who you happen to be with at the moment."[16] *The Bisexual*'s inciting breakup forces Leila to reckon with what coupled life allowed her to evade; yet her sexual camaraderie with women *and* men, necessary to make her *legible* as bi, appears to prove the "promiscuous bisexual" notion accurate. Akhavan uses the conundrum to unshoulder bisexuality's burden as the catch-all for sexual hang-ups, as in this testy exchange between flatmates:

GABE: You're the lucky one, you don't have to lock yourself down to anybody.
LEILA: Excuse me?
GABE: They don't expect you to, because there's so many people you're attracted to. [*Realizing his gaffe, he begins fumbling.*] Because of that reason, monogamy's not possible for you – which is great. You're free.
LEILA: Why are you talking to me like I'm a different species from you? You think because I'm bisexual I can just fuck any person I meet? Why are you shagging half of London, then? I've slept with three people in ten years! How many girls have you fucked off Tinder alone?

Similarly resignifying the "fickle bisexual" stereotype, Leila formulates in feminist terms her refusal of Sadie's marriage proposal: "I don't know myself outside of being yours", rejecting the proprietorial (and patriarchal) model compromising their coupling. Caught with Jon-Criss, Leila goes on to resist Sadie's resort to the "anything that moves" stereotype of bisexual insatiability by invoking the monotony of monogamy:

SADIE: Was it just sex or did you like him?
LEILA: It wasn't just sex.
SADIE: You know, it's funny, I blame myself for not being able to satisfy you. How long have you fancied men? Why didn't you tell me?
LEILA: Because it didn't matter. I was in love with you. It wasn't relevant.

SADIE: It's relevant! You will never be fully satisfied.

LEILA: You can't be with someone ten years and not want other people. No person could give another person all the things they need. You couldn't satisfy me because you stopped trying.

Even as it critiques a representational regime (and cultural norm) that conflates bisexuality with promiscuity and capriciousness, *The Bisexual* implicates Leila herself as (what a crestfallen Jon-Criss charges after she pulls back) "an emotional intimacy whore". From what we've seen of her self-involved rebounding, his words ring true; even at the risk of reinforcing bisexual stereotype, Akhavan defies demands for positive role models in favor of a complex, fully humanized characterization.

Resignifying another stereotype, *The Bisexual* exploits the adaptability pejoratively termed "bisexual privilege" to signal bisexual's then-and-now affordances for code-switching and niche-straddling. As evidenced by the series' evocation of 90s representational heyday "bisexual chic", this conduciveness to migration across audience/market demographics has led to bisexuality's frequent instrumentalization and commodification. Recalling the "twenty years too late" decree quoted at chapter's start, *The Bisexual* indulges queer nostalgia as a strategy for finally positioning bisexuality front and center, with the ultimate aim of questioning our enduring attachments to cultural texts and identity terms.

Rebooting the B Word: Resignification through Generational Change

"Bisexuality: Not Gay. Not Straight. A New Sexual Identity Emerges," proclaimed *Newsweek*'s July 17, 1995 cover. In line with popular media's penchant for claiming as "new" what was (then as now) actually re-emergent, bisexuality's most recent reboot is at once clearly cyclical and very much of the moment. Fueled by contemporary Hollywood's appetite for pre-sold properties and the 1990s nostalgia of its favored youth demographic, reboot culture provides a profitable means to update that era's *au courant* multiculturalism for today's intersectionality-informed "wokeness." Though streaming sites typically prize quantity (of offerings) over "quality TV" prestige, in co-distributing *The Bisexual* Hulu benefited from Channel 4's longtime curating of a "challenging and alternative…reputation for difference," that nonetheless stops short of the genuinely radical."[17]

The Channel 4/Hulu coupling reboots bisexuality by updating the 90s "gaystreaming" that evolved out of network TV's earlier gambit for representing queerness, "very special episodes." That format's much-deplored use of one-off characters introduced to educate the regular cast evolves in *The Bisexual* into a cross-generational, cross-cultural central ensemble of (multiple) queer representatives, permitting an individuated, affective view of the varieties of queer experience. At the same time, *The Bisexual* borrows from the "very special episode" the strategic use of a heartrending speech as plea for empathy, as when fortysomething Sadie counters thirtysomething Leila's accusation that she's "just so rigid" by revealing how her flinty demeanor serves as armor against sexism and homophobia:

> You know why I'm like that! You have to be a robot to be successful in this industry. Have you any idea what it takes to be a dyke growing up in Burnley in the '80s?...It's giving Kevin Henderson a blow job in the school car park in front of a load of kids just so they'd think you were normal and your mother could meet people's eyes in the supermarket. It was faking it, when you were fucking frightened 'cos you didn't have a fucking clue what you were doing.

Having come of age in a provincial Thatcher-era town, Sadie's Gen X experience of queer identity contrasts with Millennial Leila, with further triangulation provided by college student/Gen Z representative Francisca (Michèlle Guillot). The latter, not understanding why Leila feels the need to hide from Deniz that she's seeing Jon-Criss, questions her motives.

LEILA: It's a gay thing.
FRANCISCA: So what? I'm queer.
LEILA: Everyone under 25 thinks they're queer.
FRANCISCA: And you think they're wrong?
LEILA: No. You know what I think, I think it's different. I think when you have to fight for it, I think that being gay can become the biggest part of you. And that you're gay or straight and one comes with an entirely different lifestyle than the other. Like different clothes and different friends and you can't do both. And I don't mean to be condescending to you. I don't know what it's like to grow up with the internet. I just get the sense that it's changing your relationship to gender. And to sexuality. In a really good way but in a way that I can't relate to.

Leila's observations on queerness's political and cultural resignifications across generations point to the temporal contingency of all sexuality categories. This displacement of gender-of-object-choice determinacy in favor of circumstantial and material logics of desire, in tandem with the temporal component necessary for rendering bisexuality legible, attests to how bisexuality (and *The Bisexual*)—far from reasserting binary ways of thinking—models queer theory's Foucauldian understanding of discursively-bound subjectivity.

Representation Matters: Affective Alliance through Shared Spectatorship

In another nod to generational alliance, a scene of Leila and Gabe spontaneously reenacting the "Love Is Strange" pas de deux from 1980s urtext *Dirty Dancing* demonstrates how this shared cultural reference traverses their otherwise divergent vectors of identity—gender, ethnicity, nationality, sexuality. Further testifying to how profoundly representation matters, *The Bisexual* reflexively references pop culture's indelible imprint on Leila's nascent sexual identity. "I used to be obsessed with Tom Petty when I was a little girl," Leila reminisces, "But then I would fall asleep at night thinking about Pam Anderson playing beach volleyball." The libidinal shading of this nocturnal fantasy co-exists with the mimetic logic that also structures desire—focused, in this case, on 1990s MTV star and TV star respectively, and not incidentally both extreme figurations of whiteness.

The L Word similarly comes in for resignification in *The Bisexual*, when a table of queer women call out one of their number for aspiring to be "a Shane." After translating to Gabe, who's tagged along, the reference to the soft butch ladykiller famously a favorite of straight-identified female fans, Leila warns, "Just 'cause one person made a fucking *L Word* reference doesn't mean you get to go back to all your friends and say all lesbians do is talk about *The L Word*." With Gabe already subject to mortification for bringing up *Blue Is the Warmest Color*, here Leila imparts a lesson in straight dude decorum courtesy of lesbian screen citation. Off-screen, Akhavan used *The Bisexual*'s press junket to reproach the Showtime soap's creators for having another beloved character, Alice, as Akhavan put it, "start[] the show such a fervent defender of her bisexuality" only to denounce it—and an audience segment viewed as expendable—in dialogue that became infamous: "Well, I'm glad I finally came to my senses. Bisexuality is gross. I see that now."

The L Word's status as queer pioneer made its dismissal cut deeper than the aforementioned, as-infamous, *Sex and the City* exchange that discounts male bisexuality as "just a layover on the way to Gaytown." But even easy laughs have lasting effects. Defending her latest "sex tourist" conquest, the Shane-aspirant protests, "I think she's bisexual." "Does anyone know any actual bisexuals?" someone responds, to which an anxious-looking Leila interjects, "I'm pretty sure bisexuality is a myth that was created by ad executives to sell flavored vodka." This biphobic callback—to *30 Rock*'s Liz Lemon proclaiming "There's no such thing as bisexuality—that's just something they invented in the 90s to sell hair products—reveals Leila's slow progress toward self-acceptance.

The L Word again figures in a sequence intercutting two households "watching telly," which contrasts the medium's potential to deliver guilty pleasures *and* to talk back to power. Comforting a despondent Sadie post-breakup, ex-turned-best mate Esther (Caoilfhionn Dunne) indulges her wallowing, up to a point:

ESTHER: Oh for the love of god, I know you're going through something but I cannot watch another episode of *The L Word*. Let's go out. Season 2 is shit anyway. Tina's all boring and pregnant.

SADIE: Do you reckon if they hadn't gotten back together, Bette would have had a baby on her own?

ESTHER: Fuck no, Bette's like us. But with cleavage. It's unnatural.

SADIE: Yeah, if you're a Bette, carrying a baby's a mind-fuck. You can't be seen breast-feeding in a power suit.

ESTHER: I'd literally saw off my arm to be with her.

SADIE: [*smirking*] It'd have to be your left arm.

This ex-couple's ongoing intimacy is expressed here through one's identification with and the other's attraction to power dyke Bette, whose ill-fit as a model for lesbian maternity Esther presses upon Sadie. The sapphic soap proves no less capable of leaving an imprint on viewers as do social change documentaries such as that seen simultaneously bringing Leila to tears—despite her disgruntlement at its being made by haughty Francisca and hearing that it "changed legislation in Chile," as Gabe smugly reports. "Legal abortion is happening because of her." "I get it, she's a better person than me," responds Leila. Including such "meta" moments here and throughout *The Bisexual* underscore the powerful impressions that representation leaves not just on emotion but on self-identification (Figure 15.2).

The Bisexual' furthers its recognition of television's potential as a medium for the outrageous as well as the (self-)righteous by a sly bit of self-promotion that also nods ironically at the hypervisibility of contemporary sexual representation. Recurringly seen playing at Deniz's family's off-license is Channel 4's *Naked Attraction*, a reality dating competition series featuring fully nude contenders, hosted by TV personality Anna Richardson, one-half of a British celebrity lesbian couple. A shoutout by superfan Akhavan—who tweeted, mid-pandemic but post-2019 U.S. presidential election results, of its being "the only other thing that has brought me joy in months" (@akhavandesiree, November 7, 2019)—this embedded intertext also celebrates queer women's success in the media industry. Given that it's playing in an immigrant-owned shop managed and frequented by Deniz and Leila respectively, it suggests as well the spatial overlap of traditional and secular that informs the two women's ethnic and sexual identities.

Unpacking the Gray Areas: Resignifying (Bi)sexuality through Intersectionality

Claire Perkins points to how Akhavan's "in-between sensibility manifests as a commentary on the difficulty—and undesirability—of 'achieving' the social and temporal expectations of a range of intersecting identities."[18] Elsewhere I expand on Perkins's application of "inbetweener" as a queer conceptual framework for understanding Akhavan's own first-generation experience and her autobiographically-inscribed *Appropriate Behavior*, in which her alter ego Shirin not being out to her family is a key source of tension in both her relationship and the film.[19] With Leila's biological family absent from *The Bisexual*, it becomes her chosen family Deniz to whom Leila evades coming out as bisexual; at the same time, Deniz mirrors Shirin in also not having come out to her immigrant family. As queer women subject to Western racialization of and prejudices against Middle Eastern immigrants, Leila and Deniz are divided by another invisible marker finally confronted at the series' midpoint:

LEILA: Say it.
DENIZ: Why did you pretend to be a lesbian?
LEILA: I wasn't pretending.
DENIZ: I'm disappointed.
LEILA: I know. I'm still the same person.
DENIZ: Nobody's going to be straight up with you, but it does change things.

FIGURE 15.2 Representation matters: Bingeing *The L Word*; riveted by Francisca's social change documentary.

As before, Akhavan invokes stereotype—that of "bisexual privilege"—broaching the doubly burdensome coming out to one's queer (alongside one's biological) family that is another aspect of bisexual specificity. An episode-length flashback to Leila and Deniz first meeting at a university pub in 2005 importantly albeit subtly establishes Leila as attracted to men (Deniz's mate, in this case) yet already suppressing "the b word," as Leila's persistent attempts at befriending

FIGURE 15.3 Deniz (Saskia Chana) and Leila (Desiree Akhavan) confront their still-closeted identities as lesbian and bisexual, respectively.

Deniz bear fruit only after revealing she's dated women. "I've never met someone like me, who doesn't like boys," confesses a relieved Deniz in private; in that moment, as the expression (imperceptible to Deniz) that darts across Leila's face reveals, bisexual pride takes a backseat to a desire for acceptance and belonging (Figure 15.3).

While the prevalence of monosexist assumptions enables Leila to "pass" as lesbian during her decade-long coupledom, her cultural privilege permits her brash coming out to her family; as her university-aged self recounts, "I figured they can either disown me or get over it." Her family's absence from the present-day narrative hints that the outcome may well have been the former, and recalls Leila's earlier characterization of coming out as "hands down the worst thing I've ever had to do." Returning to their present-day confrontation in Deniz's family shop, Leila challenges her about similarly leading a double life and moreover sacrificing a career:

LEILA: Why do you get to make all the rules? Like it's not okay if I date a guy but if you give up on being a chef it's done?

DENIZ: Stop being so fucking middle-class. I can't just do whatever the fuck I want. I'm not like you.

LEILA: Not like what? You're not selfish. You don't abandon your family. You didn't even come out for their sake. I'm a shit daughter and I'm selfish as fuck. Thank god, because I have no resentments and no regrets, and I'm happy.

DENIZ: Are you saying I'm not happy?
LEILA: I'm saying it's a fucking waste that you're spending your days in this shop.
DENIZ: Leila, who the fuck are they going to get to replace me? Anyone who they've ever hired has screwed them over.
LEILA: I didn't know that…
DENIZ: Being close to my family makes me happy. Knowing that they're OK and I don't have to worry about them makes me very fucking happy. OK? What makes you so happy?

In calling upon Leila to examine her complicity in another form of privilege, Deniz's pained response rivals Sadie's account of growing up gay in 1980s Burnley in its voicing of the bitter pill proffered to those whose "choice" to come out is constrained by an entanglement of enduring homo/bi/transphobia, familial attachments, cultural heritage, precarious citizenship, and socioeconomic hardship. Again yielding the floor to another otherwise stiff-upper-lipped English lesbian, with this speech Akhavan connects the experience of a white self-proclaimed dyke in a Thatcherite town and a first-generation working-class lesbian in present-day London. As suggested by the conflicted sympathies elicited in this tearful scene, which ends with an abrupt cut to black, no clear answer or reassuring resolution regarding coming out is possible for those to whom its promised "liberation" is inaccessible.

The Queerest of Times: Bi Every Week but Still Buried too Soon

With no second season forthcoming, *The Bisexual's* exploration of the intersectional barriers to queer self-realization, scarcely underway at series' end, has been short-circuited. Nevertheless, Akhavan has brought to the episodic television projects she has since taken on as a director-for-hire her still-underrepresented perspective as a queer woman of color, gravitating to the Rosario Dawson vehicle *Briarpatch* (about a Latina policewoman's death in rural Texas); Egyptian-American comedian Ramy Youssef's acclaimed, autobiographically-inspired *Ramy* in an episode devoted to a closeted Muslim relative ("Uncle Naseem"), and an episode of the fantasy anthology series *Monsterland* featuring Kelly Marie Tran as a young woman obsessed with her enviable female friend ("Iron River, Michigan"). The two first-season episodes she directed of *Hacks* (2021-), the HBO Max hit about the reluctant pairing of a Joan Rivers-like comedian and a bisexual Millennial hired as her joke writer, registers Akhavan's sensibility subtly but especially well: in the first, the Millennial chastises her older boss for being "monosexist" ("D'Jewelry"); in the second, she awakens disturbed from having dreamed they were making out ("Tunnel of Love").

Though behind-the-scenes circumstances, soon compounded by a global pandemic, conspired to end its run, *The Bisexual*'s six episodes constitute a valuable contribution to the still lamentably small library of "for us, by us" bisexual representation. Elsewhere I explore the show's modeling of how to be "bi every week," to twist Anna McCarthy's phrase for the challenges of "everyday queerness," integrating LGBTQ+ characters and storylines within the textual fabric without universalizing or depoliticizing queerness.[20] In an ironic twist bizarre to those raised to expect queer characters to surface only during networks' sweeps weeks, we've arrived at a moment in which TV's most enduring and central bi characters are found on network series and basic cable, from Callie Torres of long-running ABC soap *Grey's Anatomy* to Rosa Diaz on Fox/NBC's *Brooklyn Nine-Nine* to both female leads in BBC's *Killing Eve*. Alongside the belated but appreciated addition of *male* bisexuality (*Crazy Ex-Girlfriend*, *Schitt's Creek*), this is the good news.

As for the bad news, the same marketplace factors that opened the floodgates for queer-themed "multicasting"—channel diversification and algorithmic marketing aimed at targeting increasingly fragmented audiences[21]—now threaten to curb the affordances that TV seriality allows bisexual representation. Instead of the TV trope that inspired fan-activists' callout of what they termed "Bury Your Gays," television's premature killing-off of queer characters has lately been motivated by the logic of renewability that leads behemoth streaming sites like Hulu and Netflix as well as prestige outlets like HBO Max to axe popular series—or keep their renewal indeterminate—with early cancellation claiming or threatening multiple bisexual protagonists (*High Fidelity*, *The Politician*, *Sally 4Ever*). Increasingly series creators combat OTT overlords' inclination to shoot down new shows just as they're gaining altitude by conceiving single-season runs as limited series, or at least shaping their first season narrative as though it may be their last. On that front, too, *The Bisexual* offers a model for resignifying not only TV's sexual and representational principles but its temporal principles as well.

Notes

1 Robyn Bahr, "'The Bisexual': TV Review," *Hollywood Reporter*, November 16, 2018, www.hollywoodreporter.com/review/bisexual-review-1161968

2 Caroline Framke, "How Bisexuality on TV Evolved from a Favorite Punchline to a Vital Storyline," *Vox*, May 16, 2018, www.vox.com/culture/2018/5/16/17339992/bisexual-representation-tv-callie-rosa-darryl.

3 Ariel Sobel, "*Cameron Post* Director: Amazon Nixed Bi Series Because of *Transparent*," *Advocate*, September 5, 2018, www.advocate.com/bisexuality/2018/9/05/cam-post-director-amazon-nixed-bi-series-because-transparent; Desiree Akhavan, "The Bisexual." Talkback, NewFest, SVA Theatre, New York, NY, October 29, 2018.

4 #StillBisexual bills itself as an "education and advocacy organization focused on empowering those who are attracted to more than one gender." See https://stillbisexual.com/

5 "Desiree Akhavan on Why TV Always Gets Bisexuality Wrong," interview by Hannah Harris Green, *Studio360*, PRX, February 14, 2019, audio, 10:24. www.pri.org/stories/2019-02-14/desiree-akhavan-why-tv-always-gets-bisexuality-wrong

6 Ibid.

7 Eleanor Stanford, "In 'The Bisexual,' Desiree Akhavan Grapples With All Kinds of Sexuality," *New York Times*, November 13, 2018, www.nytimes.com/2018/11/13/arts/television/the-bisexual-desiree-akhavan-hulu.html

8 Desiree Akhavan and Emily Danforth, "'Miseducation of Cameron Post' Creators Take Aim At Gay Conversion Therapy," interview by Terry Gross, *Fresh Air*, WHYY/NPR, July 25, 2018, www.npr.org/2018/07/25/632242898/miseducation-of-cameron-post-creators-take-aim-at-gay-conversion-therapy.

9 See Maria San Filippo, "'Just Because I'm a Lesbian Doesn't Mean I'm Evolved': The 'Bad Queer' Women's Comedic Web Series," *Bad Objects*, special issue of *The Velvet Light Trap* 85 (Spring 2020): 65–77.

10 Joy Press, "Desiree Akhavan Has a Bisexual Awakening on New Hulu Series," *Vanity Fair*, November 13, 2018, www.vanityfair.com/hollywood/2018/11/desiree-akhavan-interview-on-new-hulu-show-the-bisexual

11 Stanford, "Akhavan Grapples With All Kinds of Sexuality."

12 Ibid.; "Desiree Akhavan's The Bisexual," interview by Tobin Lo and Kathy Tu, *Nancy*, WNYC, April 22, 2019, audio, 19:09, www.wnycstudios.org/podcasts/nancy/episodes/nancy-podcast-desiree-akhavan-the-bisexual#ember5631877

13 As one example, the *Oxford Handbook of Queer Cinema* (2021) features 31 chapters of which seven single out gay, lesbian, and/or trans representation; bisexuality goes untreated.

14 Harris Green, interview.

15 Ibid.

16 Alexandra Pollard, "Desiree Akhavan Interview: 'Bisexuality Is Taboo in Both the Queer and the Straight World,'" *Independent* (UK), October 9, 2018, www.independent.co.uk/arts-entertainment/tv/desiree-akhavan-interview-the-bisexual-channel-4-cameron-post-a8570161.html

17 Martin Zeller-Jacques, "'Challenging and Alternative': Screening Queer Girls on Channel 4." In *Women on Screen: Feminism and Femininity in Visual Culture*, ed. Melanie Waters (Basingstoke: Palgrave Macmillan, 2011), 106–107.

18 Claire Perkins, "My Effortless Brilliance: Women's Mumblecore." In *Indie Reframed: Women's Filmmaking and Contemporary American Independent Cinema*, ed. Linda Badley, Claire Perkins, and Michele Schreiber (Edinburgh: Edinburgh University Press, 2016), 148-50.

19 Maria San Filippo, *Provocauteurs and Provocations: Screening Sex in 21st Century Media* (Bloomington: Indiana University Press, 2020), 252–350.

20 Maria San Filippo, "Serial Offender: *The Bisexual* (2018)," *Journal of Bisexuality* 20.3 (2020): 233-43; Anna McCarthy, A. "*Ellen*: Making Queer Television History." *GLQ* 7.4 (2001): 593-620.

21 Julia Himberg, "Multicasting: Lesbian Programming and the Changing Landscape of Cable TV," *Television & New Media* 15.4 (2014): 289-304.

16

VISUAL PLEASURE AND VIDEO-SHARING PLATFORMS

If I Was Your Girl and the Representation of Black Sexuality

Faithe J. Day

As a video-sharing site, YouTube opens up a digital space for independent content creators to produce their own web series for niche audiences and specific communities. In reference to entertainment and television, Black web series have become a popular format for content creators and consumers to engage with multiple iterations of Black identity. These representations foster identification between the audience and the portrayal of Black identity that the characters enact. In offering nuanced portrayals of Black identity, Black queer web series enact a cinematic gaze that represents queer intimacy and desire in a way that is not commonly seen within legacy network television. When viewing Black queer web series, desire is expressed in relation to the performance of gendered and sexual identity, complicating the way that we think about Black femininity as well as the construction of masculinity. In performing a textual analysis of the series *If I Was Your Girl*, the explicit representation of Black women's sexuality and engagement in sexual activities opens up a new understanding of the gaze in the study of film and television. By utilizing quare shared recognition we can also see how many Black queer web series encourage Black women to embrace different expressions of their gendered and sexual identity in order to find pleasure in looking.

Pleasure in Looking: Quare Shared Recognition in Web Series

In the article "Locating Black Queer TV," quare shared recognition is defined as a combination of E. Patrick Johnson's utilization of the term "quaring" and Patricia Hill Collin's reference to moments of "shared recognition" between Black women (Day and Christian). Quare shared recognition is the means by which one views and decodes the performance and articulation of Black queer and femme identity within texts. This concept also unpacks the ways in which those formations are utilized by Black queer people to interpret and fashion their own identity i.e. how

DOI: 10.4324/9781003109044-21

do we read each other, how do we read ourselves, and how does the reading of others influence our reading of ourselves, etc. Based on this theoretical framework, quare shared recognition combines the critical discourse and visual analysis of phenomena within online and offline setting(s), and is fundamentally an intersectional approach to studying identity and digital media. While quare shared recognition can be used to analyze multiple media texts, here quare shared recognition is used to critically examine the role of visual pleasure in Black queer web series on YouTube.

For Black and queer community members, seeing one's-self on screen is not only a moment of recognition, but a moment which is imbued with certain affective stances based on the nature of that representation. As Laura Mulvey writes in her foundational essay "Visual Pleasure and Narrative Cinema," scopophilia or the idea that there is pleasure in looking is as much a part of the experience of viewing film as analyzing the text itself (Mulvey 59–62). In describing the production of mainstream cinema, Mulvey indicates that "The magic of the Hollywood style at its best (and of all the cinema which fell within its sphere of influence) arose, not exclusively, but in one important aspect, from its skilled and satisfying manipulation of visual pleasure" (Mulvey 59). For Mulvey, the viewing and production of cinema create a space of voyeurism in which the viewer is encouraged to "focus attention on the human form" as well as being placed between moments of "recognition/misrecognition" in viewing the human form on the screen (Mulvey 60–61). Mulvey goes on to argue that the camera's gaze tends to be focused on the female body, privileging a male viewer who is encouraged to objectify the woman seen on film (61–62).

While many Black queer web series play on the "scopophilic instinct" (pleasure in looking at another person as an erotic object) and "ego libido" (forming identification processes) that Mulvey outlines for cinema, these series also eschew the male gaze by attracting a female gaze instead (Mulvey 67). In this sense, Black queer web series enact a form of quare shared recognition, or a style of looking which values and recognizes the Black queer gaze. Here quare shared recognition describes how these series encourage Black women to gaze upon the bodies of other Black women in order to garner a simultaneous pleasure in looking and moments of recognition. It is also through this use of a queer female gaze that viewers can engage with Black women's sexuality and bodies in a way that does not seek to do violence to their representation or objectify/commodify their sexual selves.

Yet, this definition of quare shared recognition and its support of the Black queer gaze is not only a reference to Mulvey's analysis of the male gaze in cinema, but also bell hooks' essay on "The Oppositional Gaze: Black Female Spectatorship." By describing how the gaze has historically been denied to Black Americans through slavery and Jim Crow, hooks argues that Black viewers were able to see through the white male gaze in cinema (hooks 207–209). Rebuking the belief in a passive audience who are inundated by media, hooks references audience members awareness of the ideological underpinnings of media narratives, by writing that:

> When most black people in the United States first had the opportunity to look at film and television, they did so fully aware that mass media was a system of knowledge and power reproducing and maintaining white supremacy. To stare at the television, or mainstream movies, to engage its images, was to engage its negation of black representation.
>
> *hooks 95*

In this sense, hooks argues that the symbolic annihilation of Black bodies on television coupled with the stereotypical representations of those who were on screen resulted in the development of the oppositional gaze for Black viewers.

The oppositional gaze also created space for creativity. Black viewers responded to the lack of representation with a desire to critique the content they saw and create representations that better reflected the intersectionality of identity. Especially for Black female viewers, hooks' intersectional analysis of Mulvey's work demonstrates that "Black female spectators, who refused to identify with white womanhood ... created a critical space where the binary opposition Mulvey posits of 'woman as image, man as bearer of the look' was continually deconstructed" (hooks 99). Not existing in the role of woman or male onlooker, the Black woman as the viewer is always already queerly positioned to deconstruct media texts based on her standpoint as an outsider in relation to much of mainstream media and societal norms. Even, as hooks points out, "Black women have written little about black female spectatorship, about our moviegoing [and television viewing] practices" (96). Although hooks states that the dissatisfaction that many Black women felt in viewing Black women on film served as a starting point for the formation of an oppositional gaze, she goes on to write that "critical black female spectatorship" emerges "as a site of resistance only when individual black women actively resist the imposition of dominant ways of knowing and looking" (hooks 103).

In viewing Black queer web series, quare shared recognition can be understood as an affective or emotional response to a lack/discovery of representation of the self within the media as well as moving cultural producers to create texts which are well received within their communities. Therefore, quare shared recognition builds on the concept of the oppositional gaze, as Black women "do more than resist. We create alternative texts that are not solely reactions. As critical spectators, black women participate in a broad range of looking relations [which] contest, resist, revision, interrogate, and invent on multiple levels" in order to create narratives that do not just inspire opposition (hooks 103). Referencing multiple Black female producers and the work of Stuart Hall, hooks points out the ways in which creating media texts outside of the mainstream imagines "new transgressive possibilities for the formulation of identity" (hooks 104). According to hooks, by focusing one's gaze to move beyond what is seen and not seen, we can critique and complicate the role that representation plays in our study of the media. Due to the lack of representations of Black queer women in mainstream media and discourse, it is important to not only take into account the types of images that are produced and represented within the media, but what those images say about popular culture and society.

Don't Kiss, Don't Tell: Queering the Sexual Politics of Network Television

In turning to the cultural politics which surround the depiction of sexuality and visual pleasure within the media, it is important to note that not all community members accept the representation of queer sexuality as a necessary component of public expression or media production. Attempting to satisfy both those who do, and do not, readily accept queer individuals, mainstream legacy television networks promote a safe and sanitized portrayal of homosexuality which leaves out much of the reality of queerness, that is, sex and sexual relationships. Instead of presenting all aspects of queer reality, which includes individuals of different racial, gendered, and class backgrounds, many networks continue to place white, upper class gay men at the center of queer narratives or as queer characters in mostly straight mediated worlds (as seen in shows like *Will & Grace* or *Modern Family*). As marriage equality became a topic of political conversation, these men were also represented in familial roles which present an understanding of queer sexuality focused on social mobility and respectability. Despite the positivity of these images, there is a clear lack of inclusion for other types of queer imagery in favor of a narrative which seeks to diminish difference and promote assimilation. Especially within queer media texts, legacy networks position certain types of queer identity as acceptable/respectable i.e. representing heterosexual norms. In contrast, other types of queer identity are viewed as inherently deviant i.e. not safe for television and mainstream viewing audiences.

As Alfred L. Martin Jr. states in the article "It's (Not) in His Kiss: Gay Kisses and Camera Angles in Contemporary US Network Television Comedy," outside of cable networks, queer individuals are rarely seen dating, hooking up, or even kissing their partners. Martin argues that we can determine how queer intimacy is viewed within network television and thereby mainstream audiences through an analysis of the camera angles and staging used to depict moments of queer intimacy (Martin 154–155). Through the strategic spacing of characters, cut-aways, and over the shoulder shots, queer intimacy is hinted at but rarely shown within network television (155–163). Instead of "dealing with the same-sex intimate relations, the implicit heteronormativity of televisual spaces becomes clear. Gay characters are allowed in these spaces but implying sexual intimacy is not" (Martin 163–164). By only engaging with the male gaze, which invites heterosexual desire and visual pleasure, the cinematic gaze of network television polices the queer gaze by only implying queer sexual intimacy instead of openly representing it. Through cutting away or lowering the lights on queer on-screen kisses, there is an implication that even as mainstream audiences recognize the existence of queer people, queer sexual acts are still viewed as taboo or something which should be hidden off screen. By limiting the portrayals of queer intimacy to mostly chaste kisses, networks do not give viewers the same opportunities to engage in desire or pleasure in looking at queer characters as they do for straight characters.

In addition to the lack of representations of queer sexuality overall, there is also a lack of diverse representations of Black queer sexuality within the mainstream media. In the article "Digital Media and the Politics of Intersectional Queer Hyper/visibility in *Between Women*," Amber Johnson and Robin M. Boylorn writes that even when there are representations of Black female sexuality within the mainstream media, they are usually "femininized and heteronormative depictions of Black female desire and desirability, [so] there are fewer representations of queer Black sexualities and Black female masculinities as sites of desire" (Johnson and Boylorn 8). In order to diverge from sexual stereotypes and controlling images, many Black content creators use digital media and video-sharing platforms to create a space to explore Black queer sexualities in ways that are not commonly shown within mainstream media.

Yet, even as video-sharing platforms create space for greater exploration of the visual representation of sexuality, like many network and cable television series, most Black queer web series do not display explicit or lengthy representations of sexual acts or romantic moments between same-sex individuals. However, within the series *If I Was Your Girl*, the representation of sexuality focuses more so on the pleasure of queer identity through the explicit representation of lesbian sex. In this sense, the performance of Black lesbian sexuality within this web series brings the role that pleasure plays into understanding quare shared recognition into sharp focus. Instead of policing the camera's gaze, *If I Was Your Girl* employs a television grammar which allows viewers to see, and take satisfaction in, the images of queer sexuality that are commonly omitted within mainstream or network television.

Reading *If I Was Your Girl*

Beginning as a spin-off of the 2012 film of the same name, *If I Was Your Girl* was created, written, and directed by Coqui Hughes. Charting the rocky relationships and ups and downs of queer women of color in an urban space, the series follows four queer women in Chicago and the drama of their relationships and friendships. After the film gained traction with viewing audiences in 2013, Hughes presented the first episode of *If I Was Your Girl* as a web series (Day and Christian). Unfortunately, the series didn't last for long, and it was canceled after only a few episodes and a season finale, and has currently been removed from YouTube (although it is available on other video streaming sites). However, during analysis of the series in 2016, episodes 1 through 3 spanned an almost 90-minute segment on YouTube and garnered well over 3 million views and 2,000 comments. While these numbers may not seem large within the context of the YouTube platform as a whole, in terms of Black queer web series *If I Was Your Girl* is a well-known and celebrated media text.

In many ways, the popularity of the series itself comes from the realistic recording of the series scenes and narrative. From the very beginning of the compilation video that encompasses episodes 1–3 of the series, the viewer is introduced to three of the four main characters (Lynne, Stacia, Toi, and Rhonda) in the narrative via explicit representations of their sexuality. The opening scene of Episode 1 depicts Lynne naked, though covered in a sheet, while simultaneously smoking a cigarette and calling Stacia. Then there is a cut to a back shot of Stacia and Toi, their heavily tattooed bodies entwined together as they writhe naked on the bed. The scenes then cut back and forth between Lynne frantically leaving a voice message and Stacia and Toi having sex with seemingly no knowledge of the drama that would unfold from Lynne's call, or their coupling (Hughes). In many ways, this portrayal of Black queer sexuality speaks back to normative representations of Black women in the media, which generally do not represent Black queer women due to the fraught relationship between beliefs about what constitutes the proper representation of Black female identity and which does not.

Right from the start, *If I Was Your Girl* pushes back against the normative representation of queer sexuality in order to actually present the viewer with not only Black queer women, but Black women engaged in queer sex. I read this opening scene as a very blatant and political move on the part of Coquie Hughes to construct the intended audience or community insiders for the series as the Black queer women she chooses to portray. By hailing a Black queer audience, Hughes signals that the series is not shy about or ashamed of the performance of Black queer women's sexuality or the representation of their pleasure. Instead of using the traditional conventions of a blank screen or cut-aways which never cut back to the establishing shot, the camera constantly returns to the scenes of sexual intimacy, lingering on the bodies of the three women portrayed in the opening scene. This lingering is what Helen Wheatley describes in the article "Visual Pleasure and Narrative Television," as "intentional erotic spectacle," which is defined as "moments, images, characters, even episodes which both seek to represent and provoke desire" within the media text (Wheatley 896). Similar to the concept of fan service in Japanese Anime, these moments are placed within the text to excite members of the audience.

In this sense, *If I Was Your Girl* utilizes intentional erotic spectacle throughout the series in order to create moments of visual pleasure for the viewer. Drawing on Mulvey's work on visual pleasure, Wheatley also points out that these moments of erotic spectacle demonstrate the important role of the voyeuristic gaze in television viewing (Wheatley 897). In her research for the book *Spectacular Television*, Wheatley found that television played a significant role in the "idea of a 'sexual awakening,' or the realization of the desiring self" for its viewers (897). This is because "At the level of address, television has become adept at speaking to diverse audiences, potentially offering 'something for everyone' when it comes to the presentation of desire and the articulation of gendered/sexual looking relations" (898). Therefore, the opening scene of *If I Was Your Girl* disrupts more conventional uses of the cinematic gaze in order to appeal to a Black queer audience in a more open and explicit manner.

In contrast to legacy film and television narratives which cover the eyes of its audience by averting the cinematic gaze of the camera during moments of queer sexual intimacy, *If I Was Your Girl* uses the visual text to illicit queer desire and scopophilia in the viewer. The erotic spectacle continues in Episode 1, as the character Lynne visits Toi in jail and offers her an indecent proposal. A portion of the conversation between the two is as follows:

TOI: Why, why do you wanna fuck me so bad Lynne? You act just like a manipulative ass, thirsty ass, disgusting ass man. I'm not interested in fucking you.
LYNNE: Me neither, I wanna fuck you.
TOI: *[rolls her eyes and lets out an exasperated sigh]*
LYNNE: Now, I know that last comment just made your pussy jump and the fact that you told me no the first time, well, that just makes you insatiably desirous. I know it's wrong, improper, it's downright bogus, but who gives a fuck. And you know I have control issues. And I don't take rejection well.
TOI: *[deep inhales and sighs again]* Fuck you Lynne.
LYNNE: *[with a smirk]* I just may let you. Now later on this morning, I meet with the state's attorney. Afterwards, anticipate being home to your son by the time the 6 o'clock news comes on. And then I expect you to meet me at the Four Seasons hotel with your body washed and your pussy shaved.
TOI: *[humph]* And what if I don't come.
LYNNE: *[looks Toi up and down]* Well that depends on how you're spelling that word. Which will determine what happens next.
TOI: *[hastily gets up from the table to leave while asking a correctional officer to take her back to her cell, dismissing Lynne with a few carefully placed expletives]*

Although Lynne notes that this conversation is meant to entice Toi, through the use of erotic language, this discourse is also introduced in order to excite the viewer. By likening Lynne's conversation to that of a man, we also see how this discourse uses the representation of queer female sexuality to disrupt traditional conventions of expressing sexual desire within a television narrative. Instead of playing a traditionally passive feminine role, through her words and her gaze Lynne openly expresses her desire for Toi and her plans to pursue her until a sexual coupling occurs. This conversation primes the viewer for the opening scene for Episode 2 of the series, when we see that despite Toi's expressed disinterest in Lynne, the two end up meeting in a hotel for a late-night rendezvous. In this hotel scene, Toi strips down to her lingerie for Lynne and proceeds to give her a lap dance. Throughout the scene, the camera plays with the expectations of mainstream media by constantly cutting to a black screen. However, instead of using this cutaway to quickly move on from the sex scene, as it is commonly seen within network television, the camera continues to come back to the women until the coupling is completed. We see this strategy again in Episode 3 when the series protagonists head out to a strip club and Toi and Stacia have sex in the bathroom of the club.

Invoking this desire in the audience also acts as a form of quare shared recognition because viewers are encouraged to look at and desire bodies which are both similar and different to themselves. As Jennifer Nash argues in *The Black Body in Ecstasy*, one of the main critiques of sexually explicit content is that it centers a male gaze and emphasizes racial/gendered differences. This observation "implicitly assumes that pleasure-in-looking hinges on difference, rather than analyzing how spectators might take pleasure in sameness, in seeing themselves—their bodies, their pleasures, their longings—projected on screen" (Nash 19). This sameness and difference specifically play out within the series representation of its characters as the main characters of *If I Was Your Girl* represent a variety of gender identities and performance. While the gender binary within normative heterosexual society creates a binary opposition between man/woman, within same-sex queer communities these differences tend to play out through a continuum from masculine to feminine (Day).

Overall, the characters in *If I Was Your Girl* offer another form of visual pleasure by allowing the viewers of the series to not only recognize their own gendered and sexual identity, but the gendered and sexual performance of the type of women that they find to be desirable. Within the series, both Lynne and Toi would be described as femme or feminine presenting, while both Stacia and Rhonda exhibit a more masculine appearance. While these representations depict a realistic portrayal of Black queer community, the authenticity in portraying a variety of gendered and sexual performances also challenges normative portrayals of Black women in the media, which are almost always feminine, and intersectional stereotypes, that is, that Black women are inherently masculine. Playing on both conceptions, the undesirability of Black female masculinity within heteronormative society is upended as the more masculine performing character Stacia is positioned as the most desirable character within the series, engaging in sexual relationships with more than one woman throughout the narrative. In addition, the femme characters balance their femininity through unique performances which do not simply recycle stereotypes of passivity or acquiescence to portray their characters. As demonstrated with both Lynne and Toi, even the more stereotypically feminine characters in the series are given the freedom to express queer sexual desire and engage in intimate acts.

Conclusion

Even as the mainstream media tends to reflect a discourse which excludes Black queer women from expressing sexual desire or intimacy, video-sharing platforms offer another space for creators and consumers to engage in narratives which defy these conventions. As Lamonda H. Stallings writes, "in order to create and sustain radical Black female sexual subjectivity," Black female cultural producers "must embrace difference as a foundation without simply reversing the established order that fosters readings of difference as deviance" (Stallings 6). Instead of simply reversing the binary that would position Black female sexuality as deviant, Stallings writes that:

> In order to disturb Western constructs of sexuality in African American cultural texts, cultural producers have to perform three specific tasks: overturn racialized sexuality, uproot the heterosexualization of desire, and explode the binary of hetero/homo in sexuality.
>
> *Stallings 158*

In this sense, Stallings calls on Black cultural producers to create media texts which reflect complex and diverse representations of Black sexuality. This is not only done through a recognition of the role that intersectionality plays in the construction and performance of sexual identity, but through acknowledging the role that queer bodies and their pleasures play into producing cultural texts.

Especially in producing Black queer web series, there is a strategic investment in the representation of different types of queer bodies, as well as voicing and depicting the pleasures and desires of queer individuals. Embracing erotic spectacle, Black female producers engage in a form of quare shared recognition, which allows them to use queer sex and the visual portrayal of pleasure in order to garner a specific audience, as well as to make room in the public imaginary for Black sexuality that does not fit into a heteronormative mold. As a form of resistance to mainstream media productions, content creators such as Coqui Hughes use web series to hail a specific queer audience (Day and Christian). Throughout the series, viewers are exposed to discourse and imagery which works against a representation of Black womanhood as proper, heteronormative, and safe. Instead, Black queer women are able to visually engage with their desires for representation and recognition, not only to claim space for themselves within the realms of queer television, but to engage in a quare shared recognition that allows Black queer women to experience pleasure within and outside of the YouTube platform.

References

Day, F. 2018. Between butch/femme: On the performance of race, gender, and sexuality in YouTube web series. *Journal of Lesbian Studies* 22 no.3. (November): 267–281. www.tandfonline.com/doi/abs/10.1080/10894160.2018.1383800

Day, F., and Aymar Jean Christian. 2017. Locating black queer TV: Fans, producers, and networked publics on YouTube. In "Queer Female Fandom," ed. by Julie Levin Russo and Eve Ng, special issue, *Transformative Works and Cultures*, no. 24. https://journal.transformativeworks.org/index.php/twc/article/view/867/826

hooks, b. 2003. "The oppositional gaze: Black female spectators." In *The feminism and visual cultural reader*, ed. A. Jones. 94–105. New York: Routledge.

Horton-Stallings, L. 2007. *Mutha' is half a word: intersections of folklore, vernacular, myth, and queerness in black female culture*. Columbus: The Ohio State University Press.

Hughes, C. 2016. "*If I was Your Girl*—WebSeries Episodes 1–3 (Full Version)" Online video. *YouTube*. April 15, 2013.

Johnson, A., & Boylorn, R. M. 2015. Digital media and the politics of intersectional queer hyper/in/visibility in *Between Women*. *Liminalities*, 11 no. 1, 1. http://liminalities.net/11-1/between.pdf

Martin, A. L. 2014. It's (not) in his kiss: gay kisses and camera angles in contemporary US network television comedy, *Popular Communication*, 12, no. 3, 153–165. https://doi.org/10.1080/15405702.2014.921921

Mulvey, Laura. 1989. Visual pleasure and narrative cinema. In *Visual and other pleasures*, 14–26. London: Palgrave Macmillan.

Nash, J. C. 2014. *The black body in ecstasy: Reading race, reading pornography*. Durham: Duke University Press.

Wheatley, H. 2015. Visual pleasure and narrative television. *Feminist Media Studies* 15 no. 5, 896–899. https://doi.org/10.1080/14680777.2015.1075276

Wheatley, H. 2016. *Spectacular television: Exploring televisual pleasure*. London: I.B. Tauris.

INDEX

www.ingramcontent.com/pod-product-compliance
Ingram Content Group UK Ltd.
Pitfield, Milton Keynes, MK11 3LW, UK
UKHW032110100125
453485UK00008B/51

9 780367 623418